Big Fish Angling

Big Fish Angling

A Specimen Hunter Reflects

TONY MILES

The Crowood Press

First published in 1990 by
The Crowood Press Ltd
Gipsy Lane, Swindon
Wiltshire SN2 6DQ

British Library Cataloguing in Publication Data

Miles, Tony *1944–*
Big fish angling.
1. Angling
I. Title
799.12

ISBN 1 85223 382 6

Dedication

I dedicate this book to my mother. The love and support she has given me throughout every aspect of my life will never be forgotten.

Acknowledgements

The photographs appearing on pages 27, 34 (bottom), 44, 46, 55, 57, 58 (bottom), 59, 60, 64, 65, 67, 73 (top), 74, 93, 101 (top), 119, 123, 125, 126, 127, 133, 135, 159, 165, 172, 180, 184, 185, 188, 192, 196, and 197 are courtesy of Trefor West; all other photographs are by the author.

Typeset by Acorn Bookwork, Salisbury, Wiltshire
Printed in Great Britain by Butler & Tanner Ltd, Frome

Contents

	Introduction	7
1	The Claydon Brook	8
2	Days at the Park	25
3	Throop Recollections	30
4	Tench Exploits	36
5	The Coventry Specimen Group	42
6	In Pursuit of Barbel	45
7	A Week in Ireland	51
8	Cherwell Days	54
9	Royalty Reminiscences	92
10	From Cuttle Mill to Cassien	96
11	Thirty Years on the Leam	116
12	Stillwater Piking	132
13	Down on the Farm	142
14	Days on the Upper Great Ouse	147
15	Hawk Lake Crucians	154
16	TC Pit	158
17	Wensum Memories	179
18	Norfolk Piking	190
19	My First Double	201
20	Three Weeks at Redmire	205
21	The Queenford Phenomenon	212
	Index	223

Introduction

This is a book about the sheer pleasure that angling for big fish has given me over the years. It is a chronicle of the good days and the bad, the hilarious and the serious and the occasionally mysterious or tragic. My angling life now stretches back over thirty years, and the highlights contained within this book will ensure that when I am able to fish no more, I will be able to look back on a treasure trove of precious memories. If I were to have one wish fulfilled, it would be that I will be able to write a sequel in another thirty years' time.

Once again, I find myself contemplating the contribution to my angling enjoyment and success that has been made by my many angling friends over the years. It would be impossible to name every one here as they are so numerous, so I will have to content myself wih expressing my special thanks to Merv Wilkinson, Phil Smith, Dave Plummer and Andy Barker. Above all, of course, my thanks must go to Trefor West. In twenty years of fishing together we have shared so many memorable days that there is simply not the space to mention them all. We have experienced together the sense of achievement as a long-awaited specimen has at last succumbed, and countless occasions when we have been so helpless with laughter that tears have rolled down our cheeks. Such friendship is beyond price. I thank Trefor also for the many photographs I have borrowed to illustrate this book.

Obviously, it would be remiss if the opportunity was not taken again to thank my wife. In twenty-five years of marriage, she has tolerated my fishing with remarkable good nature, which has been tested even more severely over the last two years when most of my spare moments have been spent writing.

The obsession with chasing big fish is one that can put intense strain on marriages, and I count myself very lucky indeed that I am blessed with a wife like Fran who is supportive of all my dreams and ambitions.

1 The Claydon Brook

EARLY DAYS

Just after I had left school in 1961, aged seventeen, and was commencing my final long holiday before starting work in September, I was fishing at Napton reservoir, near Coventry, with three school friends, Dave Beale, and Ken and Maurice Evans. It was a hot afternoon and nothing much was doing. We were lolling around on the grass, talking about fishing generally, when Ken happened to mention a farmer his father had met recently at Banbury livestock market. Ken's father was also a farmer at the village of Ladbroke, near Coventry.

Apparently, the farmer Ken's father had met, Mr Crooke, ran a large acreage at the village of Padbury in Buckinghamshire and through his land ran a tributary of the Great Ouse, a stream called the Claydon Brook. The conversation between Mr Crooke and Mr Evans had turned to fish and fishing and Mr Crooke had then mentioned that the river was teeming with big roach, some up to 2lb in weight. When Mr Evans mentioned that his sons and their friends were all mad on fishing, an invitation came straight back for us all to fish the river by appointment. Provided we obeyed his country code, we would be welcome on his land for a long fishing holidy, camping in one of his fields.

We discussed this proposition very excitedly; none of us ever having seen a roach anywhere near 2lb. I had caught the biggest two years previously at a modest 1lb 6oz. Within a fortnight, the plans had been laid and on a beautiful Friday evening in July, Mr Evans dropped us all off at the farm to commence our fishing holiday. Our first job was to become acquainted with the farmer and to listen carefully as he gave us his list of instructions: no leaving of litter; no lighting of open fires; no leaving gates open; no trampling of growing crops; and so on. That friendly lecture from a very stern old countryman did us no harm at all. It has certainly stood me in good stead throughout my adult life. We were also taken into the farmhouse kitchen to meet his housekeeper, Miss Bryant. She would keep us well supplied with fresh eggs and milk throughout our holiday, but we would have to earn them. Mr Crooke was a lover of boiled crayfish which he also supplied to friends. The Claydon Brook in those days was alive with crays and hundreds could be caught in an hour on a dropnet at almost any point along the river. If we could provide the occasional bowl of crayfish, all our eggs and milk would be free.

Our first reconnaissance along the river was daunting. Most of it was almost completely choked with rushes and lilies and the fishable areas literally consisted of tiny pockets of clear water perhaps every fifty yards. The exception was the water in the immediate vicinity of the farmhouse. Upstream of the house, a small weir and side-stream had been constructed. The bulk of the main flow went under the house to drive a mill-wheel, but the small weir also carried a mill-stream around the house to rejoin the main river in the mill-pool itself.

About 400 yards further upstream, an overflow weir and lasher were also in existence. In times of flood or high water, excess water was carried over this lasher. The water then followed a snaking side-stream around in a half-mile loop, before also rejoining the main river at the millpool.

The straight section of river above the house and upstream of the small weir was very sluggish and of uniform depth – about three feet. The surface was a mass of water lilies, but not so thick as to make fishing impossible. Under those lily leaves, we were told, was where most of the big roach that had been caught had come from. The small weir was also interesting; it was the deepest spot on the river, at about seven feet, and one or two big perch had been taken from it as well as many medium-sized pike.

What we wanted to catch most of all were the big roach we had heard so much about, so on the first full day of our trip we all went into the long, slow straight above the house wearing our swimming trunks. When we had walked the entire length of it, we had indeed found little depth variation. There were, however, three or four areas marginally deeper and it was on these that we decided to concentrate. We dragged some of the lilies out at each point to make a definite swim and baited each area with mashed bread and maggots. That same evening, I had my very first fish from the Claydon Brook, a roach of 1lb 10oz, the biggest I had ever caught. The next morning, Dave and I were up well before dawn and in the first half-hour of daylight we had two fish each. Mine both weighed 1½lb, but Dave had two weighing 1lb 14oz and 1lb 15oz. This remained a fairly constant pattern for the duration of our stay – few fish but of good quality. Obviously, our efforts were amateurish – we would have caught more had we been more experienced.

During the middle of the day when there was little doing with the roach, we used to spend our time trotting minnows round the little weir-pool for perch and pike. The pool was full of jacks weighing about a pound and we had a lot of fun with these, losing more than we landed because we did not possess any wire traces. I also had a few perch, the biggest at about a pound, but at that time I did not suspect just how big the perch grew in the river.

As well as the very big roach, we had also seen some very big chub in the heavily overgrown stretches below the house running down to the country lane about half a mile downstream. At that time the biggest chub any of us had landed was about 2½ pounds and most of the chub in the river dwarfed that. Most of our efforts to catch one ended in failure. For one thing we were far too impatient, chasing the fish with our baits and scaring them. For another, the very overgrown water meant that the occasional one we did hook had us snagged almost immediately.

That holiday, I learned many lessons very quickly; by the end of our time, we had come to the conclusion that the only way we were going to catch one of those chub was to put a bait in a clearer area and then sit and wait behind cover. The first few chub Dave and I had caught from the Leam had come on cheese, so we went into Buckingham to get some. I remember asking a shopkeeper for the smelliest cheese he had available, whereupon he disppeared into his store-room and emerged with a big lump of the foulest smelling Danish Blue I have ever handled. It really was rank – you only had to touch it for the smell to linger on your hands for hours.

Back at the campsite, Dave and I worked the cheese into the most evil paste imaginable – surely every chub in the river would home in on it. We also decided to have fun with it. When we had arrived back at the tents, Ken was asleep in the sun, dead to the world. He was attempting to grow a moustache at that time and it really was a pathetic wisp of a thing. Carefully, Dave smeared a little of our cheese paste thinly on the whiskers and then we went off to fish, leaving him sleeping peacefully. It was about two hours later that Ken came down the bank, his nose wrinkling in disgust. 'I don't know what Mr Crooke is doing in that farmyard,' he said 'but there's the most foul smell in the air.' We agreed with him and let him carry on moaning all day, until we finally let him in on the secret at dusk. He was not amused.

The highlight of the trip was to come during the next afternoon. Dave and I were lying on the bank again with two enormous chunks of our paste in position, when Dave's rod almost flew into the river. After a terrific struggle, we had one of those magnificent fish in the net at long last. It weighed 4½lb – a fish beyond our wildest dreams.

Later that night I was to achieve something – my first ever chub on crayfish. It was not a big chub admittedly, a fish of about two pounds only, but I was very pleased with it. It was the most exciting take I had ever experienced and showed me how big a bait even a modest fish can engulf quite easily. Those Claydon Brook crays were monsters, frequently being over 4in long.

In celebration of the day's events, we all made our way to the village pub. We were all under age, but got away with it, getting totally legless on draught cider. That was the first time I said 'never again'!

Only a couple of weeks after that first trip, I was to catch my first ever 5lb chub, from Throop on a family holiday, and I soon went on to take my first five-pounder from Padbury. In the late autumn the river at Padbury was dredged and, knowing what I know now, the dredging was very sympathetic to the environment. It was carried out by a private contractor who left all the bushes and trees intact and just removed a sufficient amount of the clogging rushes to open the river up and alleviate flooding. There is no doubt at all that this initial dredging had a profound effect on my fishing. For a start, a great many areas were now available that had hitherto been inaccessible. Also, because there was now a temporary shortage of natural food, the fish were quite easy to catch for a while.

The winter of 1961 saw a bonanza, with a great many catches of chub over 4lb and two over 5lb. For the first time ever, the side-stream (from the lasher to the mill-pool) was fishable. Before the dredging this had been blocked from bank to bank by rushes and was a total non-starter for angling. We could now see that it was in fact a very attractive little fishery in its own right, with variations from gravel shallows to steady runs with a maximum depth of about four feet. In normal water conditions this stream was virtually stagnant as all the flow went over the mill-wheel and the house weir. When the level rose, however, the stream used to flow. The first winter the stream was fishable, we had many chub and big roach from it, free-lining lobs. We also saw a chub of quite breath-taking proportions, a fish we all said must have weighed at least 6lb. That was our first sighting of one of the leviathans.

SMALL STREAM PERCH – A LOVE AFFAIR

Although we had been told about big perch on our first trip to Padbury and had caught a few weighing up to 1lb on minnows, we had not given much serious thought to fishing for them deliberately. All was to change on a hot July morning in 1962.

Over the previous two weeks I had taken

several nice roach on stewed wheat and that was how I was fishing that day, laying on in a mid-river cabbage patch. This had become one of my favourite areas. It was one of the steadier and deeper swims on the fishery at four feet. As well as thick clumps of cabbages, there were also mid-river rush beds at both the upstream and downsteam extremities. Head-high marginal rushes grew wildly and in great profusion along the bank from which I was fishing. The most obvious feature, however, was the twenty yards of tangled alders and blackthorns which lined the opposite bank. The foliage from these trees overhung the river by about three feet, their outer branches touching the water surface. The far-bank tunnel which was created by these trees was in a state of permanent semi-darkness and was virtually weed-free. This was, understandably, a favourite haunt of big chub and I had taken several from there the previous winter. There were three narrow gaps in the outer branches – each only about a foot wide – and an accurate cast from the opposite bank could place a bait right under the cover.

Upstream of the line of trees the deeper water was confined to a run about four feet wide under the same bank. This deep water stretched for about thirty yards until some gravel shallows were reached which were only inches deep. From the bank I was fishing and upstream of the swim to the shallows was a solid mass of rushes and lilies in two feet of water. At one point only there was a gap in the rushes where it was possible to cast across and present a bait in the far-bank run.

On the July day in question there was an additional factor to take into account. A few hot, dry weeks had seen a steady accumulation of surface algae and scum and rafts of it were caught up around the weed beds and overhanging branches. Since the flow in the far-bank run was steady and the alder and thorn bushes acted as a downstream brake, its entire length was covered in an algal raft.

That morning my red-tipped porcupine float had not moved for over two hours since the sun had become hot. I was just contemplating whether to cross the river and present a chub bait under the algae when there was an upheaval under the scum. A momentary clear patch appeared in the sea of green and several minnows cleared the water. A few moments later it happened again and this time I had a clear sight of a very large prickly dorsal. My decision had been made for me. Within a few minutes, I was in position. After I had carefully poked a small hole in the algae with the handle of my landing net, I lowered a slow-sinking lobworm through on a size 8 hook under my porcupine float. I did not have long to wait. Within a minute the float tilted and shot away and I found myself playing a very powerful adversary indeed. For a long while I was sure that I had hooked a good chub, but when the fish eventually appeared from the depths I could see that it was, after all, a very big perch indeed. It weighed 2lb 10oz, by far the biggest I had ever seen and I can still remember how monstrous it looked as it lay on my landing net, its fins glowing bright scarlet in the strong sunlight.

During the next hour there were to be four more bites to the same presentation which yielded a brace of 1½-pounders, one missed bite and a big fish pricked and lost which signalled the end of the action. Little did I realise it at the time, but I had stumbled across the combination of circumstances which allows specimen perch from small, shallow streams to be a viable proposition in the heat of a summer day. Being extremely light-sensitive, the perch were encouraged to feed avidly in the sombre conditions under the algal raft much later than they would usually have done. Under normal conditions, a bright summer morning would see the bigger perch go off feed no more than about three hours after dawn. I took several good bags of perch from these algae-covered areas, but there is one particular catch that I remember even now.

It was one of my wife's first ever fishing trips with me and it could not have been better scripted. From first light until mid-afternoon, fish came steadily and when we eventually packed up I had taken no fewer than five 2lb perch in a total bag of over thirty fish. There was also a terrific bonus in the shape of a 5½ pound chub.

For quite some time, that first big perch from Padbury remained my best, although a month after that capture I was to lose a much bigger fish on my roach tackle. I was fishing the same cabbage patch, laying on with maggots right under the pads. At about mid-morning Dave came sprinting up the field to borrow my landing net. In the weir-pool, about 400 yards away, Ken was into a good pike. As soon as Dave was out of sight, sod's law was to prevail. I had a good lift of the float and as I struck there was an almighty boil on the surface as a very big perch rolled and shot off through the cabbages. I played that fish very carefully, all the time yelling for the net back. Eventually, the fish was beaten, but I had no way of landing it – even my keep net was ten yards away. With no sign of Dave, I tried to land that perch by hand. As I gingerly slipped my fingers under its body and began to lift, it flipped back into the water, the tiny hook pulled free and my prize, with a new-found burst of energy, rocketed across river into the rushes. I really could have cried and called Dave all the names I could lay my tongue to. At the time I entered in my diary that I had lost a perch possibly as heavy as 4lb. I do not think that I was far out because, a few years later and having by then taken several three-pounders, I believe I saw that fish again.

On that occasion I had brought a good friend, the now sadly departed Peter Rayment, who had never caught a perch as heavy as 2lb. I had put Pete into the best swim at dawn, the run where I had taken my first big perch under the algal raft, but by mid-morning he had not had a bite. This was very unusual since conditions were excellent and I had caught a couple of nice fish further upstream in a far more inconsistent area. As we sat together discussing his lack of action, his float slid away at long last. There were no preliminaries. One moment it was lying at half cock alongside the rushes, the next the rush stems were swaying as a big fish forced its way through them.

Immediately he struck, Pete was well tangled and I grabbed the landing net and waded out to the edge of the rush bed to free the line. In that I was successful and I caught a substantial flash of gold deep down as the fish came out of the rushes again. My first thought was tench, as I had caught several up to and over 4lb from that swim over the years. As Pete increased the pressure on the fish it came to the surface and rolled only a few feet from me. It was a huge perch, certainly well over 4lb. Pete never had a good look at the fish, but I made the mistake of telling him how big it was. At this I think Pete tried to be too cautious; he eased up the tension, with the result that the perch was able to reach the sanctuary of the lily roots in mid-river. We did not see that fish again. Everything went ominously taut and then the float shot out of the water minus the hook. Before his untimely death earlier this year, Pete told me that he had never gotten over the loss of that perch.

Another method of taking good perch at Padbury that evolved by accident was fishing the gravel shallows just before and after dawn. I had decided on an all-night session to see if I could tempt out a big chub that I had found sitting tight under the alders. I felt that he might venture into the shallows to feed at night. Not only did I catch the fish I was after, but at dawn the following morning I was fascinated to observe several dorsals arrowing through the shallow water as perch harassed shoals of minnows. I had a couple of perch on that occasion to just over 2lb on lobs, but soon found that the best bait in those circumstances was, not surprisingly, a loose-lined minnow.

This is possibly the most exciting form of small-river perch fishing of all, the restriction being that it is only effective in the period of half-light around day-break. As soon as it is fully light, the perch depart the shallows. For the method to be at its most effective, I used to like a completely still night so there were no ripples from the wind on the water. I would be in position at least two hours before dawn, sitting as close to the surface of the water as possible. I had to keep very still as the fishing was at very short range and the fish therefore easily spooked. Not long after the first swirl was observed, the activity would build up to a peak until the light intensity reached a certain level and then it would stop just as suddenly.

During that magic hour, I would cast to the swirls, either legering the minnow with a single swan shot, or using an AAA to give a little casting weight, and would fish the minnow on the move. Takes were spectacular with either presentation, with perch smashing ferociously into the bait. This was the biggest problem. If you were

Four perch caught at dawn – three of them weighing over 2lb.

An early morning catch from the shallows using free-lined minnows.

unprepared for the savagery of the take and could not give a little slack line immeditely the first pluck was felt, bite after bite would be missed. The best perch I ever took with this method was 2lb 14oz and that fish gave me a memorable struggle in the shallow water. It reached the deep water downstream of the shallows and I got two wet feet landing the fish, but it was well worth it.

The run from the shallows to the blackthorns was undoubtedly the most reliable perch swim on the entire fishery and, apart from the special circumstance of algal concentrations already discussed, I learned many valuable lessons in small-stream perch fishing in several happy seasons. The first one was that the most predictable time to catch a specimen was at dawn in the summer. On a bright morning, every hour of daylight that passed lessened the chances of taking good fish and on the vast majority of occasions, the first bite yielded the biggest fish. So overwhelming is the evidence of this from my own records that it cannot be coincidence. I came to the conclusion that, as well as light intensity being a very important factor, the fish are so voracious at first light that they lose much of their customary caution. I have used this fact to my advantage in the years since those days in locating big perch in other streams. If a swim is fished at dawn for a couple of days without response, or with just small perch resulting, I discount the area for that season.

Earlier, I mentioned the importance of light intensity and how perch dislike strong light. For this reason, as soon as the dawn half-light period was over, I found that it was necessary to present my baits as close to the weed beds as possible. Arranging for the float to actually touch the rushes or fishing in tiny gaps in the midst of dense lilies meant that the feeding period was extended. The bigger fish obviously hide themselves away in the foliage where they are perfectly camouflaged, venturing out to intercept anything that has the temerity to come too close. This was very important. Many times a bait remained untouched when presented only inches away from rushes, but if I re-cast such that the float was touching them a bite resulted immediately.

One occasion stands out in my mind. I took a neighbour to fish the river, set him up with the correct gear in the swim and then left him to it. My parting instructions were to lay on lobworms as close to the mid-river rush bed as he could get them. I wandered a long way upstream to investigate a new swim I had found and it was perhaps two hours after day-break when I popped back to see how Bob was doing. He was sitting there quite happily and patiently, but reported that he had not as yet had any bites. The quill float was lying at half cock a good foot away from those all-important rushes and I suggested that he re-cast his tackle much closer. His first cast was perfect, the float settling right among the outer stems. He was about to place the rod in its rest when the float shot up in the water, lay flat and then disappeared into the foliage. Pretty soon, I was netting a personal best of 2lb 2oz for him. The next cast was a repeat performance with a perch 2oz less. He looked at me as if I were some kind of magician. It is great when an angling principle can be practically demonstrated so graphically.

The laid-on lob was the presentation which produced most of my summer fish from the Claydon Brook, but it always paid to keep an open mind. There were days, admittedly rare, when whole lobs would not be taken properly and I had to revert to scraps of lob or redworms on smaller hooks to get positive takes. More common was the necessity to change the presentation during a session. It was common to take two or three fish quickly on the laid-on bait and then find it ignored thereafter. A change to an off-bottom trotted bait usually yielded an extra bite or two. My biggest fish from my favourite run was caught this way. Within half an hour of day-break, I had taken fish of 2lb 4oz and 1lb 14oz on laid-on lobs and then the swim died for an hour. I then pushed the float down a foot and moved the single swan shot under the float to present a slow-sinking and moving bait. The second trot down the edge of the rushes with this presentation yielded a tremendous perch of 3lb 6oz.

An area where trotting tactics really came into their own was immediately downstream of the gravel shallows where the water deepened quite suddenly and there was a pronounced undercut under the steep near bank. A deadly presentation was to trot lobs or minnows along the near-bank fringe, holding the float back periodically to allow the bait to swing under the cover. This area was particularly good when there was extra water in the river and a fond memory is of a miserable drizzly August morning when my first three trots resulted

A plump 2½-pounder.

in perch of 2lb 11oz, 2lb 13oz and 3lb 2oz. When I think of the state of the Claydon Brook today after several murderous dredgings, substantial water abstraction and regular pollution over the last few years, it brings a lump to my throat.

Although the summer was always my favourite time to search for those perch, my three biggest catches came in the winter months, as did my first three-pounder. These all came from the little backwater, up to a distance of 100 yards or so upstream of its confluence with the mill-pool. When the backwater had first been opened up by the initial dredging, I had adopted the same tactic that I had used on my first visit to the river – that of walking in the river in swimming trunks looking for depth variations. This revealed three quite pronounced depressions around a right-angled bend. One of these, right on the bend itself, was especially interesting since a good bed of cabbages grew there, effectively disguising the existence of the depression to the casual observer. Knowledge of this feature in the winter when the water rose and coloured up was an important advantage. As I had walked the river, I knew exactly where to place my bait to fish it right amongst those lily roots. Just as summer fishing demanded that the bait be hard against the rushes, it also had to be positioned exactly in the winter for consistent success.

On a mild December morning I found the river a foot up and coloured. The backwater was flowing steadily and after a couple of fruitless hours chubbing, I arrived at the bend swim and laid on a large lob amongst those lily roots. To hold the bait in position required a float carrying two swan shot, fished about two feet overdepth. There were three bites that day: a small roach; a perch of 1½lb; and then at about midday, the fish I had been waiting for – a lovely perch of 3lb 2oz.

As if that were not exciting enough, the following weekend was to result in a capture that I still rank as one of the most notable captures of my career. I returned to fish the same swim, but when I started I realised that laying on would be impossible. The river was much faster and dirtier, although not appreciably higher. If I had been fishing a near-bank run, I could have used a heavy float, but holding a bait in the mid-river depression demanded the use of leger tackle. I had never been very successful with tight-line legering for perch. I could get bites all right, but most were missed. The perch seemed very intolerant of resistance and dropped a bait as soon as it was felt. To try and alleviate this problem, I set up with the rod pointing straight down the line at the bait – a lob anchored in position by a three-swan sliding link – and held about three feet of slack line in my left hand. The idea was to give line as soon as I felt any indication and the method quickly proved its efficiency when I had fish of 1lb and 1½lb not long after starting to fish.

A nice brace. The roach weighed 1lb 15oz and the perch showed 2lb 7oz on the scales.

As the morning wore on, the conditions rapidly deteriorated. There was a definite lowering of temperature and by early afternoon the light drizzle had turned to steady sleet. I was wet, cold and uncomfortable and was thinking about packing up early when there was a sharp jab on the rod top and the line was pulled through my numb fingers. The line began to move upstream and I set the hook into a perch that certainly did itself no justice in so far as the fight was concerned. It was landed very quickly indeed, but when I lifted it out in the landing net I caught my breath in excitement – it was enormous, and when I registered a weight of 3lb 14oz I just could not believe it. The sleet (which was falling more and more heavily) was forgotten as I gazed at that magnificent creature before slipping it back. Without a second thought I packed up there and then, a very happy man indeed.

Almost exactly a year to the day after I caught that perch, I had another from the same swim of 3lb 13oz, to be followed a few weeks later by another of 3lb 10oz. I am sure that all three captures were of the same fish. I was looking forward to making its acquaintance when it went over 4lb, but sadly the terrible perch disease put an end to that dream, as well as marking the beginning of the end of my relationship with the Claydon Brook.

Returning a small pike to my favourite perch swim.

BIG CHUB

During my summer fishing on the Claydon Brook, my normal approach was to fish for perch for the first few hours of daylight and as soon as they had gone off, revert to chubbing with natural baits. After the dredging in 1961, I had been lucky enough to take two five-pounders during the winter, the best at 5lb 4oz. We had all fished for the very big fish we had seen in the backwater, but to no avail. In June 1962 the areas of the river that had been choked with rushes from bank to bank the previous summer were now much more open and consequently the chub were much easier to spot.

It was at about midday on my second trip of the season that I caught sight of an absolutely monstrous fish over the gravel, close to a small road bridge. This particular area was always frequented by a shoal of chub, but I had never spotted this individual before. I felt that he could weigh over 7lb. That first occasion in fact gave me an excellent chance of catching him, since he was on his own and there would be no competition for the bait from lesser fish. Being careful to stay as unobtrusive as possible, I flicked out a large black slug and, perhaps surprisingly under the circumstances, the cast was perfect – the slug landed about two yards upstream of the fish. By the time the bait had settled it was no more than a foot from the chub's nose. It was then that I believe my inexperience cost me a chance at the fish. The chub very slowly sidled up to the bait and gave it the tiniest nudge before departing from the swim. A short while later he had circled the swim and returned to the bait. Again he was hesitant and as he once again shied away, there was a savage lunge on the rod top and a small pike left the water with my slug firmly clamped in his jaws. The chub disappeared. I now know, after a great many more years of chubbing, that slugs are a much more effective bait when fished on the move. Had I twitched the bait after it had come to rest, I may well have induced a bite from the fish.

A few weeks later I was to be foiled again by a small fish taking a bait intended for the leviathan. I had found him in the company

Slipping back one of my first Claydon Brook five-pounders.

of a few other chub and had risked a cast. Predictably, one of the smaller fish got to the lobworms first and my chance was gone. I cursed myself for my impatience, but it was a mistake I would not make again.

I was given a golden opportunity in the late autumn, when I spotted the fish again in the same swim and this time he was alone. Two lobs landed almost on his nose, promoting the most savage reaction. In a blur he had engulfed the lobs and rocketed into the far-bank rushes with them. Everything was solid. Telling myself to keep calm, I carefully waded across the stream to the rushes. If I could extricate the line from the stems without alarming the fish, I would have an excellent chance of landing him. I nearly succeeded. Just as the line came free, there was a tremendous swirl and the chub shot through the other side of the rush bed. There was a sudden lessening of tension and then the limp line came fluttering back to me. I had never felt more devastated in my angling career.

During the following close season, I had two reconnaissance trips to the river with my parents and both were memorable. On the first I saw what were undoubtedly the two biggest fish I ever found. In the narrow mill-race almost under the farmhouse two huge chub lay together in the current. My father and I watched them for ages and I will state emphatically that the bigger of the pair could well have weighed 8lb. I was never to see them again. On the second trip I found my old adversary, in the usual station by the bridge, and plans were laid to capture him on opening morning.

Before light on 16 June I tackled up with lunker gear, 8lb line and a size 2 hook adorned with the biggest slug I could find. Positioning myself behind the head-high rushes adjacent to the clear gravel holding area, I tossed the bait over the rushes and heard it 'plop' into the water. I waited expectantly.

No more than a couple of minutes after the bait had come to rest there was a terrific lunge on the rod top. As I struck and scrambled to my feet, a very heavy fish shot downstream towards the shallows. Heart pounding with excitement, I played that fish very carefully – all the snags were successfully negotiated and before long a big chub sagged heavily in the landing net. Even in the dawn half-light I could see that the fish was a personal best and thought that it could go as much as 6lb. In actual fact he weighed 5lb 10oz, and was in pristine condition – short, deep and without a scale out of place. For a time I thought that fish was the one I had been after, which made my original estimate way off the target. It was when I put the fish back on the shallows after day-break that I realised that it was a different specimen. It was too short; the chub I had been chasing for over a season was at least 2in longer and appeared a lot paler in the water.

July came and went and then, in the second week of August, I found the chub again, this time in the company of five much lesser companions. I remembered the lesson I had learned the previous summer and resisted the temptation to fish for him with those smaller fish in such close attendance. Without showing myself, I wandered upstream. I checked periodically to see if I could find the fish on his own.

In early afternoon decision time came. I arrived back at the swim to find the big fish lying in the clear water over the mid-stream gravel and could only see one other chub with him. The second fish was a yard downstream and closer in to my bank, so I decided to risk a cast upstream of the big one. In the event, I badly miscast and instead of the bait landing nicely upstream of the lunker, it actually fell between the chub. For a second my heart sank, but for a change the gods were on my side that day. The small fish shot forward, but before he could intercept the double lobworm offering, the big fellow had whirled round and engulfed it in one savage movement.

As he had done the previous time I had hooked him, the chub shot across the river, seeking the sanctuary of the far-bank rushes. This time, however, I was prepared. It was not for nothing I was using 8lb line and a size 2 hook. I clamped the reel, stopping the fish dead in his tracks. For a second or two he thrashed at the surface and then gave it up, preferring to make for the mid-river cabbages downstream of me instead. Again I held him hard, not allowing an inch of line. I knew that once he reached the lily roots it could be game, set and match and I would rather lose him now than be forced to pull for a break, hopelessly snagged. But the tackle was sound, there were no mistakes and before long an absolutely monstrous chub was being swung over the marginal irises. The first thing I noticed about the fish was the poor condition it was in which was very unusual for the Claydon Brook in those days – all the fish were usually immaculate. I put it down as a very old fish that had probably weighed a lot more in its time. One of my biggest regrets is that I did not take length and girth measurements, but I did record the weight. That chub registered 6lb 12oz, still my best ever by a long way and, as I cannot get interested in stillwater chubbing, it is probably destined to be the biggest chub I will ever catch in my lifetime.

Almost a year later to the day, I was to take another very big chub, this time weighing 5lb 14oz from a swim I called the Sheep Dip – the river at that point was adjacent to a pen the farmer used as (not surprisingly) a sheep dip. I was actually roach fishing that morning. Of all the swims on the river, I had consistently spotted the biggest roach in the Sheep Dip, which was a beautiful steady glide harbouring a dense mid-stream cabbage patch. As I remember, I was fishing stewed wheat which was my favourite big roach bait in those days. I had only taken two average fish when, at about mid-morning, a colossal chub drifted into view, picked up a couple of grains of wheat and then disappeared back into the aquatic undergrowth.

There was a quick change of plan. Off came my 2lb line, to be replaced by a spool of 6lb line and soon two lobworms were waiting in ambush amongst the grains of wheat. I sat back behind some willow herb to wait quietly and patiently and then, to my chagrin, I saw two swans rapidly bearing down on my swim from downstream. Hoping they would go through my swim without stopping I sat in silence but, to my annoyance, one of them found the wheat on the exposed gravel when they were opposite me. Within seconds both were feeding with gusto. My line lifted sharply and in disgust I began to wind in; the last thing I wanted was a foul-hooked swan. I was taken completely by surprise when there was a sudden vicious lunge on the rod and then the lilies parted as a big fish ploughed downstream through them. By the time I had scrambled to my feet, the fish was in the clear water over the shallow cattle drink and I could see that I had been very lucky. Instead of being inextricably tangled in the cabbages as I should have been, the line had somehow lifted straight through them and I was still in direct contact. With the fish fighting far away from any dangerous snags, the outcome of the battle was never in any further doubt and a few minutes later I was admiring the second biggest chub of my career.

I am almost certain that I made the acquaintance of that same fish twice more during the 1966/1967 season and both times it weighed 6lb 4oz. The first time, in July, was on a day that was memorable for a different reason in that it was the first occasion when I caught two chub both over 5lb in a session. In fact, I never expect to better the catch of chub I had that day. I caught eight fish that weighed 3lb 4oz, 3lb 6oz, 3lb 14oz, 4lb 6oz, 4lb 8oz, 4lb 10oz, 5lb 4oz and 6lb 4oz; a red-letter day indeed.

When I caught the big one again in January it was the result of stubborness (or

A four-pounder is returned.

An early four-pounder.

stupidity) as much as anything else. I remember that I had been quite ill over the Christmas period and although I was still feeling a bit rough, I decided to go for a day's chubbing in Buckinghamshire. Almost as soon as I arrived I knew that it was a mistake. I felt terrible all day, but stuck it out until mid-afternoon when the cold drizzle turned to much heavier and more persistent rain. All day I sat in one swim, the tail of the thorn bushes under a raft of debris and had only one bite to show for it, on legered lob. But it was well worth the discomfort and I packed up early quite happily. What would I give nowadays to catch one six-pounder in a season, let alone two?

Although I have no way of proving it, I do believe that I met up with that chub for a fourth and last time in February 1971, when he weighed 5lb 14oz again. Coincidentally, he figured again as the starring role in a duo of five-pounders, his co-star being a 5¼-pounder. That was another day which stands out in my diary. As well as the two five-pounders, there were also two four-pounders, a roach of 1lb 10oz and a brace of 2lb perch for good measure.

Space forbids describing the numerous other captures of chub between 5lb and 5lb 8oz I made in those halcyon days of the sixties and early seventies. I did not realise at the time quite how incredible was the quality of the chubbing I was enjoying; I do now. When I look at the pitiful wreck my beloved stretch of the Claydon Brook has become following dredging, pollution and a lowering of the water table by abstraction,

Merv Wilkinson with a Claydon Brook perch weighing just under 2lb.

I really could cry. Now that I am middle aged I can appreciate what Dick Walker meant when he said that you should never go back to the scene of a past angling triumph. You should be content to rest with your memories.

I will end this section on a lighter note. It was a cold, wet day in November 1967 and Mervyn Wilkinson had come with me for one of his first visits to Padbury. At about mid-morning my legered lob was picked up by a fish that shot under the opposite bank in very purposeful manner. I managed to haul it out but then the fish, which I could now see was a double-figure pike, became snared in the mid-river cabbage roots. Seeing that I was into a good fish, Merv came along to lend a hand. The bank at that point was quite high and slippery and following the persistent rain it was easy to lose one's footing. Carefully, Merv picked his way to the water's edge and waited with the net.

I leaned into the pike; still it refused to budge, but as the pressure was increased it suddenly came free and shot off upstream. The slackening of tension was enough to unbalance me from my already precarious foothold and I fell backwards, my feet shooting from under me. As they did so, the toes of both my boots caught Merv very neatly up the backside, propelling him gracefully into four feet of icy cold water. When he eventually stood on the bank next to me (which took several minutes as he lost his grip twice and slid back in, and I was too busy laughing to be capable of helping him) he made a comical spectacle, covered from head to toe in mud and slime. It was the first time I had actually seen anyone purple-faced with rage, and I thought he was going to burst a blood vessel. After directing a torrent of invective in my direction (including several interesting and new words, which roughly translated suggested I should be more careful in future) Merv calmed down and saw the humour of the situation. More than twenty years later, I can still laugh at that memory. It was like a Laurel and Hardy sketch.

THE PLAYFUL BULL

One of the hazards of fishing the Claydon Brook was that the bulk of the farm land was devoted to cattle, both beef and dairy. All anglers know what an absolute pain inquisitive cattle can be when you are trying to fish. They are forever crowding around, slobbering over everything in sight and generally making a nuisance of themselves. I remember having a pair of rubber overtrousers ripped clean off one day when a particularly persistent Friesian took a liking to them! Very rarely, however, are cattle dangerous with the obvious exception of a stud bull, but it does pay to treat them with respect. I will never forget an incident that happened only a few years ago at a local carp water.

There were about thirty bullocks in the field and a pair of swans and four cygnets were preening on the bank, quite a distance from the water. Without warning the bullock nearest the swans set off straight for them at a gallop. This seemed to trigger a case of mass hysteria, for within seconds there was a headlong stampede towards the lake. The swans scattered, five of the six making it back to the water safely. The remaining cygnet, in his panic however, went the wrong way. Instead of heading for the water, he went along the field towards the hedge. His wings were not yet very strong and he half ran and half flew until he was trapped against the fence. The bullocks were on him in an instant. There were quite a few of us watching the incident and until now it had appeared quite funny. But we all went very quiet when the cattle continually reared on their hind legs and stamped the poor cygnet to pulp. It was a chastening experience. Naturalists tell us that gang violence is not confined to humans and that was a vivid example of exactly that type of behaviour.

In the mid-sixties the farmer had a particularly skittish herd of bullocks in residence in the meadow bordering the best chub stretch. On my first two or three trips that summer those bullocks almost made serious angling impossible as I was continually checking their whereabouts to make sure that my tackle was not being demolished. By about mid-July, however, they had become used to me and from then on treated me as they did the farm hands – they totally ignored me!

There was, however, one notable exception. One of the bullocks, whom I called Ferdinand but who had been named Ebenezer by the farmer, was totally crazy. He was always charging around the field, kicking his feet in the air, dashing in and out of the shallow water and generally livening up the proceedings. Whenever he saw me enter his field, he would gallop towards me at break-neck speed, bellowing as loudly as his lungs would let him. It was quite a nerve-racking sight, but he was only exuberant – he would always stop short of a collision with me and would lick my jacket with that great rough tongue of his. He liked nothing better than to be stroked on the head like a dog and would follow me round for the first half-hour or so. After that he calmed down and left me in peace. Ebenezer and I became firm friends that summer and despite his initially threatening appearance, he was as gentle as a lamb.

One day in August, I took a work colleague down to the Claydon Brook to try and catch him his first chub. Ian had not been fishing very long, but was as keen as mustard and had been wanting to have a session with me for weeks. It never occurred to me to warn Ian about Ebenezer; in fact I never realised that he, being city-born and bred, was terrified of farm animals. He was paranoid about it. Anyway, just after dawn we climbed the stile and made our way across the wet grass towards the river. Ebenezer was about a hundred yards away. He looked up and on seeing us let off a thunderous bellow and set off on a mad dash across the meadow, grunting and snorting as he ran. I never had time to explain. With a scream Ian was off, dropping his tackle and heading for the river some thirty yards away. He never even hesitated. Upon reaching the bank, he dived across the marginal reed mace into about three feet of water and flailed his way to the far shore. He was like a man possessed, with arms whirling like windmill blades and his face a picture of abject terror. I can never remember being so helpless with laughter as I was that morning. Ian, however, never quite got over the experience.

2 Days at the Park

CRUCIANS THAT LIKED BLOOD

In the mid-sixties most of my tench fishing activities centred around Fawsley, a park complex in Northamptonshire. There were three pools at Fawsley, all containing good fish of many species and we used to concentrate most of our efforts at the largest of the trio. The dam end of that water was very popular with tench anglers, and plenty of average fish were taken. The water also had a reputation for big pike and some very big eels, as well as very elusive large roach. I never did manage to take a large catch or any exceptionally big tench, but had a lot of fun for several years taking two or three nice fish most times I went there.

During the mid-sixties I took this roach from Fawsley – my first big one at 1lb 10oz.

One very hot summer afternoon I went for a stroll round the smallest of the three lakes which was largely neglected by anglers as it was very choked with lilies. The intimacy of this water appealed to me and I decided that on my next visit to the park I would bring a drag and create a small swim in the midst of the cabbages. The following weekend, three of us had decided to make it a team effort and after an hour of hard labour, we had made a swim big enough to fish side by side, using one rod apiece. The standard groundbait for tench in those days was the old faithful, bread and bran and this is what we used on that day, plus about 100 assorted worms. That first morning in the new swim gave us the biggest catch of tench we were ever to enjoy – about twenty fish between us to a maximum weight of nearly four pounds. I also hooked, and lost, one of the water's few and very elusive mirror carp.

After a few weeks the catches started to tail off and we began to give thought to our baiting procedure. One of my companions came up with the idea of incorporating blood in the bait, following an article we had read about tench's liking for this particular delicacy! His uncle could obtain the blood from the local abattoir and we all agreed that it was worth a try. My worst fears were realised. Using blood in the groundbait was indeed a messy, disgusting business, but the first time we used it we certainly caught more tench than we had for several weeks. The bites on blood-soaked bread paste (which most of the fish came on) were very bold, socking the float away with no preliminaries. One day, however, I started to experience frustrating tiny lifts and trembles on my large baits that I simply could not connect with. In the middle of these incessant indications, I did have two confident bites and duly landed two tench. I put the small bites down to the tench wising up to our tactics.

The next weekend, however, the small bites started to get to us all. I scaled right down to 2lb line, used a small lift float shotted right down by only a single AA, and baited a size 16 hook with a tiny scrap of my blood paste. Within a few minutes of making this modification, I had a lovely slow lift and struck into a fish that fought much differently to a tench. Whatever I had hooked scampered around the swim very energetically and I was amazed eventually to see a lovely crucian carp in the net. The biggest crucian I had ever caught until then had been a fish weighing about a pound from the Oxford Canal, so this specimen of 2lb 2oz was a delightful and unexpected bonus. At the end of the day I had taken two more weighing 1¼ pounds and one of my companions had caught a fish of 1lb 13oz. We determined that on our next session we would fish for those crucians from the off.

That next trip was to produce a crucian that is still my personal best some twenty-five years later. We started fishing at the crack of dawn with our lift tackle and initially landed a run of hard-fighting tench that took ages to land on the light gear. At about mid-morning, my friend Ken had a crucian of exactly 2lb and that was the signal for a spate of bites in the next couple of hours. Most of the action was experienced by Ken at first and neither Dave nor I had even seen a crucian when Ken was landing his fourth – a magnificent 3¼-pounder. I was just wondering what I had to do to get a bite, when my float lifted gracefully in the water, lay flat and began to move towards the lilies to my left. The fight was dogged on the 2lb line and I played that fish very carefully. I could obviously feel its weight and also knew that it was not a tench. Very early on in the fight I had seen a broad flash of brassy gold. Thankfully, all the lily roots were safely negotiated and I soon landed a crucian that took my breath away. It was almost the twin of Ken's big fish, weighing

1oz less at 3lb 3oz. After taking that fish I caught three others, one of which was over 2lb and Ken took two more nice fish as well.

Throughout the following week we counted the hours until we could renew our acquaintance with those beautiful little carp, but we were never to catch one again. Several more sessions that summer failed to produce another bite and the following year we never did find them. Shortly afterwards that lovely lake was netted and turned into a trout fishery and those super crucians were lost for ever.

BIG ROACH AT NIGHT

The Fawsley Park pools had long held a reputation for containing large roach, although they were caught very rarely and in the late seventies Trefor and I decided to have a crack at them. The few big roach that had been landed had always come at night and so that is when we decided we would fish for them. The plan was to arrive at the water about an hour before sunset to give us time to pre-bait and tackle up and then fish into the early hours of the morning.

Our initial sessions were very interesting but also very frustrating. We obviously started off with legering tactics, using swingtips fitted with Betalights, but soon found that the roach bites were almost impossible to connect with. There were many times during those nights when the tip would rise to the horizontal and hold there, but still the majority of bites were missed.

One night in particular nearly drove us crazy – Trefor and I must have had over

Trefor with a magnificent roach weighing 2lb 9oz.

thirty good indications between us and landed the princely sum of three roach, one to me and two to Trefor. All the bites came to large pieces of bread flake, the most consistent bait of all for big roach and we thought that perhaps our large baits were responsible for the missed bites. They may have been, but the fact remains that scaling down to smaller fragments of bread or maggots never gave us a bite from a large roach while small fish became a nuisance. It was obvious that the problem lay in the bait presentation and on one session Trefor and I thought up different ways of solving it.

Trefor's was the more obvious solution and, as it turned out, the more effective. He float fished with a torch beam directed on the float and on the first night caught three nice roach that way. The bites were beauties with the float lifting and sailing away very confidently. I was not too happy about using a torch, and tried to figure out a way of making the legered presentation more efficient. What I came up with was, I suppose, a version of a hair rig. I tied up my normal end tackle using a size 10 hook with a good chunk of flake and then, off the bend of the hook I tied in an inch of 2lb line, carrying a size 18 and baited with a fragment of crust. I was trying to imitate the appearance of a piece of bread from which a small scrap had broken away. It was a very fiddly rig to tie up and I only ever used it the one night. The only bite I had resulted in a fish very badly hooked with both hooks and the idea was abandoned.

By the following summer, I had equipped myself with a home-made two swan-shot sliding float, equipped with a built-in Betalight and so I was then able to enjoy fairly consistent sport. I only had a few sessions, but they all saw one or two good roach come to net. It took me some time to get used to the bites to expect using the Betalight, because the light reflections were initially very confusing. It was best employed on a calm night, otherwise the wind-ripple made the distorted light reflections very difficult to concentrate on. The technique was to use an AAA very close to the bait (about two inches away at most) and fish one swan shot and one AAA about three feet up the line. By fishing overdepth, the float would of course cock very high in the water. After dark this would appear as two streaks of light separated by a wide black band. When the rod was placed in two rests and the line tightened, that black band would gradually narrow until it disappeared altogether. At that stage, the Betalight was obviously flush with water and the float at its correct fishing position. This tight line presentation was deadly and extremely sensitive – the slightest lift of the float, which may have been difficult to detect in daylight, became very obvious as a narrow black band re-appeared between the two halves of the light.

I did not need to detect any such minor indications during my sessions – the bites were very easy to see and to hit once the basic presentation had been worked out. The normal lift-and-lay flat type of bite gave an unmistakable indication: the dark band widened very rapidly and then the two halves of the light seemed to fall towards one another, in an ever-narrowing angle as the float keeled over. It was a fascinating way of fishing and I really ought to do a lot more of it. Of course, if the float went under, the light (being twice as long because of its own reflection) seemed to disappear twice as fast as normal. This effect led to some incredible optical effects – one second there would be a bright streak twenty yards out in the blackness, the next it had disappeared. It was as if someone had thrown a switch.

I became side-tracked from that highly entertaining roach fishing by some big gravel pit tench before I managed to catch a two-pounder. My best over those two summers was 1lb 14oz – I believe that Trefor's best was 1oz bigger.

I have often thought about devoting another summer to those big roach as there are certainly bigger ones that we never caught, but something else always seems to take precedence. Whether I ever go back or not, I will always look back on those nocturnal excursions in that beautiful park with a great deal of affection.

A GHOULISH REPAST

The old bailiff at Fawsley was one of the greatest characters I have met during my angling career. He was a real old countryman with a gnarled and ruddy complexion and, I would think, well into his eighties at the time of the incident I am about to relate. Although he was quite a likeable old boy he was also, at times, quite the most cantankerous man I have every met. Woe betide anyone who did not have the correct licence, or who parked their car in the wrong place.

He was a very keen angler himself (although I believe that the only water he ever fished was Fawsley) and every weekend you could find him in his favourite swim in the corner of the dam, fishing for the tench. Most weekends he had his friend with him, an invalid who fished out of his wheelchair, and I can still see the bailiff's rickety old van crossing the field, bringing his companion down to the water's edge.

They always had a filthy, decrepit old paraffin stove with them and a motley assortment of ancient iron cooking utensils; story had it that they ate everything they caught, be it roach, bream, tench or whatever. I had never been quite sure whether to believe some of the wilder stories, although the bailiff had twice begged small pike from me which I had caught in the winter.

One summer's evening I was settling down to an all-night session after the tench and, just before dark, the bailiff came round for a chat. Night fishing was not officially allowed, but those anglers who were regulars and whom he knew could behave themselves were allowed to fish after dark. During the conversation (or at least that part of the conversation I could comprehend through the filthy pipe that was permanently jammed between his black teeth) the bailiff explained to me that it had been a long time since he had tasted eel which apparently was his favourite meal. As he noticed I was using lobworms, he asked if I would keep any eels I caught for him. I was happy enough to comply with this, although I had never taken an eel from the lake before. That night I had several fair tench, a 1½lb roach and, as luck would have it, a good eel of 3lb 10oz which I killed.

At about 9 a.m. the next morning I went round to their swim, taking the eel with me. I arrived just as they were about to prepare breakfast and watched with horrified fascination at what followed. The bailiff put about a pound of lard in the old cast iron frying pan which he placed on the grimy stove until the fat was hot and sizzling. At that point he picked up the eel and laid it in the pan. It was neither beheaded, gutted nor even washed. It just went in as it was – covered in blood, slime, bits of mud and grass. As if that were not enough, the two occupants of his keep net – a tench of about two pounds and a ¾ pound crucian – were summarily hit on the head and laid to rest alongside the eel.

After about ten minutes this gastronomic delight was judged fit for consumption and the two gourmets tucked in with relish. At the end of the repast the entire contents of the pan had been devoured and I felt physically sick. As the bailiff wiped his greasy mouth on his sleeve and grinned at me with those horrible discoloured teeth, it was not difficult to believe that I may just have been watching something from a horror film!

3 Throop Recollections

Without a doubt, the Dorset Stour is one of my favourite rivers and for many years I devoted a high proportion of my fishing time to the famous Throop Fishery. The first time I ever fished there was during a two-week holiday with my parents in 1961, staying at the caravan park above Iford Bridge. It took me quite a few days to come to terms with the streamy water and the characteristics that were totally different to those I was used to on the more sedate Midland rivers. My catches during that holiday reflected my inexperience and I caught very few fish of any reasonable size. There was, however, one notable exception. At dusk one day, I was legering a large chunk of cheese paste about fifty yards below the small weir and my one and only bite produced a chub of 5lb 2oz, which was the first five-pounder I had ever taken.

That big chub was obviously exciting enough, but what made the holiday even more memorable was that I saw my first ever barbel. Towards the end of my stay, another angler fishing nearby caught two fish of over 7lb in quick succession. Those barbel had a profound effect on me. I just had to catch one and so I decided that on my last day I would fish the weir-pool from dawn till dark.

I was settled in the swim long before daylight and cast out an enormous lump of cheese paste. For hour after hour I sat there biteless but eventually, at about midday, I had a savage pull on the rod top. I can still remember how excited I was as I played that fish, but the excitement did not last long. It turned out to be an eel weighing 3lb 12oz, still my biggest of the species. I have detested eels ever since.

It was actually not until several years later that I landed my first Throop barbel. During the early days of the Coventry Specimen Group, we all made regular pilgrimages to the water for the barbel fishing and most of us had one or two fish. The best I managed was a shade under 8lb. Those early Throop trips were a lot of fun, with time spent learning the art of catching a fish which was quite new to the majority of us. There were quite a few laughs as well and one incident in particular still makes me chuckle now.

On our trips to Dorset we used to sleep rough, parking in a quiet country lane and either sleeping as best we could in the cramped cars, or on bedchairs under our umbrellas. One Friday night it was exceptionally foggy, with literally only a couple of yards visibility. I was with a colleague Mick Jelfs in his rickety old Ford Anglia and we crawled along a narrow lane for what seemed hours in the dark and the fog, looking for a safe place to park for the night. Eventually, the verge suddenly opened out on our left to a wide, flat, grassy area – a perfect place to pull the car off the road. On a previous trip we had both tried to get comfortable in the front seats of the Anglia and as they did not recline, that was an impossible job. So this time we had come equipped with bedchairs and sleeping bags. In no time at all, two umbrellas had been erected and we were settled down for the night. I was the first to awake on a lovely bright sunny morning. I rolled over in my bag and found myself looking straight into someone's front window, barely five yards away. A face was looking back at me, with an expression of absolute horror. That flat grassy area was in fact a beautifully maintained front lawn, or had been until Mick had put tyre tracks right across the middle of it! In the circumstances, the owners of the property were quite understanding, but Mick and I had to endure a verbal barrage initially.

In September 1972, I caught a barbel from Throop that was to remain my personal best for the species for fifteen years. We had been concentrating on the swims immediately upstream of the bypass bridge – swims that had the reputation of holding barbel of larger than average size. My swim consisted of a deep glide of uniform, steady flow upstream of gravel shallows with large beds of streamer under the near bank. I settled into the swim about two hours before dark and for about an hour and a half I fed the swim steadily with free samples of luncheon meat, legering a 1in cube of meat under the streamer fronds. Tackle was a two swan-shot link leger, stopped 18in from a size 4 Au Lion d'Or hook to 8lb Maxima. The rod I was using at the time was an 11-foot Oliver's glass Avon.

Just as the light was beginning to fade there were a series of small taps on the rod top. The sensation on my finger was like a rasping as the line continually tightened and slackened. I do not know why I struck when I did, because I had ignored several other small plucks which I had attributed to dace. The indication was just different somehow. When I struck I was convinced I was snagged, since whatever I had hooked was totally unmoving. After a few minutes I got off my seat and went downstream to pull from a different angle. Suddenly the rod was slammed over and the clutch screamed as a powerful fish shot out to mid-river. I called out to Trefor, who was fishing thirty yards upstream, to come and watch the fun. It was a dogged rather than spectacular fight and for some time it was stalemate. When eventually Trefor netted the fish for me it was completely dark and in the torchlight we were both convinced it was a double. The scales, however, confirmed that it was 4oz short, at 9lb 12oz. That fish still remains one of only a small number of barbel that have given me any bite indication other than a strong pull.

Another very interesting session in the same swim occurred just a fortnight before I caught the nine-pounder. Trefor and I were fishing together again and in the early evening he shouted to say that he was into a good fish. I got up to go and watch and assist in the netting. As I walked towards him, I was looking directly into a very brilliant setting sun and, temporarily blinded, I walked straight into the river! At that point there was about seven feet of water which was moving quite strongly. It was a nasty moment and Trefor, who was naturally concerned for my safety, shouted 'Stop thrashing about, or you'll spook the barbel!'. When I had scrambled out, the only thing that was not soaked was my hat but, getting priorities right, I netted Trefor's fish for him, a plump eight-pounder.

I then made my sodden way back to the car to rustle up what dry clothing I could. I had no spare underwear or socks and when I eventually resumed fishing my sole attire was a tatty old jumper, a pair of lightweight rubber overtrousers, a fishing hat and carpet slippers! I fished like that until after dark and believe me, it got bloody cold! My persistence, courage and fortitude (stupidity for short) paid off at dusk when a tremendous wrench on the rod heralded the arrival of a barbel of 7½ pounds. Even more memorable than the fishing was having the gall to go and sit in a restaurant at night for a meal – still dressed the same way!

Three seasons later, once again in September, I had a good catch of Throop barbel on a weekend when conditions can only be described as diabolical. They were, without doubt, the worst weather conditions I have ever fished through. It rained non-stop for the two days and most of the time it was torrential. Coupled with this were severe, storm-force winds blowing in from the South Coast which made the use of an umbrella absolutely impossible. Fishing conditions were therefore uncomfortable to say the least. Consequently the river was very high and coloured and carrying tons of debris – which even included a garden shed! Submerged clumps of weed were the most troublesome items of debris – every few minutes the rod top would slowly bend round as the line became fouled and I was continually winding in to clear the tackle. This kept happening even though I was fishing my meat baits only inches from the near bank.

On the Saturday evening that same weekend I spent the last hour of daylight fishing the famous Barbel Bend area and just before dark managed my only fish of the day, a nice catch at 7lb 10oz. On the Sunday morning the conditions were laughable. Water was in all the fields and the river was full of fallen trees. The wind was so strong that it was difficult to walk against and all in all it was crazy to even contemplate fishing. But I had travelled a long way to fish Throop and was determined to give it a go. All morning, I wandered up and down the river, searching for a swim I could fish in comfort, but everywhere it was the same story – the bait hardly touched the bottom before the rod bent round as another clump of debris fouled the line. By about midday, I had not caught a thing and had convinced myself that it was probably hopeless attempting to fish on. I was on the point of packing up when the rod top slowly bent round, as it had a hundred times before. As I tried to wind in, everything was solid and immovable. After a couple of minutes pulling from different directions, I decided to pull for a break. As I did so there was a vicious tug which took me completely unawares and something powerful shot off downstream. Hurriedly I got the rod point up and after a very exciting fight in the heavy current, I landed a barbel of 7lb 9oz. That fish was caught from the Willow Tree swim, upstream of the School Bridge.

After landing that barbel I decided to fish on until dark and I was glad that I did, for the afternoon and evening were memorable. I spent another hour in the Willow Tree swim and then I had an unmistakable barbel bite, the kind of arm-wrenching thump I love so much. That fish took about fifteen minutes to land in the floodwater as it had the assistance of a pile of floating weed that became fouled during the fight. It was another splendidly-conditioned barbel of 7lb 4oz.

At about 4.30 p.m. I was back at Barbel Bend and thankfully the rain had now eased to a normal steady downpour. In the space of half an hour in the new swim I had another barbel and saw two anglers go in the river, both of whom could easily have drowned. An angler fishing opposite, who had the wind behind him, was vainly trying to use his umbrella, obviously without guy ropes. Eventually he hit upon the idea of sitting with the umbrella shaft across his lap, lashed to one of the legs of his fishing stool. You can probably guess what happened. Two or three minutes after he had settled down he must have lifted his weight momentarily from the stool to adjust his tackle. This allowed the wind to get undë his umbrella, which blew over his head and neatly catapulted him straight into the river. He scrambled out all right, but he never did recover his chair and umbrella.

Just after that entertaining little diversion, my rod nearly took off as a barbel decided it would rather eat my meat in Christchurch Harbour. I then had a real fight on my hands. The swims around Barbel Bend in those days were very fast and powerful in normal conditions, but with the river brimming to the top of the bank I was playing a big fish at the bottom of 14ft of extremely fast and turbulent floodwater. In fact, so fast was the current that I doubt whether I would have landed the fish without the arrival of another angler to lend a hand. The problem was that my big net was being continually swept away by the fast current as I tried to control it with my left hand, while simultaneously straining to hold the barbel against the torrent with my right. As it was the barbel was landed successfully and found to weigh 8lb 2oz.

Just after I had returned the fish the next drama occurred. My new-found compan-

Trefor caught this 5lb 2oz chub using trotted bread flake.

A five-pounder taken on crust.

My best Throop chub which weighed in at 5lb 6oz.

ion was standing chatting with his back to the river, when the bank collapsed and he disappeared into the deep floodwater. Fortunately my landing net was right to hand and I was able to haul him out. He was a very lucky man indeed. I last saw him squelching off into the distance. An hour later, about twenty yards upstream, I caught my last barbel at 7lb 7oz – this completed a very interesting, if wet, session.

As well as containing many big barbel, Throop is of course a superb chub fishery. Throughout the seventies, Trefor and I spent much of our winter fishing time there and we had countless large catches of good fish. One of the most memorable is a weekend in 1972 when Trefor had two five-

A nice eight-pounder is returned.

pounders, a 5lb 2oz sample on trotted flake and one at 5lb 8oz on legered crust. They were the highlights of a catch that included no fewer than thirteen fish weighing over 4lb between us, and thirty-three chub in all. That weekend my biggest weighed in at 4lb 14oz.

A Throop session that stands out in my diaries above all others is a three-day trip taken in March 1974 which turned out to be both very successful and yet heart-breaking at the same time; let me explain.

I was fishing the river with a match fishing friend who had expressed a desire to learn somethng about specimen hunting tactics. Fred was a very accomplished angler indeed and adapted well to the Stour, which was a very different river from those to which he was accustomed. I had a lot of fun watching his delight as he caught several chub bigger than he had ever taken before, with fish weighing up to 4½lb coming to his net. It was also great to see his almost childlike excitement when I caught a 7lb barbel, the first one he had ever seen.

Over our three days there, the conditions remained perfect, the chub fed well and by the evening of the last day I had taken nineteen chub with nine over 4lb, the top specimen again being 4lb 14oz. For the last hour or so Fred and I sat side by side at the tail of Pig Island. After about forty minutes of steady feeding and searching around with my crust baits, I eventually had a good pull which, after a stirring scrap, resulted in a huge chub of 5lb 6oz – a perfect end to any season.

After taking a few shots the light was fading fast and we were on the point of packing up when Fred struck at a good pull, fleetingly felt a fair fish and then it was gone. After that he wanted to fish for another ten minutes and so I also re-cast, this time with a large piece of cheese paste. To this day, I do not know why I baited with cheese instead of crust, but the fact remains that within seconds of the bait coming to rest in mid-river, there was an almighty lunge on the rod and a barbel raced downstream with the clutch buzzing angrily. After that initial savage run, the fish allowed itself to be led upstream quite easily. Perhaps a minute after it had been hooked, it rolled on the surface in front of me, giving me a very good look at itself – this was a barbel that was every ounce of 13lb. I was not to see it again, for it shot across the strong flow with great power and acceleration and tried to bury itself under the opposite bank; this is when tragedy struck. Somehow the line became caught fast under a large clay boulder where part of the bank had fallen in during the floods. For a minute or so there was a stalemate, with neither I nor the fish able to give or take line. A terrific bow wave then took off downstream and the line parted with a noise like a pistol shot. The last half-hour had aptly summed up the highs and lows of specimen hunting and the fine line that separates exultation and despair.

4 Tench Exploits

RESERVOIR TENCH – THE LEARNING YEARS

The first reservoir I ever fished as a child was Napton near Coventry, when I was taken there for a day's tench fishing by a neighbour who was a very keen angler. I was sixteen, had never before caught a tench, and the thing that stands out most in my mind is the groundbait we took with us. The traditional bread and bran was not for Bill, he had with him a sackful of the most foul-smelling manure which was absolutely seething with redworms and brandlings. Having set up shop to fish close to the rushes on the smaller of the two reservoirs, Bill proceeded to ladle in that stomach-wrenching slop, telling me in no uncertain terms to dip my hands in and help. My hands stank for weeks. Because of the nature of the 'feed', we were forced to fish at close range – no more than two rod lengths out – and Bill set us both up with a crude lift-float arrangement, the first time I had ever fished in that style.

All morning the surface of the water over the bait seethed and frothed so that it was a mass of bubbles. I am not sure whether it was tench bubbling or simply an advanced state of fermentation! Despite the activity we had but two bites each on redworms. All mine produced were a missed bite and a small roach, but Bill was able to show me two nice tench about 3½ pounds apiece. I remember marvelling at their velvety smoothness as I picked them up – tench have been one of my favourite fish ever since.

Another memorable night at Napton was when I took my first catch of tench there, in June 1964. It was my wife's second fishing trip with me and she had expressed a hope that there would be no disasters this time. On our first trip (to the Cherwell) the session had ended with myself being tossed over a fence by a bull. I promised my wife that no such misadventure was possible at Napton and in the early evening we settled down alongside the rushes at the smaller reservoir for a few relaxing hours in the late sunlight. For about two hours all was blissfully peaceful. I had managed my first two Napton tench, both of about 2½ pounds, and Fran then broke out the picnic basket she had brought, full of goodies like strawberry jam sandwiches and cream cakes. That was the signal for bedlam to break out. Within minutes of biting into our first sandwich we were surrounded by hundreds of wasps. I had set up over a nest! Leaping to her feet Fran yelled something at me about never asking her to go fishing with me again and then ran off screaming down the bank. That was the end of the tench fishing for that evening!

In the early days of the Coventry Specimen Group we all did a fair amount of tenching at Napton, never catching anything except very average fish, and in 1969 we were introduced to Clattercote Reservoir, near Banbury by Edwin Grant, a local angler who knew a lot about the water and who is sadly no longer with us. Clattercote produced a lot of 4lb tench and the occasional five-pounder, fish that were a class above those we were catching from Napton and so we set about coming to grips with this new water. I will never forget my first session there.

A fellow group member, Terry Jones and myself decided that we would fish the water from 16 June, that we would first create a brand new swim in the close season and that we would pre-bait it heavily and hopefully we would enjoy tench fishing of a quality we had never experienced before. We selected an area about half-way down the right-hand bank from the dam where it was very heavily overgrown, and for weeks we worked at removing rushes, cutting fallen trees and making a section of the bank fishable. After the swim had been created it was time to decide on the baiting programme, and I reverted to the principle my neighbour had employed at Napton – that of baiting with manure saturated with worms. It was Merv Wilkinson who came up with the bright idea of digging in a sewage farm and we made several trips there, filling large plastic sacks with the most unmentionable material which did, however, contain worms by the thousand. Several more trips were made to the reservoir to deposit this unsavoury mixture into the chosen area. This was a back-breaking job since the nearest car access point was a good half mile from the water and the heavy sacks had to be manhandled over quite a steep hill to get there.

At long last, 15 June arrived and at the stroke of midnight Terry and I cast out our baits. The time had come to enjoy the fruits of our labours. Dawn came and went and then Terry had the first bite – a lovely lift-and-sail-away affair. He missed it, but we were not despondent. The tench were obviously there and it was simply a matter of time before we caught any. All of a sudden, there was a commotion behind us and a very irate farmer appeared, shouting and waving his arms about. When I had calmed him down, it transpired that where we were fishing was actually out of bounds. The farmer allowed no fishing from that bank and no amount of pleading made the slightest difference. We would have to go there and then; all those hours of back-breaking graft only resulted in a few hour's fishing and one missed bite!

Clattercote Reservoir did teach me the efficiency of the swimfeeder for tench fishing and I had several good catches off the dam wall to this method. The best technique for consistent catches there, however, was undoubtedly the sliding float. Merv Wilkinson was again the master exponent of this method, showing us all how to go about it. I had never before fished a slider on the lift method in twenty feet of water, but once the technique was mastered it was deadly. That reservoir also taught me how important feeding is for maintaining the interest of estate lake or reservoir tench. The method was to re-cast the float every ten minutes or so and each time it settled, to catapult a pouchful of maggots around it. The number of times a bite followed quickly after the loose feed had touched the bottom cannot have been coincidence.

Tench up to low five-pounders were landed from Clattercote and it was soon time to move on again. Rumours were rife about a water that was producing not only 5lb tench, but occasionally ones over 6lb. This was barely credible, since a 6lb tench in those days was an almost impossible dream. We were assured it was genuine, however, so we all joined the club controlling this new tench Mecca, Sywell Reservoir near Northampton.

On one of my earliest trips to this new water I was pleased to witness Trefor West's new personal best – a tench of 5lb 10oz. Again, there was a change of style needed to tackle this water. Fish were caught at much longer range than on our previous waters, so legering was the order of the day. The

Trefor with a lovely 5lb 10oz Sywell fish.

feeder was again a popular method, but Trefor and I initially tackled the water with bigger baits such as flake and lobs, fished in conjunction with swingtips. We did very well, catching tench regularly, but not as well as Phil Smith who stunned the group members one day with a mammoth tench of 6lb 10oz, a fish we were all convinced none of us would ever surpass.

My biggest tench from Sywell, also weighing 5lb 10oz, came the season before Trefor and I moved on to TC and was caught on the second of two days that began disastrously. On the first day I was trying out some new size 12 hooks. They were aimed at the specialist angler and were supposed to be super-strong and I was fishing them on two matched swimfeeder rigs. Sod's law was to prevail that day as I had left my box containing all my other hooks in my garage at home. The significance of that remark will soon become clear. On that first day I had more tench bites than on any other day at Sywell. At least a dozen times the swingtip went up positively and I found myself attached to heavy tench. Twice the tench were lost very early by diving into the weed and there was little I could do to prevent that. But every other fish was lost after a few minutes by the hook pulling out. In each case, when the tackle was retrieved, the hook was found to have opened out. By the end of the day, I was nearly demented with frustration. Another lesson learned the hard way. I had not tested the hooks before coming fishing, had I?

The following morning I consigned the whole batch of hooks to the dustbin and was on my usual pattern – as you might expect, I had only one bite all day. The size of the fish made up for everything though, and I went home that night a happy man after all. Not, however, before I had made a complete fool of myself. When I had that solitary bite, I was actually talking to two girls who were walking their dog along the bank. When the swingtip shot up without any preliminary warning, I struck so hard that the back of the folding chair I was sitting on could not take the strain, and collapsed under the pressure. The tubular aluminium snapped, resulting in my rolling over backwards and landing in my bath of groundbait. The girls went off sniggering to themselves, leaving me to shake all the breadcrumbs out of my hair and land the tench which by some miracle was still attached.

THE TENCH OF THE CASTLES

In the summer of 1967 I bought my first house, on the outskirts of Nuneaton in Warwickshire and during investigations of the countryside surrounding my new home, I came across two very intimate and mysterious looking waters. They were both mature and fairly neglected estate lakes, one in the grounds of an old castle and one behind an old baronial hall. I soon found out that both waters were actually leased by small local angling clubs, but the nature of the banks suggested to me that both were very little fished.

I had a good look around the castle lake first. It was a tench water straight out of every textbook, about three acres in extent, surrounded by trees and bushes and almost entirely covered by water lilies. Its position meant that it was hardly affected by wind and it had a very brooding quality. On my first serious reconnaissance I was to spot some very big tench, silently gliding between the lily stems. At the time I had yet to take my first five-pounder and I remember thinking clearly that some of the fish before me could easily weigh in excess of 6lb. Having wormed my way into the club controlling the water, I could not wait for my first crack at it.

Long before dawn on a bright July morning, I groundbaited a hole in the lilies I had already prepared the previous evening and impatiently awaited day-break. As soon as there was sufficient light, a red-tipped quill was sitting at half cock alongside the lily stems with a large, lively lobworm in position. I was fishing one large shot only so that a bite would be immediately apparent – the float would lie flat if the bait was lifted a fraction.

Three hours of daylight passed and, with the sun becoming very warm, I was thinking my chance had gone when the float suddenly disappeared. There were no preliminaries, none of the normal foreplay with the bait that often characterises tench bites in estate lakes. One minute the float was still, the next the rod was disappearing off the rest. Whatever I hooked that morning was big – a very large tench was the

The beautiful lake in the grounds of the castle.

Three plump tench taken from the lake at the castle.

obvious guess, but I was never to see it. Within a few minutes it was totally immovable, buried in a mass of lily roots and I eventually was forced to pull for a break. During the drive home I was really wound up. I could not wait for my next crack at the water.

Three mornings later I was back for a short early session before work and this time I achieved modest success. I had baited the previous night with 2lb of stewed wheat and fished with a single grain of the seed on a size 10 hook. There were three bites in those few hours, yielding lovely tench of between 3½ pounds and 4½ pounds. Remember, this was 1967 and a 4lb tench was a big fish.

Over the next few years I was to use the water in the same way – for the occasional summer session before work in mid-week – and caught many more tench and a few good roach. It was by no means an easy water, however, and blanks were quite frequent. I never did catch one of the giant tench I had seen, the biggest I caught weighed a modest 4lb 10oz, but did lose several bigger fish in the weeds. On one of my few evening sessions, however, I did manage to gain a clue as to the possible identity of the big fish I had lost on my first trip.

I arrived after tea one day in August for a pre-baiting session prior to fishing the next morning and met the first other angler on the water I had seen since I had joined the club almost two years previously. We sat talking and I looked with interest at the rod he was using. It was a 13-foot split-cane rod of extremely doubtful pedigree and was unusual in that all the slivers of cane had become unglued; it was held together by the occasional loop of cotton! I said to him 'I hope you don't hook a really big fish on that rod, it will collapse under the strain!' The words had hardly left my mouth when his float dipped and he struck into a fish that took off for the centre of the lake like a scalded cat. As the rod bent, there was an ominous creaking and groaning and bits of cotton began to fly off in all directions. About thirty yards out, a double-figure carp swirled at the surface and that was the signal for the rod to give up the ghost. It just disintegrated and the angler was left clutching a useless collection of firewood. As he stood muttering darkly about smart young upstarts, I beat a hasty retreat!

The hall lake proved to be a water which I had access to for only one season – the club I joined lost the rights to the fishing and the water reverted to private ownership. It was a water of two halves, long and narrow and only fishable from one bank. The private bank was very heavily covered in lilies, while the road bank was barren of weed and down the middle of the lake there was a very sudden division between the two. It was almost as if the water had been specially dragged to create exactly that effect. It took me many trips before I had my first bite from this water and the bait had to be tight against those mid-water lily pads to have any chance. Apart from one nice rudd at 1½ pounds, all I caught were blackish tench, seldom exceeding 2lb in weight and I soon lost interest in it. The last session I ever had there, however, was one of the most frustrating of my career and still remains the only day in over thirty years when I have used potatoes as hookbait.

I had been told that the water contained some very big carp that were often seen but never caught. Rumour had it that these fish weighed up to well over 20lb and my wife and I spent a week making evening trips to the water, which was only about three miles away, to pre-bait with small, cooked, whole potatoes. I fished it all day from dawn until dusk one Thursday, having taken a day off from work, using a size 2 hook to 10lb line. In view of the fact that all the tench had been caught very close to the lily pads, I had made the mistake of pre-baiting with the potatoes in the same area and the events of that day taught me the value of thinking ahead before embarking on any plan of action.

Four times during the day line streaked off the reel as big carp galloped away with my bait and each time the fish was buried deep in the lilies before I had even set the hook. The result was predictable. On each occasion, I was hopelessly snagged within seconds and twice had the small consolation of seeing large common carp thrash at the surface before the hook pulled out. Four times that day I was forced to pull for a break and I went home that night a sadder but wiser man.

5 The Coventry Specimen Group

During the mid- to late sixties all the friends I had fished with since childhood were rapidly losing interest, other than for the very occasional far-from-serious excursion. On the other hand I was becoming more and more obsessed with the search for big fish, consequently spending an increasing amount of time fishing on my own. That in itself did not bother me, having always been quite content with my own company, but I did realise that the learning process would be slower than if I were fishing in the company of like-minded anglers.

I was already an avid reader of everything published on angling and one of the monthlies carried an article by Peter Butler which made the first reference I had seen to a specimen group. Peter, Herbie Green and a few others had formed the London Specimen Group and the pooled knowledge had led to them taking some tremendous catches of specimen fish – big roach from the London reservoirs in particular.

I read and re-read that article and realised that this was what I had been looking for. I would start the Coventry Specimen Group, but how did I go about it? Coincidentally, I was in my final degree year at college in Coventry at that time and whilst there had first made the acquaintance of an extrovert by the name of Ray Brown, or 'Crazy Horse' to his friends! Ray was as nuts about his fishing as I was and equally as excited about a Coventry group. He was already a member of the National Anguilla Club and knew Dave Ball who was involved with the newly-formed Leicester Specimen Group. He had also met Pete Rayment who was secretary of the Birmingham Specimen Group.

In early 1967 Ray contacted Pete Rayment which resulted in a meeting taking place at Ray's house comprising Ray and myself, together with Pete and his friend Don Stockton. Sadly, Pete and Don are no longer with us. We all became very good friends at that meeting and Pete and Don gave us some valuable advice on the way the Birmingham group was run and what had already been achieved since its formation.

Following that initial meeting, we decided to advertise in the angling press for members for the new group. The first advert went into *Angling Times* in June 1967 after our final college examinations. Surprisingly we only received one reply from that initial advert, but it turned out to be from the right man, Mervyn Wilkinson. Although I had by then taken many big fish, Merv was a few years older and had considerably more experience over a wider field. He was also, and still is, a superb angler, carrying considerable respect in the big fish world and was chiefly responsible for the growth in the group over the months that followed.

Ray and I met Merv on the banks of a local carp lake in July and I was taken with the man immediately. We shook hands, and the Coventry Specimen Group was born. In the weeks that followed, we all fished together as often as possible, talking to other anglers we met on the bank about the new group. Our activities were somewhat curtailed in the early winter months of 1967 by the fishing ban on the Midlands rivers caused by the foot-and-mouth disease outbreak, but on our first trip after the ban was lifted, we met a young man on the Cherwell who has since become a household name in big fish circles, Phil Smith. He told us that he had not been fishing very long, but was obviously extremely enthusiastic about catching specimen fish. That day he was fishing with his father, Bill and a friend, Graham Twizzle and all three were invited to Merv's house the following week for the first official group meeting. Also present was another Coventry angler who had expressed interest in joining, Terry Jones. At that meeting we took the first steps to put together some rules and guide-lines and I was elected as the first group secretary and treasurer.

Before the end of that first season, serious rifts were starting to appear. Ray Brown received some very bad publicity about live-baiting on the fens using four rods at once – this attracted much adverse comment about the group in general. It was not so much what Ray was getting up to in his pike fishing, but more the way it was being splashed over the pages of the angling press that upset the other members of the group. Ray was asked to resign and he went on to form the Coventry Circus. Despite that Ray and I remained friends, even though it had fallen to me to ask for his resignation.

At one of the earliest group meetings of 1968 there were two more newcomers, both from contact with Merv who were two of the best anglers I know, Mick Nicholls and Trefor West. Trefor in particular was an enigma – an ex-professional footballer who had been selected to play for England by Sir Alf Ramsay before an injury

Two of my earliest Cherwell chub which I caught after I met Merv Wilkinson in 1967.

cruelly ended his career. Trefor was outspoken to the point of arrogance, totally self-confident and by far the most intense man as far as big fish angling was concerned. He could not have been more unlike me as far as temperament was concerned, but I liked the guy. Like Merv, he always told the truth (if a little bluntly at times) and you always knew where you stood with him. One of my strengths – which I have had to develop in my career in sales – is that I can be diplomatic when need be. Trefor and Merv have no such hang-ups!

By the end of that summer Mick Jelfs had joined us and the following season, by which time Merv had taken over from me as group secretary, Bill Robinson and John

The winter of 1970 and a 19lb Cherwell pike for Trefor.

Taylor became members. Although other members came and went, the ones mentioned formed the backbone of the Coventry Specimen Group.

Over the five years between the group's formation and its disbanding, the results we achieved were outstanding in many spheres of big fish angling. The teamwork of those days resulted in us making very rapid strides forward in our understanding of the problems of specimen hunting and laid the foundations for the success that has been achieved by the group members as individuals ever since. After the break-up of the group, Merv and Phil continued to fish together as a team, as did Trefor and I and it says a lot for the camaraderie of those formative years that we are all still friends. Mick Nicholls, Trefor and I are all part of the Midland region of the Barbel Catchers Club, while Phil Smith and I now work together and are in close liaison with waters like Queenford, both of us being involved in the first explorations of that exciting water. Merv tends to fish on his own these days, but we keep in contact with him regularly through his connection with Joe Taylor's tackle shop in Bicester. Mervyn will always be associated with the famous Coventry Specimen Group stag nights which made their humble beginnings in 1969 with a small gathering of Midland groups. In later years invitations were sent out to big fish anglers throughout the country and the Coventry Rugby Club, where the event was staged, was invariably packed. The catering and entertainment was always left for Merv to organise and the mountain of good food provided has become legendary. We have had some top quality comedians and Merv has always managed to organise outstanding entertainment.

I owe the Coventry Specimen Group a great deal. Through my involvement with the group, I have developed my angling expertise in a way that would not have been possible otherwise. I know that all the old group members share that conviction and I look back on those years as the most important of my angling career.

6 In Pursuit of Barbel

EARLY THAMES BARBEL

My meeting with Merv Wilkinson in the early days of the Coventry Specimen Group was directly responsible for my catching my first ever barbel, a burning ambition I had held for seven years, since I saw my first one at Throop in 1961. I had fished the Thames several times on my own at Rushey Weir, which was a well-known venue for Coventry anglers, but had never got to grips with one of those streamlined battlers. In the summer of 1967, I went to Rushey with Merv for the first time and his advice brought me the fish I craved.

We started off well above the weir-pool fishing several swims from which Merv had taken barbel in the past, but to no avail and at about midday we arrived back at the weir. It was then that Merv introduced me to the swim that was apparently always a banker. In the back current under the right-hand wall only a few yards down from the weir sill, there was a large dock plant growing out from the brickwork with the trailing roots of an alder at the same position. Under the foliage, close in to the bank, was a favoured holding spot and Merv suggested that I should fish that swim. He promised me that I would catch my first barbel.

We were using half a beef sausage as bait, a very popular offering with Thames barbel anglers in those days, and the first bait I lowered alongside the dock leaves was taken with such savagery and so quickly that I was taken completely unawares. I missed the bite. Excitedly, I re-baited with another half-sausage and this time was prepared. There was another vicious lunge on the rod and again I missed totally. This was mortifying. When I missed for the third time it was time to ask serious questions about my technique and only then did I realise that the skin on the sausage was impeding the penetration of the hook point – a stupid oversight which I should have noticed earlier. The next bait was hooked in such a way that the hook was standing

My first ever barbel from Rushey Weir.

Trefor slams into a good Thames barbel.

proud of the sausage and the fourth bite led to a fish being solidly hooked. That was my initiation into the fighting abilities of a barbel and for many arm-aching minutes I battled with that powerful adversary in the heavy flowing waters of that Thames weir-pool. Twice I was convinced I was snagged as the barbel hugged the bottom and refused to be shifted, and the longer the fight went on the more convinced I became that I would soon see a fish weighing well over 10lb. When Merv eventually slipped the net under it for me, however, there in the mesh lay a fish which was only of average size – 6lb 12oz to be exact. Even to this day, it is impossible for me to be accurate about the weight of a hooked barbel. Even a small one will give a terrific account of itself.

It would not be until the following June before I was to fish the swim again and this time I definitely lost a very big barbel indeed. I had arrived well before light to secure the swim and had quickly taken one of the biggest Thames chub I have ever caught – a specimen of 4lb 12oz – on sausage-meat. Before long I caught a second weighing just under 4lb and then, at long last, I was locked in an exciting conflict with a barbel. It fought in the white water with great power and tenacity but there was never any doubt about the eventual outcome and I soon increased my personal best on the Thames to 7lb 6oz.

Shortly after landing that fish, I lost a medium-sized chub on a long trailing tree root which was well submerged; this particular snag was to become a real pain. I had to put a bait near it to get a bite and yet was becoming regularly hung up. The problem was that the root whipped around in the strong flow and gave an indication on the rod top just like a barbel bite and eventually it fouled the line. I had twice played that root for some time before realising that it was not a big fish after all. When the rod hammered around yet again and I played something that refused to come off the bottom for over ten minutes, I convinced myself that it was that infernal root again, probably hooked at its thickest point thus making it difficult to draw to the surface. I began to pull and heave for all I was worth and ended up applying a direct pull along the line. All of a sudden the hook pulled free and I retrieved it. Imagine my dismay when I also retrieved a huge barbel scale, firmly embedded on the point. All right, maybe the barbel had been foul-hooked, but with a scale that size I would have been mighty interested to meet its owner!

I would like to be able to relate a story of a big Thames barbel, but I cannot as that seven-pounder from Rushey remains the biggest I have ever taken from the river. I can, however, tell of a very entertaining evening at Port Meadow near Godstow when I was settling down for an all-night session. The meadow is a public park, the upstream extremity of which is the famous swimming pool area, where Fred J Taylor took his eleven-pounder many years ago. I was fishing a very well-known swim at the tail of the straight just upstream of the entry of the mill-stream. It was early evening and very humid after a hot day. One or two chub were showing themselves around the branches of the large willow under the opposite bank and I was looking forward to sunset. There were a lot of children playing in the field and people walking dogs passed by continually – this was an occupational hazard with that particular fishery and one that I had learned to ignore. After dark, when fishing would begin in earnest, such disturbances would be rare. It was perhaps for this reason that I ignored two young ladies who sat down on the bank about ten yards from me and lay in the sun for a while. With a lack of interest from the chub and barbel, my attention started to wander and I then became aware of the girls. Perhaps it was coincidental, or possibly because they saw me looking at them, but they whispered together before getting to their feet and performing a slow strip-tease. Once down to their underwear, they lay down again for another ten minutes sunbathing. It was now difficult to concentrate and it became impossible to do so when they got to their feet again and took off what remained of their clothing. They slowly walked towards me and when only feet away they suddenly dived into the river. They spent the next few minutes swimming around in front of me before emerging once again, whereupon they quickly got dried and dressed, and ran away up the bank, laughing to themselves. It was several hours before the appeal of barbel fishing had fully returned!

SEVERN BARBEL

The River Severn is one that has never really fired me with the same enthusiasm that smaller, more intimate rivers do and for this reason I have largely neglected it. There are, however, two incidents involving this river from my angling career that are memorable and the first of these concerns the Snag swim. This was a swim on the Severn near Berrington that Trefor first discovered in 1978 when he was taking a very long walk along the bank looking for areas that received little attention from anglers. In the middle of the river, in a stretch where the flow was deep and powerful, the only clue to the swim was in the form of a branch that

A small barbel from the Snag swim.

protruded above the surface. Such snags always hold attraction for barbel and as Trefor stood on the bank looking at it, a very big barbel obligingly rolled right alongside it. Not only was it a definite double, but Trefor was convinced that it could weigh as much as 12lb. Obviously, having found a fish of that calibre Trefor fished the swim often, but for whatever reason, the snag totally frustrated any attempts to land a big fish. A few smaller barbel were landed, but he had to fish close to the snag to get a bite and in so doing risked losing every big fish that was hooked. Whatever was submerged under the nine feet of heavy water was totally immovable.

The summer following Trefor's first excursions to the swim, I joined him and we fished the swim together. The snag was very substantial, whatever it was, and was at least twenty yards long. On my very first day I caught nothing, but still had a taste of what Trefor had been going through. I hooked a fish that was undeniably huge but, despite heavy pressure from the word go, it reached the obstruction and I was forced to pull for a break. I had been using my standard barbel gear of a 1¼lb test curve rod coupled with 8lb line, but losing that fish made me decide to step up to a carp rod and 12lb line on my next trip.

The following week Trefor and I decided on a weekend session when we would fish through the dark hours. We hoped that the barbel might possibly move a little closer to the bank under cover of darkness, thus giving us a better chance of landing one. In actual fact, that was a forlorn hope. The only place I could get a bite (as during daylight) was right alongside that snag – I landed every fish I hooked, probably more through good luck than judgement, although they were all only small barbel. I had a string of fish up to only about five pounds.

Not long after day-break came the highlight of that particular session. I had a strong pull and struck into a fish that was obviously much bigger than anything I had yet connected with. Immediately I felt it, I used the tackle strength at my disposal and really leaned into the fish, not allowing an inch of line to be taken. The rod bent right round to the corks and then I felt the fish yielding. Suddenly it gave up trying to attain the sanctuary of the cover and surged upstream out of harm's way. At that, I jumped off my seat and followed the fish upstream from where I could play it normally and be in the best position to prevent it trying to re-enter the snaggy area. Both Trefor and I were now very excited. The curvature in the carp rod told us that a big fish was on the end, and as we had not yet caught a sight of it, we naturally assumed that I was firmly attached to the double-figure barbel that Trefor had seen. It was therefore both surprising and a little disappointing when the net eventually closed round the fish and we could see for the first time what I had hooked. There in the net lay an immaculate common carp of just over 10lb. That fish obviously gave us food for thought. Perhaps all the big fish that had been lost over the previous months were carp rather than big barbel, although the first fish that Trefor had spotted had undeniably been a barbel.

As the weeks wore on no more big fish were caught from the swim, although several more were lost in the snag. By the following June, Trefor had become obsessed with cracking that swim and had determined to shift at least part of the snag to give himself more chance. We were convinced that it was a fallen tree with an accumulation of submerged debris and certainly several sets of lost tackle attached to it. Determined to do the job properly, Trefor had equipped himself with a boat and in the early part of the season we rowed out until we were alongside the branch and then lowered a large and strong drag into the water. The first few sweeps with the drag brought a collection of sticks and larger pieces of wood to the surface, which we ferried away and disposed of on the bank, and the next sortie revealed two discarded and lethal looking eel traps. A terminal rig dropping into one of those stood no chance. The third sweep with the drag solved the mystery. The drag snagged solidly, and although we heaved on the rope as hard as we dare, nothing shifted. We were in grave danger of swamping the boat. Suddenly something broke away deep down and we lifted a dead weight to the surface, something that swung around alarmingly in the brisk current. We soon found that it was a complete car door, and by diving in the river to have a look, Trefor soon confirmed that the rest of the car was also there. That was the signal to give up! No wonder we kept losing fish – they were probably conger eels!

I have only fished the River Severn for one day in recent seasons, although some massive fish that are putting in regular

The double-figure common carp that took me by surprise.

appearances at the moment could persuade me to renew my acquaintance with it. In 1984, the river around Worcester and Upton featured in the angling press most weeks, with double-figure barbel coming out to both pleasure and match anglers. As my earliest experiences with the river had been with very small barbel and as it had never given me a seven-pounder, I had to be interested and decided that I would spend a day on the day-ticket water at Upton to see if I could find out what all the excitement was about.

When I arrived at dawn, there was the promise of a nice day with the river at normal summer level, and I was soon ensconsed in one of the 'stones' swims just inside the public park stretch. That area is characterised by very steep clay banks, and the swim I was fishing was no exception with a sheer wall of clay at least fifteen feet high behind me. When the rain started

Trefor prepares to dive under to investigate the nature of the snag.

shortly after I made my first cast, it never occurred to me what problems I might incur later. The early light rain soon gave way to a much more persistent downpour and this continued unabated all day – as the wind had picked up force considerably and was blowing directly in my face, it was quite uncomfortable. The quality of the fishing, however, made up for the weather. It was slow to start with as I gradually built up the swim with hemp and corn, but after possibly two hours' fishing, I had my first bite. I was actually destined to lose that first barbel but, after having modified my terminal rig to include a short hair, I went on to take nine barbel during the day. Of those fish, four were over 7lb with a fifth over 8lb – fabulous barbel fishing from any river and particularly so from the Severn, which I had never rated for really big fish.

I had actually intended to fish well after dark that night, but as my waterproof suit had proved itself ineffective and I was drenched, I decided to call it a day at dusk. It may sound overly dramatic, but that decision may have saved my life. For the past two hours, I had noticed that the river was rising quite steadily. From a mark on the stone in front of me, I knew that it had risen at least six inches in an hour and that rate of rise was increasing quickly when I packed my gear. That is when I discovered my dilemma. The wall of clay behind me was now glassy smooth from the impact of the incessant rain and was totally unclimbable. I must have struggled for over half an hour but had to give it up. I could not climb it myself, let alone heave my gear up it. I was now becoming very concerned – it was pitch black, and as the stones I had been sitting among only hours earlier were totally submerged I was rapidly becoming trapped. I had to do something and quickly.

About fifty yards downstream there were thick alders and thorn bushes growing out from the bank. They looked totally impenetrable, but I realised that they would provide the only possible foothold – it was my only hope. Very gingerly, I picked my way through the water over the marginal rocks until I stood under the foliage. With no tools on me, I had to tear a path through the branches and thorns with my bare hands and within seconds they were a mass of blood. Eventually, however, I succeeded in my task and some two hours after I had decided to pack up I stood safely on top of the bank at long last. I breathed a long sigh of relief. I was to find out later that no more than two hours after my departure that night, the river had risen no less than ten feet. It is a chastening thought to contemplate what might have happened had I made a different decision that evening.

7 A Week in Ireland

When I first met Merv Wilkinson he used to spend a week every close season seeking the bream and tench of Lough Ree in southern Ireland, in a large bay known as Garnafailagh Lake. The fishery was near the town of Athlone and he always stayed at Fred Carter's guest house on the banks of the water. Some of his catches of bream had been tremendous and when he asked me if I fancied a trip with him in May 1968, I jumped at the chance.

It transpired that our timing for the bream fishing could not have been worse as the fish began spawning in earnest on the day of our arrival. So the plan we followed for the duration of our stay was to fish for the tench of Garnafailagh early and late and to spend the middle part of the day searching for the big rudd of Lough Killinure, which was a very shallow, reedy bay. This entailed a row of half an hour across Lough Ree itself.

Garnafailagh Lake was a beautiful fishery, heavily reeded and with the bottom seductively adorned with scattered cabbage patches. One of the immediate things that struck me on our first morning was the astonishing clarity of the water. At a depth of eight feet, tench could actually be watched taking the bait. The fishing was well controlled, all the best swims being marked with permanent stakes driven in to the lake bed and it was a simple matter to tie up the boat fore and aft to these stakes.

Merv and I fished the same tench swim for the entire week, Merv fishing a cabbage patch at the prow of the punt and I a similar feature at the stern. Although our tench catches were certainly not spectacular, we took fish steadily, roughly equally shared and each managed one tench of exactly 5lb. Remember that this was 1968, when a five-pounder was still a huge tench, so we were quite happy with our results.

The one incident from the tench fishing that stands out in my memory occurred on the second morning. Merv was using two

A catch of Irish tench taken in early June 1968. The biggest weighed almost five pounds.

rods, one for tench and one for completely uninterested bream. After a while, he realised he was wasting his time trying to catch a bream and wound that rod in and rested it on the gunwhale adjacent to his tench rod. The tench were also particularly unresponsive – the sun had climbed quite high in the sky and we were still biteless. Merv then whispered that he had a bite. I turned around to watch the action. His float was making those little movements so indicative of tench in natural lakes. There were small lifts, bobs and sideways movements, while masses of needle bubbles rose all round. For several minutes these maddeningly indecisive indications continued and Merv became more and more tensed up. Suddenly the float lifted and lay flat. Instantly he struck, but much harder than was warranted considering the short range at which he was fishing. The next second I was seeing stars as a jet-propelled lump of split cane hit me straight in the mouth. You have guessed it – Merv had struck the wrong rod! I was dizzy for at least two hours and Merv missed the tench.

The rudd fishing on Lough Killinure was fascinating. We were blessed with incredibly sunny, warm and calm weather, and the rudd shoals were easy to locate in the crystal clear water. The technique was simplicity itself. We very quietly poled around the lough until we spotted the dorsals of priming rudd. The anchor would be lowered at least thirty yards away and then we fished for them using bubble floats with bread crust on the surface. Some of the takes were spectacular and we had many fine rudd

Killinure rudd weighing 1lb 15oz and 2lb.

weighing up to just over 2lb. One thing we found was that you had to take advantage of the opportunities when they presented themselves. After perhaps two or three casts, or after a couple of fish had been taken, the shoal would move away, very agitated. It was then time to up anchor and search for other fish.

As well as the rudd, the shallow bays like Killinure were also ideal for the many big pike that lurked there and Merv and I spotted many tremendous fish lying partly-concealed in the marginal rushes. We never actually tried for them ourselves but were privileged to be present when that fine Irish angler, George Higgins, took a great fish weighing over 29lb on a trolled plug.

As well as being a first class, all-round angler and good friend, Merv is also well renowned for his liking of practical jokes and for his mastery of the wind-up. One of his jokes in Ireland was to have very painful repercussions for him. During our stay, we made the acquaintance of four Londoners who were great characters. Every breakfast time there was playful banter and twice it became quite heated. Only on one early morning session did Merv fail to catch a tench and over the meal he took some unmerciful verbal abuse over that. He decided to get his own back and that night we packed up fishing earlier than usual and Merv crept into their bedroom and rigged up some kind of booby trap. I am not sure what it was, but the lads were not at all pleased the next morning, although they were soon laughing with Merv about it.

As the week drew to a close, the weather became hotter and hotter and by the last day the midday temperature was well over ninety degrees Fahrenheit. I recorded a water temperature of 81°F (27°C), incredible for May. The combination of early mornings, late nights, little sleep and hot sun had made us very torpid and one day, in the middle of the afternoon, both Merv and I fell asleep in the boat (Merv had made the serious mistake of removing his shoes and socks). I was first to awake and even in the bright sun I could see that Merv's feet were the most vivid scarlet colour. They really were very badly burned indeed and for the rest of the evening he was in great discomfort.

At the dining table that night, you could tell that every movement was agony and we were all suitably sympathetic. As we were all returning home early the next morning, we went up to bed immediately after the meal with Merv drawing up the rear, hobbling gingerly on tiptoe. In our bedroom, he undressed and then very carefully climbed into bed. Slowly, he slid his scorched feet down under the cool sheets and then, all of a sudden, gave out a thunderous bellow. In one movement, he had leaped out of bed and stormed out of the bedroom, cursing and swearing, his burnt feet temporarily forgotten. The next minute, bedlam broke out in the next room where the Londoners were billeted. Puzzled, I had a look in the bottom of Merv's bed – it was full of nettles! The lads had got their revenge!

8 Cherwell Days

A SUMMER CHUBBING PARADISE

During my formative years on the Claydon Brook, which was a lovely clear, shallow and heavily overgrown stream, I developed a deep love of summer chub fishing. The excitement of actually being able to see the quarry, perhaps in a very inaccessible spot and persuading it to take a bait without alarming it, appealed to my latent hunting instinct. Watching a big chub savagely engulf a slug or crayfish, gills flaring, is still a sight I find tremendously exciting, despite my thirty years' experience and the hundreds of chub I have taken in this way.

With the dissolution of the Coventry Specimen Group in the early seventies, Trefor and I formed a close relationship that still endures today and one of our first objectives was to get to grips with the chub of the Oxfordshire Cherwell. The group members had taken many good fish from several areas of the river, but many other stretches of unknown potential had been all but ignored. These were the areas we decided we would investigate and we would start off in the summer months, when plotting the contours of the river bed would be easier and the fish would be more visible.

Some of the stretches we found were very reminiscent of my beloved Claydon Brook, being beautifully clear over sparkling gravel and heavily overgrown with rushes and

My first Cherwell 'five', weighing 5lb 1oz.

Trefor's first Cherwell five-pounder – it weighed in at 5lb 4oz.

sedge. There were beds of lilies, lush mats of ranunculus and deep, mysterious glides overhung by bankside foliage. Many stretches were totally neglected, the banks being a riotous jungle of dense woodland where fallen trees at regular intervals formed the nuclei for numerous inviting rafts. And everywhere we went we found chub – not one or two but hundreds and many of them were very big fish indeed. The lessons we learned in those days have proved invaluable. We learned a lot about their shoaling behaviour and how the extra-large fish is often a loner. We observed their feeding patterns and noted how the biggest fish in any small group is often the last to commence feeding on loose feed. This knowledge has proved so important on many winter fishing sorties and has enabled us to establish techniques that largely avoid catching small chub. We also learned how many chub could hide themselves in an astonishingly small area and that big fish could be taken in very shallow water. On more occasions than I care to remember, as many as twenty chub have been disturbed from under weed cover as little as two feet square.

Most important of all, however, was that we mapped all the areas which consistently contained chub, taking particular note of the location of the biggest. As well as that, the surrounding river bed topography was carefully examined so that we not only knew where the chub would be found in the winter, but where they would be most likely to move to with the onset of higher water.

I already knew, from my many years on the Claydon Brook and Upper Ouse, how

A summer fish that fell to floating crust.

deadly natural bait fishing for summer chub was and Trefor and I began our Cherwell campaign with substantial naturals such as crayfish, slugs and lobworms. We soon found that the river was alive with crays and for the first two or three seasons we caught a colossal number of chub on these freshwater crustacea. It was obvious that rarely had they been fished for in that way, so uninhibited was the manner in which fish after fish would smash into the bait. There were so many outstanding days of summer chubbing at that time that it is difficult to select any one as being particularly memorable. There was the day when Trefor went to a new stretch on his own and caught thirty-three chub, with an average weight of over 3lb, all on crayfish. I doubt that any angler living has taken a greater haul of summer chub on naturals in a single day. I have never approached that total, but my biggest single-day catch was nineteen fish, taken on either crays, slugs or lobs and which included three four-pounders.

One of my more interesting summer chubbing sessions (because it sums up many of the techniques that Trefor and I perfected over the years) was condensed into only about four hours of a blazing hot July afternoon. I was actually returning home after a singularly unproductive Thames barbel session and decided to drop off at the Cherwell for a couple of hours to see if I could put a bend in the rod. The river was very low and clear that summer, heavily overgrown and the chub were easy to spot. I had only walked the first hundred yards and was already becoming very excited about the prospects. Chub were in evidence everywhere I looked and all appeared to be actively foraging for food. I had several sweaty pieces of luncheon meat with me and these free offerings were devoured greedily. Two of the fish looked every ounce of 5lb and the session had now changed from being a pleasant way to spend a couple of hours to something much more serious.

Back at the car, I tackled up with a 6lb freeline to a size 4 Au Lion d'Or and then waded out on the stony shallows by the road bridge to search for crayfish. That area had regularly proved reliable for crays, its characteristics being absolutely perfect. It was not too shallow at about eighteen inches and had a lively current to quickly wash away any disturbed silt that would otherwise hinder visibility. The fine gravel on the river bed was littered with small- to medium-sized stones and the depressions scoured under these stones were where the crayfish lived. Carefully lifting up each stone as I came to it, I was soon able to accumulate a dozen crays in my bait bucket and it was soon time to make my first cast.

The first two chub I had spotted were lying under the far bank, between a mid-river bed of ranunculus and an overhanging clump of brambles. They were stationed over clear gravel in nine inches of water and would be very easy to frighten, so the approach and the cast had to be perfect. Quietly and cautiously I approached the swim from upstream until I was within

A lovely summer five-pounder for Trefor.

The deadliest natural bait of them all.

casting range. Crouching behind the head-high willow herb, I selected a crayfish and then made my cast, upstream and across, aiming so that the bait would land adjacent to those trailing brambles, two yards upstream of the chub. For a moment I thought that I had blown it as the crayfish actually alighted on the brambles. But I was lucky, only a slight twitch was required to free the bait without unduly shaking the branches and it 'plopped' into the water about three feet upstream of the bigger of the two fish.

There was a tremendous puff of silt as the chub accelerated and hammered into that crayfish and, as I struck, an almighty boil appeared on the surface as the fish rocketed under the sanctuary of those brambles. I was prepared for that manoeuvre and lay the rod over so that it was parallel to the

A free-lined crayfish tempted this fine 4lb 1oz sample.

Another chub finds a crayfish irresistible.

water, clamping the reel to prevent the fish taking line and applying maximum side-strain. I can still see the violent thrashing under those brambles as the chub fought for a few seconds against the restraint I was applying. But then he suddenly gave up the struggle, came out at great speed and dived into the mid-stream streamer. Once he was away from those dangerous bramble roots, there was never any doubt about the eventual outcome and I was soon admiring my first chub of the day. What a first fish it was, a totally unmarked specimen of 4lb 13oz and a fish that definitely would weigh well over 5lb at the back end of the season.

Not surprisingly, the other fish had disappeared and after returning the four-pounder, I made my way forty yards or so upstream, where there had been a shoal of six chub occupying a small clearing in mid-river, in a stretch where there were dense rushes all around. I was to have four takes in that clearing, landing fish from three of them, the last being particularly interesting. The first two casts had resulted in immediate takes exactly as previously described and two fish of about 3½ pounds had been weighed and returned well away from the swim. I made a complete mess of the third cast and a large loop of line flew up from the bale-arm, making the cray drop hopelessly short so that it landed only inches over the rushes and well away from the chub I had actually aimed at.

I started to wind in when there was a vicious tug that took me completely by surprise. I instinctively struck, which I knew immediately was the wrong thing to do on a tight line. Sure enough the line fell slack and I retrieved the tail of the crayfish. It had been bitten clean in two. Over the years, I had learned that you must leave a little slack for the chub to take up whenever using crayfish. The incredible savagery with which they attack crays means that a tight line invites either a devastating smash or, as I had just experienced, a severed bait. One day on Dick Walker's stretch of the Ouse, I had four crayfish bitten in half in this manner in four consecutive casts, a lesson which would never be forgotten.

Once the bird's nest of line had been unravelled, I tossed a crayfish to the far side of the clearing towards the bigger of two fish that lay side by side under some broken rush stems. Once again, my cast was slightly wayward. Instead of the bait landing ahead of the fish, as intended, it landed right on top of the chub's tail. In an instant the chub had whipped round and snapped the cray, half leaving the water as it did so. What a dramatic couple of seconds that was. That fish (which tipped the scales at 4lb 6oz) was memorable in as much as it was one of the first chub I took by landing the bait on its tail, albeit accidentally in this case. Dick Walker had often written and indeed had said to me on the Ouse, that this presentation was one of the most deadly. Almost every time I had tried it previously, it had resulted in the fish bolting, but this was a notable exception. Since that four-pounder, I have taken many more chub using the same approach, but have to admit that I have also had lots of refusals. It is part of the repertoire I now reserve for those occasions when a more orthodox approach has failed.

What I know to be the most effective presentation for summer chubbing (that of inducing a take with a moving bait) was to result in my fifth chub and third four-pounder at 4lb 10oz from the next swim I

A plump 4½-pounder.

fished. I was walking past a dense streamer bed when I noticed a great black tail protruding from under the tresses in mid-river. I had intended to land the bait just over the streamer clump so that the lively current would carry it under the fronds where the chub lay. In actual fact, it landed about a foot short on the clear gravel on my side of the streamer. When the bait had settled, I estimated that it lay probably two feet and slightly upstream of the head of the fish.

The crayfish lay there for perhaps three minutes and still the chub had not moved, so I took a yard of slack line in my left hand and gave the line to the bait a sharp jerk of about six inches which made the crayfish rise off the bottom and move quickly a little upstream. A small cloud of sediment rose as it did so. The result was electric – a grey torpedo launched itself from under the tresses and the crayfish disappeared in an impressive swirl. It was as well I had taken the precaution of holding some slack, or I feel that the line may well have broken on the bite. While I realise that readers who have studied my writings over the years will have heard of induced takes *ad nauseam*, I will repeat it again here: any angler who does not utilise this technique is missing a lot of fish and a lot of fun from what undoubtedly produces savage bites.

In the next half-hour I had two more takes from casting directly at individual fish in non-descript swims – a sixth chub of 3lb 14oz and a bite off from a mid-four-pounder. I then arrived at a substantial near-

Action on a summer morning.

A 4¾-pounder with a liking for slugs.

bank raft where a thick mat of algae was caught around trailing willow branches. At both the upstream and downstream extremities of the raft, the river bed was carpeted with thick cabbages and the chub under the willow were entitled to feel secure. Several fish were milling around at the upstream edge and my first cast resulted in an immediate smash-and-grab take from a two-pounder. After the commotion that fish created, which was out of all proportion to its size, the other chub retreated under the cover. I would now have to fish blind.

Casting a cray to land right at the extremity of the algae allowed it to sink very slowly, drifting under the raft as the steady current took it. It settled on the bottom without response. I left it to lie there for only about thirty seconds before I gently lifted it to the surface and then allowed it to sink naturally once again. Again the bait settled undisturbed, but when the sink-and-draw tactic was repeated there was a different end result. As the crayfish was drawn to the top for the second time I could see clearly white lips following and, just under the surface, it was taken by a fish that looked all of 5lb. I struck, there was a swirl and then I got the bare hook back. Ten minutes later the same tactics resulted in another almost identical take but this time the fish did not come adrift. Once again I weighed a chub of over 4lb – 4lb 9oz this time to be exact which continued a quite remarkable average weight.

Before leaving that raft I threw half a dozen lumps of luncheon meat under the algae as I decided it would be worth spending half an hour fishing a static bait to see whether the big one would put in another appearance. In that I was disappointed. Although two more chub would be caught on meat from that swim before I left, they both only weighed about three pounds. The five-pounder was earmarked for a future occasion.

With one crayfish left, I wandered about another two hundred yards. Several small chub were ignored, but then I spotted a decent one lying in a very awkward position in a little bay in the marginal rushes on the opposite bank; this entailed a cast over very thick streamer weed. Before baiting up I greased the line quite heavily as I could not afford for it to sink through the intervening snags. For once my cast was spot on, the crayfish landing sweetly six inches ahead of the chub. It was the kind of cast I can never achieve when someone is watching! The chub saw the cray and, quite nonchalantly, swam up to it and sucked it in. Upon feeling the line it woke up and bolted downstream, making the greased line shoot across the surface very excitingly. That chub fought well, becoming solidly snagged in the streamer and eventually I was forced to go in and retrieve it. Before long I was back on dry land with only one boot full of water and returned a very plump fish of 3lb 12oz.

The eleven fish I had that day, including four four-pounders, make it one of the best short sessions I have ever experienced but I never did catch that five-pounder under the raft.

As well as the tremendous fun we had with crayfish on the Cherwell, many good

A free-lined slug scores again.

Another big chub in the bag.

chub also fell to large black slugs (one of the deadliest of all baits) and bullheads. Like the crays, bullheads were also best fished on the move but where a truly static bait was called for, I always found lobworms were more productive. After the first two seasons, the stretches that had received most attention became quite unproductive on crays, the chub bolting in alarm as soon as they saw one. Those same chub would, however, accept a slug greedily and in one season in particular I had several big fish using the sink-and-draw style. As with crayfish, the takes were savage in the extreme and it was very exciting fishing.

The other technique that Trefor and I perfected during those years was the use of floating crust. All our favourite Cherwell stretches featured many areas of fast, gravelly shallows leading in to deeper, steadier pools. These were ideal areas for the presentation of a surface bait and, like trouting with a dry fly, it was wonderfully exciting visual fishing. As with natural bait fishing there were so many good sessions that it is difficult to pick one out as being any better than another. Instead I have selected one typical day when, although the chub were not particularly big, the fishing was extremely interesting in terms of the constantly varied bait presentation that was necessary.

The head of the swim was barely ankle-deep over clean, fine gravel and was quite rapid even in the drought conditions we were experiencing in the summer of 1976. A few yards downstream of the cattle drink

A 4¾-pounder taken on surface crust.

A big fish moves towards a piece of floating crust.

access point to these shallows, the river, still fast and shallow, was flanked by head-high rushes. The river gradually deepened to about two feet, still carrying a lively current and lilies were in evidence among the marginal rushes. Towards the end of the swim this marginal vegetation became increasingly densely interwoven with algae as the current speed gradually diminished. That summer thick algal rafts were a particular feature of many Cherwell swims and indeed, a very extensive mat was trapped around the trailing branches of the large willow that marked the downstream extremity of the swim. Under that raft the water dropped to about four feet and the current was very steady.

On a hot July afternoon I waded out to mid-river at the head of those shallows, with the tops of my waders stuffed with loose crusts. I was using my usual 6lb Maxima and a size 6 hook and the line was very heavily greased for about twenty yards. Floating-crust presentation for summer chub in shallow, clear water has to be perfect if it is to be effective. Comfortably positioned in mid-river, I scattered six loose pieces of crust across the current at my feet and watched their progress downstream. Just at the point where the water began to deepen alongside the rushes by the left-hand bank, one of the loose offerings was taken in an exciting swirl. One minute it was there, the next only a vortex in the water marked its passing. That was good enough for me and the next piece of crust that drifted towards that spot had my hook in it. It was quite a difficult presentation that afternoon since it was quite a breezy day and so I needed to have exactly the right amount of line out. Although the greased line was obviously preventing the line sinking and associated problems of drag, the wind meant that surface drag would be a problem if too much line were allowed out. On the other hand if line was not paid out fast enough, the crust would be presented at a slower pace than the current, thus causing a wake. My first drift down was obviously satisfactory as the bait disappeared right on cue, at exactly the same spot as had the previous offering. The greased line slithered across the surface as I struck and soon I landed a particularly acrobatic 2½-pounder. It was disappointing as the swirl when the first crust had been taken had led me to mistakenly believe that a much bigger fish was responsible.

I continued to drift baits down that first half of the run for about another half-hour but it became quite trying. The wind was becoming difficult and as there was a very slight bend in the river at the point where I had caught the chub, I was continually becoming caught up on the rushes and dragging the bait across the current. It was small wonder I had no more offers from that position.

It was time to change the point of attack and so I reverted to fishing from the bank, creeping down to stand adjacent the point where I caught the fish – behind the head-high rushes along the left bank. From this position I had a straight drift to that downstream willow, while being completely hidden from view. I peered over the rushes from my new vantage point immediately and was encouraged to see one of my previous crust offerings (which was lodged up against the algal raft around the willow branches) disappear silently. A big black tail broke the surface momentarily as the chub turned back down with his prize. There appeared no other loose crusts in evidence and so I introduced another half-dozen, again scattering them across the flow and waiting on events. Once more a piece was taken under the left-hand bank, but I was not able to catch that fish. Trying to drift a bait close to my own bank was virtually impossible – the wind constantly blew the line into the marginal rushes, making the bait behave most unnaturally. Not surprisingly, it was refused and in frustration I abandoned the attempt. In the meantime, two or three crusts had been taken alongside the raft in mid-stream and this is where my next offering headed. This time there were no mistakes and the bait drifted perfectly to cross the exact spot I wanted. Sure enough it was taken confidently by a lovely short, stocky specimen of 3lb 12oz.

After landing that chub there were still fish taking crusts at the edge of the raft, but in the next half-hour all I had were two baits destroyed by fish that continually swirled at them without taking them properly. The chub were wising up rapidly. I overcame this with a trick that Trefor and I had employed on many similar occasions. Chub that behave in this way are becoming nervous of floating bread, but will readily devour any pieces that sink. We had often watched crusts at close range being knocked about by a chub that would not take the floating bread, but as soon as a small piece became detached and began to sink, the chub would dart in and eat it confidently. With this in mind, I pinched on a swan shot and baited with a piece of crust big enough so that it only just sank under the weight of the shot. It was cast a few feet short of the hot spot and then allowed to drift the rest of the way naturally, sinking slowly as it went. The bite was savage and immediate and soon I was releasing another three-pounder.

There were to be no more takes to crust in that swim although I did take a fourth chub later on a piece of luncheon meat, free-lined under the raft. The catch had been nothing out of the ordinary yet it had demonstrated how important it is to achieve the correct bait presentation in successful chubbing.

Floating crust led to this chub's downfall.

Fishing for chub with floating crust in clear, shallow water demands perfection; make your hookbait behave in any way unnaturally and the fish will have none of it.

A PAINFUL PICNIC

One Cherwell chub session that I will never forget is the first day I ever took my wife fishing. Fran had prepared an absolutely enormous picnic hamper and when I saw it I had to abandon any plans I had for a mobile day! Instead I took her to a stretch I knew well where one particular swim not only contained a good head of fish, but had a comfortable grassy bank to sit on.

When we arrived and had crossed two fields and a five-bar gate, Fran got out the tablecloth (I kid you not) while I tackled up – never before had fishing been quite this civilised! Soon I was fishing happily away, munching a salmon batch; the sun was shining and I was at peace with the world. Then the cows moved in. Fran, I then discovered, did not like cows and asked if I would please shoo them away. One, it appeared, was definitely threatening the individual trifles! So I handed her the rod and drove the herd a hundred yards or so up the field.

When I arrived back she was shouting excitedly and I eventually found her at the water's edge, hanging on for grim death to a rod that was bent round in quite an alarming fashion. Before long we had a 3lb chub in the net but by the time the chub was unhooked, weighed and returned, the cows were back and this time the big black cow with the ring in his nose did not appear to relish being shooed. It was then that I noticed for the first time that there was a bull in the field and, having been brought up in the country, I knew that a stud bull in a field with a herd of cows was not to be treated lightly. In fact, not to put too fine a point on it, it would be as well to get the hell out of there! The bull pawed the ground in a most bad-tempered manner and started towards us. He was obviously working himself up and it was only a matter of time before he charged. I was not happy! Trying to appear calm for Fran's benefit, I quickly unscrewed my landing net handle and brandished it at the bull, trying to appear as aggressive as my quaking knees would allow. This ploy fortunately kept the bull at a respectful distance while Fran quickly packed our gear.

Slowly we backed to the five-bar gate with the bull following, always keeping about ten yards away. His snorting and pawing was becoming more insistent and I was now very concerned for our safety. While I faced the bull, Fran quickly got herself and the gear over the gate, out of harm's way. I then backed to the gate to find myself in an unpleasant dilemma. The only thing preventing the bull charging was the landing net handle which he was obviously unsure of and yet I found it impossible to wave the thing while climbing the gate backwards and one-handed. It certainly was a frightening couple of minutes; I knew I eventually had to turn my back on the animal to climb the gate, yet I also knew that the instant I did so he would charge. However, I had no alternative and so, taking a deep breath, I whirled round and scaled the gate as fast as I could. No sooner was my back turned than I heard the thunder of hooves and then felt a sharp pain in my backside as a horn caught me. Had I hit the gate and fallen back on the same side as the bull I dread to think of the outcome, but I was lucky. All that happened was that I was tumbled over the gate in a most undignified fashion to land in a heap, face-down in the smelliest black mud imaginable.

Fran and I often talk about that day on the Cherwell and have a good laugh. But I can tell you that it was not funny in the slightest at the time!

SOME FABULOUS CHUB WINTERS

Without exaggerating I can say that I have enjoyed so many memorable days of winter fishing on the Cherwell that it is difficult to know which ones to discuss. Quite literally they could fill a book on their own. It is only natural that the first one that always comes to mind is the day when the biggest fish was landed – it is no different in the case of my best Cherwell chub of 5lb 14oz. That day was one of the very few occasions in my angling career when I was actually fishing for a known big fish. Two years previously I had weighed the only 6lb Cherwell chub I know to be genuine, a magnificent 6lb 4oz specimen for that fine and unassuming angler Dave South. The sight of that chub took my breath away, so scale-perfect and impressive did it look in the winter sunshine. I promised myself that I would catch it one day and in February 1984 I was to keep that date with destiny.

The strange thing was that on the day in question I was on the stretch almost by accident. I had fished it the previous day under bitterly cold, frosty conditions and, although I had taken some nice fish, had decided that the next day I would go to a more prolific stretch where I could be more active, perhaps have more bites and keep a lot warmer. I had set off from home with a particular area in mind but half-way along my journey I was overwhelmed by the most powerful premonition. I knew that if I went back to the big fish stretch, something very special would happen. Such feelings come over me quite frequently in fishing and they are never ignored. Following my instincts

This catch of chub came on legered crust on a bitterly cold February day.

The bitter cold did not prevent this 4½-pounder picking up a large piece of crust.

has caught me more specimen fish than I care to remember. So insistent was the feeling that morning that I literally did a U-turn in the middle of the road and headed off in a totally different direction.

It was another clear, cold and very frosty morning and my breath formed great white clouds in the still air as I walked briskly down from the bridge to my intended start point, a lovely raft on a slight right-hand bend. Some 200 yards from my objective, the old instincts went into overdrive once again and I stopped quite abruptly at the head of a group of six pollarded willows. The eighty-yard glide always looked good, but in fact I had always been singularly unsuccessful there. However, today was going to be different – I could sense it.

After mashing up two stale loaves, I deposited four large handfuls of feed almost at my feet at the point of a small promontory and watched the feed sink slowly as it drifted down and slightly across to mid-river. A pair of swans took most of the floating bits, but as the river was about five feet deep at that point I was not unduly worried about them. Before starting to fish, I wandered downstream and baited another three swims.

On my return, I put another handful of mashed bread at my feet and then set up the gear – my normal simple arrangement of a two swan-shot link to 6lb Maxima, baiting a big piece of crust on a size 6 Au Lion d'Or. I swung the crust out to land at about mid-stream ten yards down and the link weight was such as to ensure that the terminal rig swung around to settle along the line of the loose feed. The bait must actually have settled right underneath the two swans who were waiting expectantly for some more goodies to come floating down. I had literally only seconds to wait. Almost in slow motion the quivertip bent round in a most determined fashion and I set the hook into a chub I knew instantly was something out of the ordinary. On feeling the hook, it swirled at the surface before making an irresistible run across to the far bank. That initial sighting was sufficient for me to know that I had hooked the long sought after six-pounder. I was only using a 14oz test curve rod that day, a real wand of a thing and I had to play that chub very carefully. They were a heart-stopping few minutes, but eventually the fish was mine and triumphantly I swung him over the marginal rushes. For a while I stared at that magnificent deep flank and rich navy back colouring and then the all-important weighing ceremony took place. It had never entered my head that the fish would not weigh 6lb, but it was impossible to be disappointed with a reading of 5lb 14oz. It

My personal best from the Cherwell – 5lb 14oz.

was still my biggest Cherwell chub by some considerable margin.

About three-quarters of a mile further upstream from the swim where that big fish was taken was a terrific looking swim that had been an enigma to me for years. A steady, smooth glide emptied into a deep pool before the river made an abrupt left-hand turn. There were two very pronounced creases in that pool, as well as one in the run in and it looked a superb chub area. However, I had only ever caught one average fish in all the countless hours I had fished there. Despite that, it had to contain good chub at some time and I knew it would only be a matter of time before I took one.

When success eventually came (in the shape of a fish that was my Cherwell best at the time) it was an accidental capture again in many ways as I was only fishing that particular stretch as it was as far away from other people as I could get. That day will never leave my memory for a reason other than the big fish I caught – it was the day following my father's funeral. His untimely death at such a young age had hit me very hard indeed, especially as he had died in the street and I had undergone the trauma of having to identify him in the mortuary. The only way I felt I could cope with my loss was to be totally alone for a day and that was the sole reason why I slowly walked the banks of the Cherwell on that grey morning in early March 1983.

I did not intend to fish the pool. My intention was to spend a day in the spinney well upstream, surrounded by the wildlife that my father had loved so much; there was a breeding pair of kingfishers in that spinney, one of Dad's favourite birds. As I approached the pool, however, that old feeling took over despite my plans and I knew I had to fish the long run in. I did not fight it and placed my box at the head of the run, adjacent to some dead rushes and set up my gear. The solitude was more important than the fishing and I could not be bothered to undertake any fancy swim preparation. I simply baited with a chunk of bread crust, threw three handfuls of squeezed breadcrumbs into the main flow alongside the crease and followed that with the hookbait. When the bait had settled I placed the rod on a rest, which I never do normally for chub fishing and sat back on my chair with a fresh cup of tea in my hand.

Within a few minutes of sitting down, fishing was the furthest thing from my mind and I am not ashamed to admit that I gave way to my grief for a while. Had there been anyone there to see, they would have observed a very forlorn figure indeed.

I do not know quite how long the rod had been pulling round when I finally came back to reality, but I remember it sliding off the rest just before I grabbed it. A chub had obviously hooked itself and the clutch buzzed angrily as I tried to get myself together. It was not until the chub was boring away in the deep water of the pool that I was fully in control of the situation and that scrap has to be one of the most memorable I have ever had with a chub. There were no snags to worry about, however, and after an exciting few minutes of strenuous pulling from both sides, there could only be one victor. As I peeled back the folds of the net, I could see an immaculate chub indeed – very short and fat. I am convinced that it had never been caught before and there is no doubt that this chub, a specimen of 5lb 5oz, had a tremendously therapeutic effect on me. Not long after catching it, I was packing the car to return home. Those few hours and that super fish had done the trick. I was mentally prepared to face the world again.

I consider one of my most memorable Cherwell days in recent years to be one which happened only three winters ago when I had decided to have one of my all too infrequent sessions trotting. I was fishing a stretch where even my unpractised trotting arm could achieve a half-decent presentation and I had selected two lovely steady glides alongside dense near-bank rush beds. The first of the two entailed a walk of at least a mile and by the time I had reached the swim on that clear frosty morning, I was melting. Because of the cold, I had put on my thermal suit under my wax jacket, very warm and cosy but hardly ideal hiking attire.

After I had deposited four large handfuls of mashed bread a couple of yards out from the rushes, I set up my float rod with 4lb line straight through to a size 8 hook baited with flake. The float was a two swan chubber with all the weight concentrated a few inches from the hook – I am far from being a sophisticated float angler! On the first trot down, I thought I had set the float too deep as it sank out of sight after travelling only about six feet. As I lifted the rod point to retrieve it, I realised the error of my diagnosis – a powerful fish shot ten yards downstream. There followed a good tussle for a while and then the first chub of the day sagged heavily in the net, a solid specimen of 4lb 10oz.

I trotted that swim for another hour and had only one other bite, from a 1lb roach. I then latched into my second chub of the morning, which was exactly the same weight as the first – what a super brace. Apart from a scar on one gill cover, the two chub could have been twins.

It was mid-afternoon before I was to have further success. The second of my pre-selected swims had proved to be barren and I was guiding my float down the crease created by a large near-bank tree stump. On the third trot the float had just reached the outermost branches of a large willow when it disappeared. The greased line etched the water surface very excitingly as another energetic chub fought for his freedom and I was soon weighing another cracking fish an ounce heavier than the other two at 4lb 11oz.

It was now late afternoon and I had decided to spend my remaining time legering a 100 yard stretch of overhanging willows which lined the far bank. After depositing loose feed in four areas, I set up my standard terminal rig using three swan-shot which would enable me to hold a substantial bait under the branches. Before I left for

Unhooking a four-pounder.

A nice Cherwell roach weighing 1lb 15oz.

home that night, I caught one fish from each of the four areas – two average roach and two more chub of 4lb 12oz and 4lb 14oz. To catch five chub all weighing over 4½ pounds and in such a narrow weight band is a remarkable statistic, as I am sure you will agree – a day's fishing I shall never forget.

When I was collating information for use in this chapter, I realised how many of my Cherwell 5lb chub were either accidental or unexpected captures. That is certainly true of the first two I caught which were both taken from one of the stretches in which I fish for barbel today and which is not known for big chub. In fact, the only other five-pounder I know to have been caught there was taken by Trefor West. In our deliberate searches for our first Cherwell 'five', Trefor and I had discounted this particular stretch as it always yielded lots of fish of between 2lb and 3lb, a discouraging indication if the bigger fish are the target.

However, when my interest in the river's barbel was kindled in the early eighties, the stretch in question took on a new meaning and I began to fish it regularly. During the winter months I reserved the stretch for those days when the river was carrying extra height and colour, conditions which I felt would give me the greatest opportunity of making the acquaintance of one of the elusive barbel. Consequently I headed there one day after a week of very heavy rain but found on my arrival that I had wrongly assessed the impact of the rain. Although the river had risen slightly there was only the merest tinge of colour and it was obvious that the conditions were far more

A 5¼-pounder is returned.

conducive for chub fishing than for barbel. It was disappointing so I decided to confine my barbel fishing entirely to the dark hours and to spend the daylight hours chubbing. Before I started I selected a couple of swims where I felt the chances of a night-time barbel were good and throughout the day baited each area periodically with several pieces of luncheon meat.

A little before dusk I had already taken eleven mainly small chub and arrived at the first barbel swim – a deep, steady glide under the near bank flanked by dense cabbages. Sitting well back from the water's edge, I lowered a large piece of meat a rod's length out so that it came to rest adjacent to the roots. As is often the case with a swim that has been pre-baited and left alone for hours, the first bite was immediate. Within seconds of settling back in my chair, the rod top hammered round towards the water and a big fish rocketed across the current. I knew almost immediately that it was not a barbel even though it fought tremendously hard and eventually I swung a chub ashore that looked all of 5½ pounds. Its appearance was deceptive, however, as it was badly out of condition, but it did still weigh 5lb 1oz. It was a shame the fish was so flabby, but it was still my first Cherwell five-pounder and it was an exciting evening.

Out of condition and flabby are descriptions that can certainly not be applied to my second Cherwell five-pounder which weighed 5lb exactly and which was taken under almost identical circumstances. Once more I was fishing for barbel with meat but at midday this time and on a river that was

Another muscular five-pounder for Trefor.

well up and coloured. A good pull in a strong current saw me attached to a muscular adversary that fought with great vigour and which fooled me for a while into thinking that I was attached to an average-sized barbel. When that fish was on the bank I then underestimated it, thinking that it weighed about 4½ pounds. It was, however, as solid as a rock, with great thick shoulders and as I have said it weighed 5lb exactly.

Over the last few winters the amount of time I have spent chub fishing has been very strictly limited as I am devoting more time to pike, roach and barbel. Therefore, when I do go chub fishing it is for bigger than average specimens and I have been working on some ideas to make the fishing more selective. Even on the better stretches, the normal approach to a day's chub fishing will produce fish of all sizes, the big one coming along occasionally purely as a result of the law of averages. There is nothing wrong with that if there is plenty of time available, but what I wanted was a technique that avoided catching small to average fish and which only resulted in fish of 4lb or more if that were possible. The more I thought about it, the more I became convinced that the answer to the problem lay in the loose-feeding technique. In almost any pre-baiting operation it will be the smaller fish that respond first and therefore these are the first to get caught. Catching the biggest fish in residence is a matter of wading through all the lesser individuals first, which often results in the big fish being scared off anyway. When I pre-baited for summer barbel I could see the reaction of both chub and barbel to the feed and this gave me the answer. I noticed that the bigger fish were always more sedate and measured in the way they approached a baited area whereas the others were more inclined to dash around, picking off all the stray food items. It occurred to me that if I mixed my normal mashed bread feed in a special way, I could possibly achieve segregation of the chub in certain swims. If the swims were left in peace long enough after the baiting, a sufficient number of the lesser fish should have moved to make the odds of catching the biggest member of the shoal much more favourable.

One day in January 1988 I arrived at the Cherwell to put my theory to the test. I had deliberately selected an area which contained a good head of fish, but where I had only taken the occasional four-pounder. I had never taken a five-pounder from that stretch and my best stood at 4lb 6oz. The important thing, however, was that the average chub for that area was about three pounds. If I could substantially improve on that average, my theory would have definite possibilities. I selected six areas having one characteristic in common; a steady area where heavy loose feed would settle, but which was in close proximity to faster flows. I would also not be fishing at all for several hours – for my plan to work, I had to devote a lot of time to the baiting programme I had mapped out.

The first essential was the correct loose feed mix. Three loaves were mashed up but plenty of crust fragments were left intact so that the loose-feed would float. Several handfuls of dry fresh breadcrumbs were added to this pulp – the idea was that this feed would ensure that bread scattered far and wide upon its introduction. The heavier mash would tend to congregate in the slower run, wheras the crumb and crust fragments would be free to follow whatever current variations existed. I wanted the feed to continually disperse particles into the faster flows when the smaller, more impetuous fish would hopefully be encouraged to chase them. If my theory were correct, the bigger and lazier the chub in residence, the more likely it was that they would be content to take the line of least resistance and feed on the mash lying conveniently in the steady flow.

I baited each of the six swims three times in rotation over the first three hours of the morning. In each case I placed two handfuls of feed directly in the steady water where I would eventually place the hookbait and introduced other handfuls of feed both upstream and across, so that bread was drifting down along a broad path.

Some four hours after my arrival I was ready to commence fishing and was very keyed up as I lowered my usual crust bait into the first designated area. I always get a tremendous kick out of trying a new approach and this time I did not have long to wait. The efficiency of pre-baiting was demonstrated once again when the quivertip bent round almost immediately the bait had settled. There was a solid thump as the hook went home and after a good scrap I was admiring a lovely fish of 4lb 9oz, the biggest chub I had ever caught from that stretch – an excellent start and a tremendous confidence booster.

The next two bites were both from good roach each weighing about 1¾ pounds – as they were also exceptionally big fish for the stretch this suggested that my new selective approach could prove very useful for roach as well as chub. It was some time before I had another chub bite, but on my first cast into the third prepared swim I hooked a chub that dashed off with great speed and power. After taking about five yards of line, it fought deep and slow and for a time was very reluctant to come off the bottom. I became more and more excited during the fight and sure enough, when the chub finally surfaced, I could see that I had a five-pounder. In the same way as my first ever Cherwell five-pounder, this was a very big fish indeed with the potential to weigh much more than the recorded 5lb 1oz.

The rest of the day followed exactly the same pattern and by the end of the session I had taken other chub of 4lb 2oz and 3lb 14oz. That day was a very significant step forward in my searches for big chub. I had taken only four fish, many less than a more orthodox approach would have achieved, but the average weight was outstanding – in the region of 4½ pounds. Days like that, when I can learn something really significant, ensure that I will never lose my fascination with specimen hunting.

CHERWELL BARBEL – A NEW QUEST

As I write it is late October and I have just returned from my latest barbel session on the Cherwell – several weeks of quite spectacular success which have proved an exciting culmination of five years' intense pursuit of the species from the river. Before I tell you about the tremendous events of this season, let us go back to 1981, when my interest in the Cherwell barbel was first triggered.

During the early part of that season, Trefor and I were involved in our TC bream quest (TC pit is a premier big bream water) and one of the Oxford-based anglers who was also fishing the water mentioned the capture of an 11lb barbel from the Cherwell. Trefor and I had known for some time that the river contained barbel, in fact I had first seen two small ones back in the sixties. But this was the first time we had ever heard of a fish of anywhere near this size. The stretch where the eleven-pounder had been taken was well known to us through our chub exploits and we made several visits to the river, usually on our way home from TC for spotting sessions. I never saw any barbel that season, but on one occasion when Trefor went on his own and left me to look after both sets of tackle at TC, he spotted an enormous fish partly concealed under a clump of streamer. It was at fairly

A 5lb 6oz Cherwell bream.

close range and Trefor was able to study it for some time. During that time, he became convinced that the fish could not weigh less than 12lb.

When he eventually arrived back at TC, he was bursting with the news and was very undecided as to whether to pack up there and then and forget about the bream and instead fish for that barbel throughout the evening and night. In the end he decided against it. It was getting quite late and all the bait was prepared for the bream session, so he decided that he would stop off at the Cherwell on his way home the next day and have a crack at the big fish. He never found the fish again; in fact we have never seen that very big barbel since. We have often wondered what might have happened if Trefor had followed his instincts, had taken the trouble to pack up all the bream gear and had driven back to the Cherwell on the same evening he had found the fish.

What that initial sighting did do, however, was to instil in us a strong desire to catch one of these big Cherwell barbel. The barbel is our favourite species and to catch one from the Cherwell, our home river, appealed enormously. We decided that next summer we would embark on a determined campaign to catch one.

Two things happened in 1982 that changed our plans and led to me ignoring the Cherwell fish again until 1984. Firstly, after several weeks of effort we were no nearer to capturing the fish we were after. It is true that we had located some barbel, but they were so very elusive and nor were they that big. I never had a chance at one at all that year and all that Trefor managed was two fish weighing 5lb and 6lb. Both of those came on free-lined lobs in successive casts one sunny afternoon. Secondly, Dave Plummer (who had recently moved to Norfolk) had told us about the fabulous barbel he had found on the Wensum. Several doubles had been taken, both by him and others and this seemed a better prospect for the fish we were after than the Cherwell. The latter river was once again relegated with comments that began 'one of these days . . . '.

My meeting and growing friendship with Alastair Nicholson in 1984 was responsible for my interest in the Cherwell barbel being rekindled. During a conversation he mentioned that recently he had walked the banks of the Cherwell near his home, had located several barbel (many of them big ones) and he even described one as a monster. He said that he thought a weight of 14lb was possible. I was sceptical about that, but it was obvious that Alastair had seen a barbel that I would not object to reposing in my landing net. He said that I should come down and have a try for it, and in August I did just that.

The stretch where the fish had been located (which was not the one where the eleven-pounder had been caught) was again a stretch with which Trefor and I were very familiar. We had devoted a lot of summer chubbing effort here and I found it amazing that, if there were as many barbel as Alastair had indicated, Trefor and I had missed seeing them in the low, clear water of summer.

That sunny August morning I searched a long stretch of the river without seeing anything except the usual hordes of chub. And then I came to a large, very overgrown thicket which I admit I had often walked straight past in previous trips. This time I forced my way through it and eventually stood on the bank by a large fallen tree, positioned perfectly for climbing and therefore also perfect for spotting. Once I was safely ensconsed in the branches, I could clearly see that the tree overhung an absolutely classic swim. Right under the bole, tight under my own bank, there was a deep steady run which continued upstream for several yards before gradually shallowing and emptying into a wide pool. Downstream of the run the bed shelved up quite gradually over clear gravel for a few yards, until it was only about two feet deep and clothed with lush streamer weed. In mid-stream the river was far shallower than under the tree and in fact it was only ankle deep by the far bank. The area from the far bank to mid-stream was thickly overgrown with cabbages.

As I balanced in that tree looking directly beneath me, I spotted a large shoal of chub immediately, which contained one individual I shall never forget. He looked every ounce of 5lb, but bore on his head the most hideous growth I have ever seen on a fish. It was the size and colour of a small orange. I never did catch that chub, but then I never wanted to. I was also interested to see several bream and although most looked about three pounds, there was one that must have been every ounce of 7lb. There were also one or two large roach and it was obvious the run was a natural holding area for several species.

For several minutes there was no sign of barbel, but once when my eyes wandered to the downstream streamer I caught a flash of orange pectorals. I watched the streamer bed intently thereafter and within a few minutes a big barbel nosed its way from under the sanctuary and slowly swam upstream towards me. That fish must have been all of 10lb and when I saw four more following it I could hardly believe it. None of them were really small fish and two of the four appeared to be well over 8lb.

Later that day (in a torrential thunderstorm) I was to catch my first ever Cherwell barbel – probably the smallest one present at 6lb 1oz – as well as losing one of the big ones in the tree roots. I had caught many barbel much bigger than this during my career, but I was absolutely over the moon with this one. Somehow there was something very special about a Cherwell barbel. That day I also learned other important lessons, not least about the problems of nuisance fish. I had taken several chub, bream and roach and realised that I needed to give more thought to my baiting technique and bait presentation to avoid this problem as much as possible.

During my angling career (which now spans over thirty years) I have had very few frightening experiences that could be attributed to anything but entirely natural causes. I have always found ghost stories great fun and although I certainly have never discounted the possibility of a spirit world, either for good or malign intent, none of my countless night-fishing sorties had ever been disturbed by spectres or things that went bump. I have always found that the countryside is a very friendly and benign place at night. During the eighties, however, I have experienced two nights when the events that occurred have no satisfactory explanation. One of those nights (which you will read about later) happened in the Evening Pitch at Redmire, but the other took place in that barbel swim on the last day of August, 1984. I have never been as frightened, either before or since, as I was that night.

The night was totally breathless with not the slighest hint of a breeze and, as it was beautifully clear and starry, it was not excessively dark. I had not seen a soul all day and complete silence reigned all around me. I was completely relaxed, watching my glowtip intently when quite suddenly the quiet was disturbed by loud clumsy footsteps and distinct heavy breathing sounds. I was not at all concerned. The noises were so loud I knew they had to be caused by someone walking up to me and was certain that Alastair had come down to see how I was faring. I actually spoke out loud to him, but thought it strange that I had not heard him wading through the shallow water that had to be crossed to reach the swim. There was no answer and yet the breathing noises continued, so I picked up my torch and searched the bushes behind me, fully expecting one of my friends to spring out at me. But there was no one there and my little copse was deserted. I even waded back across the small side-stream to the field beyond and searched both upstream and downstream for some explanation, but could find none. There were not even any cattle in the field that I might have heard.

It was once again totally silent when I reentered the copse, as indeed it had been in the open field, and I half-convinced myself that I had imagined it. It was most odd. However, within only a minute or two of resuming fishing, the rustling and heavy breathing sounds started again – so loud that they could not possibly have been imagined and I was now becoming quite apprehensive. Cracking noises right behind me prompted me once again to search the thicket with my large torch and before long I stood at the edge of the open field again, having once more reconfirmed that the bank was deserted except for myself. I remember taking a deep breath and telling myself very firmly to ignore the strange sounds. Somehow there had to be a logical explanation although I was hard pressed to find one.

I went back to my tackle again, turned off my torch and broke out my flask for a welcome cup of tea; I never did drink that tea. Within perhaps half a minute of pouring it, there was a terrific crash in the undergrowth that sounded right next to me. I can tell you that I was getting scared now and with more than a little trepidation I searched the area once again. This time I knew that I would find nothing, but what I did realise was that the thicket had quite suddenly become cloaked in a cold, clammy, swirling mist. Everywhere I walked the heavy breathing accompanied me and I knew that further fishing was impossible.

The visibility was down to only a few yards as I half-waded, half-stumbled across the side-stream, and when I stood on the open field something else struck me as being highly unusual. The only area where there was any mist was that little thicket. Over the rest of the river and the fields there was none, and the night was as beautifully clear as it had always been. That made no sense whatsoever.

My heart was still pounding with nervous exhaustion as I packed the car and as I drove out of the lay-by that night, I vowed that I would never night-fish that swim again. I never have.

In the four years that followed that bizarre night I did make many visits to the swim, always leaving at dusk, and caught quite a few more barbel from it. I was never destined to land one of the bigger fish, losing no less than four monsters in the snags. The best I ever took there was 7lb 13oz. At about the time I caught that fish, the swim had been discovered by many other anglers, and I abandoned it in 1987 and started my search for pastures new.

In early September of that year my many hours of walking and watching were rewarded when, on a little-fished stretch, I located a barbel of about seven pounds in a near-bank cabbage patch. On that first trip I failed to get a bite from the fish and did not locate any others, but it was a good enough starting point. My Cherwell barbel campaign would recommence in earnest.

The following week I was back in the swim, and this time there were three barbel in evidence – although none looked particularly big, it was very encouraging. I had a different plan in mind, one designed to encourage confident feeding in the barbel before attempting to fish for them. I baited the swim very heavily with hemp seeds and then left it alone for several hours to settle. I went and fished elsewhere, and in so doing located two more swims that contained one small barbel apiece. It seemed as though I had found what I had been looking for. I did not bother baiting these two swims, as the barbel looked as if they weighed only about three pounds.

At about 2 p.m. I crept into position in the prepared pitch and peered over the high rushes. My heart nearly stopped when I spotted no less than five barbel feeding over the hemp with gay abandon. One of the fish was a belter, easily 10lb and I tried hard to contain my excitement.

Carefully, I lowered a cube of luncheon meat into the swim. This made the barbel temporarily agitated, but before long they were feeding happily again and I sat in impatient expectation – it was surely only a matter of time. I was, however, to be sadly disappointed. For hours those barbel flashed over the gravel, digging up the hemp seeds, but not once did one look even likely to pick up the meat. I continued fishing well after dark, but finally had to pack up biteless and totally frustrated.

On my next trip I decided that it was the large bait that had been the problem. The barbel had been so preoccupied with feeding on the hemp that I felt they had not recognised the meat as food. So on this trip I decided that I would use a particle hookbait and I arrived armed with not only two gallons of hemp but also plentiful supplies of corn and casters. I had taken many barbel on the hemp/corn combination and that was to be my first plan of attack.

For the first two hours I walked the bank, baiting several areas with hemp and corn, and eventually barbel were feeding in three separate swims. Two of those three swims contained fish of the size I was after, and those were where I decided to concentrate my attention. I would fish each in rotation, periodically topping up the loose feed in each swim. Again, the first few hours were sheer frustration as the barbel seemed oblivious to the corn. As with the meat the previous week, it was as though the hook-bait did not exist and the barbel simply ignored it. After I had spent a considerable amount of time in each swim and had tried the corn counter-balanced, mounted on a buoyant hook and mounted on a hair rig – all with negative results – it was time for a serious rethink.

After a short tea break back at the car I decided to introduce some more hemp into each swim, but this time to add two or three droppers of casters also. My intention was to bait with a bunch of casters on a large hook; perhaps that would be different enough to tempt one of those barbel. When I arrived back at the river, to my chagrin, one of my pre-baited swims was occupied by another angler and I had to be content with the one. It was the swim in which I had fished for the five fish the previous week. After I baited up again, I deposited my gear in the swim and went for a short walk to allow the fish to settle. It was then that it occurred to me that I was missing the obvious. These barbel were very rarely, if ever, fished for and the best bait for them would possibly be the most natural. I had some lobs in the car and I decided that on my first cast in the swim, the offering would be double lobworm on a size 4 hook.

At about 2 p.m. I hid in the marginal rushes watching five barbel flashing over the hemp. I waited patiently until the fish had made one of their regular exits and then carefully lowered the worms to lie adjacent to the gap in the cabbages, from where the barbel always re-entered the swim to start feeding. I sat back and tried to relax. Within two minutes, the barbel were back and no sooner had I caught sight of them when the line lifted, the quivertip thumped round and the smallest barbel in the swim scampered into the cabbages, making the clutch sing. It was not a very protracted fight. The strong tackle was too much for this fish, even though he fought gamely and I was soon well upstream, returning a fish of just under 5lb. As my first barbel from a new stretch of river, it was immensely satisfying.

I had already worked out my plan of action should I catch a fish and now was the time to put it into operation. I would now introduce three more droppers of hemp, more casters and rest the swim for half an hour to give the remaining barbel time to recover from the disturbance. After a sandwich and a leisurely cup of tea, I carefully swung out another double lob offering, and this time the bite was literally instantaneous. The bait can hardly have settled when the rod lurched round in my hand and I was firmly attached to a second barbel – this one eventually pulled the scales down to 5lb 15oz. That was the second smallest in the shoal – I was certainly doing things the hard way.

After another deliberate break, a third bait was taken in an identical manner, and this time the barbel that graced my net weighed 6lb 10oz. They were slowly getting larger and the only two fish left in the swim were now big fish. I estimated one at about 8½ pounds and the other was a possible double. When I came back to the swim after returning the six-pounder, I could see the remaining two barbel still feeding furiously on the hemp as though nothing untoward had happened, and I therefore decided to introduce another hookbait immediately. I regretted that decision almost instantly because the fish disappeared and for about fifteen minutes the swim was barren. I really thought that I had blown my chance with my impatience.

I need not have worried. The pulling power of the hemp was too great and before long the barbel were back over it. I could not see my bait at all from my crouched position behind the rushes as it was obscured by a lily leaf which I did not dare to move. As the bigger of the two barbel shoved his snout under the same leaf, I am sure that I stopped breathing and then there was a large puff of silt as the fish rocketed downstream, dragging my rod after him. As I scrambled to my feet, the clutch whined and the barbel ploughed about twenty yards through the cabbages, only stopping when it was deeply immersed in the roots. Without hesitation I plunged into the river which was luckily only about three feet deep at that point as it would have been heart-breaking to lose yet another monstrous Cherwell barbel. Once I managed to get a different angle of pull I was lucky in that the barbel came clear quite easily, but there followed a pulsating scrap, during which the fish twice more had me snagged. Eventually, however, it was beaten and over the net he came. As he folded into its capacious mesh, my feelings of elation are difficult to describe. Once on the bank I thought the fish would probably go to about 9½ pounds as it was quite short and stocky. So when the needle steadied at 10lb 3oz, my joy was complete. Days later I still could not believe that I had actually landed a Cherwell double.

The following week I returned for another session, after which I thought that I would move on again. I honestly thought that I had caught the biggest barbel in the stretch. Looking in the same swim on my arrival, I was astonished to see no fewer than seven barbel in the swim, four of them being new fish. The two smallest fish I had taken the previous week were not present but I was pleased to see the ten-pounder again. Barbel fight themselves to a standstill and it is always comforting to have confirmation that no permanent damage has been inflicted. An eighth fish drifted into view then – this barbel was monstrous. It appeared several inches longer than the ten-pounder and so I estimated that it could be as much as 13lb. This was altogether a different dimension; I had stumbled across a totally neglected gold-mine.

For the remainder of that summer and autumn, I fished the stretch as often as possible and never had another bite from a barbel.

On the day I found it, the monster lay looking at two lobworms for hour after hour without showing the slightest intention of eating them, and I was not to see the fish again for two years. Within two weeks of its discovery, the autumn rains had heightened and coloured the river and visual location became impossible. Without being able to see the fish, Cherwell barbel fishing is a complete lottery.

During the 1988/1989 season, the poor summer meant that it was the most frustrating season on that stretch. On every trip there was too much colour to spot any fish, and although I fished very hard in all the areas in which barbel had previously been located, I never had a bite to show for my efforts. There is one incident, however, that is very worthy of recounting.

I had spent the day fishing the known barbel swims during a high autumn flood and had caught one small chub when I decided to leave early. On my walk back to the car I noticed a large moth struggling in the fast water, just behind a large far-bank raft. All of a sudden, there was a boil and a very large chub engulfed the unfortunate insect. Just for fun, I decided to try a floating bait for that fish – it certainly looked big enough to partially recompense me for the lack of barbel activity. I had no bait other than meat or lobs with me, so I reverted to a weightless line and air injected two lobworms so they floated for quite a few yards before the weight of the large hook slowly began to submerge them.

The very first cast led to success. The worms alighted just clear of the branches and had only drifted about two yards when they disappeared in an exciting swirl which resulted in a nice chub of about 3½ pounds. Two more chub soon followed to the same presentation and I was thoroughly enjoying myself. The fourth cast met with no response and the worms drifted out towards mid-stream, slowly sinking as they went. Suddenly, there was a vicious tug and I found myself playing a powerful fish that felt like a shark in the heavy flow. It took me a long time to subdue that barbel, and when I landed a seven-pounder, I was very surprised that it was not a lot larger. That fish was a total fluke, of course, and I can claim no credit for it whatsoever, but it was extremely interesting. Those worms still had to be very close to the surface when they were taken.

So we come to August 1989. I had taken my twelve-year-old daughter Jacqueline for a day's chubbing on the barbel stretch where the chub are very visible and therefore there is more interest for a child. At about mid-afternoon I was showing her a shoal of chub under the branches of a trailing willow when a movement right under my own bank caught the corner of my eye. I was standing on a high bank, about four feet above the water, which was clothed with dense brambles and sharp thorn bushes. This tangle of vegetation overhung a 30yd-length of bank by about two yards, creating a mysterious near-bank tunnel. I watched intently the spot at the outer edge of the branches where I had detected the movement, and within a minute it was repeated. Under a single frond of ranunculus, which was wafting around in the steady current, there was the most enormous barbel tail. I did not need to see the rest of the fish to know that it was a good double. As I watched, more of the fish came into view and then I became very excited indeed. There, right beneath me, was the enormous fish I had first located two years previously.

I had no equipment with me that day which would make the swim slightly more accessible, so I had no choice but to fish over the brambles and thorns. My long-handled landing net would give me a sporting chance of landing the fish despite the snags. I decided to give the fish plenty of bait over a three-hour period, topping up at regular intervals to encourage it to feed confidently. During that period I never attempted to fish the swim, but contented myself with chubbing elsewhere.

At long last, at about 5 p.m., I swung out a size 4 Au Lion d'Or to 8lb Maxima, baited with four grains of corn. The bait landed perfectly, just inches away from those overhanging brambles. Within seconds the rod hammered round and a lively chub sprinted across river with great alacrity. It was not a very big fish, about three pounds, but the trouble I had netting it over those brambles warned me of what to expect if I were to hook that barbel. At that moment it was obvious that I may have to take my life in my hands and leap into the river over those sharp bank-side bushes if that were to happen.

With another bait in position, Jacqui and I sat for about twenty minutes, demolishing the remainder of our sandwiches. Just before 5.30 p.m., the quivertip gave a sharp jab and then pulled round in very determined fashion. I struck and then all hell let loose. There was an almighty swirl under the brambles and an impressive vortex appeared as a gigantic barbel shot upstream past me. I had a close look at the fish and I thought it could be as heavy as 13lb. Seconds after I had hooked it, it turned abruptly downstream again to dive back under the brambles from whence it came. Everything went ominously solid and I could feel a horrible grating sensation on the line. Just as I was bracing myself for that leap into the river (which would certainly have scratched me to shreds) there was another strong lunge and the line parted. I was devastated and sat for several minutes in total silence, looking sadly at the broken line fluttering in the warm evening breeze. At that moment I vowed that I would return to the fishery as often as it took, until that great barbel at last rested in my landing net.

The following week I returned with a set plan of action. I had equipped myself with a new pair of breast waders and at mid-morning I went into the river with secateurs with the aim of making an access point large enough to allow me an unhindered entry to the river from the fishing position. For several hours I worked in the 4ft-deep swim, and at the end of it had created a 3ft-wide gap with a step just above the water. It would be a simple matter to slide down on to that step if a big fish was on the end of my line. I also cut a large clump of willow with which to disguise the new swim on my departure.

Obviously the swim required some time to settle after I had completed my task, but before I went off to fish elsewhere I deposited ten droppers of hemp and two of sweetcorn on the clean gravel at the downstream extremity of the gap I had created. It was several hours later when I returned to look and I was gratified to see several chub feeding vigorously, but there was no sign of barbel. Nevertheless I felt there had to be barbel under the brambles somewhere and in late afternoon the first bait, again a bunch of sweetcorn, came to rest over my hemp carpet. Again the chub were on to the bait immediately and I was very surprised that they were all I caught that evening although I fished well after dark. When I packed up I was very disappointed although I had taken

Four four-pounders are included in this winter catch.

A lovely 10lb 1oz Cherwell specimen.

four nice chub – the top sample was an absolute cracker of 4lb 14oz. Actually, that chub is my biggest ever from that stretch of the Cherwell and I should have been over the moon with it. I was, however, totally obsessed with thoughts of the massive barbel I had lost.

On my arrival the following Thursday, I walked the entire stretch and baited all the areas where I had ever seen barbel, together with many where I had not. It was a possibility that the big one had moved again and I would feel far more confident if I could locate it first before fishing. About two gallons of hemp and four tins of corn later, I found barbel in three swims. My new swim contained a fish I put at about eight pounds, but in another area I caught a glimpse of a much bigger individual. It was not the monster but it certainly may have been a double and I decided he would be my first target.

A little after 2 p.m. I settled behind the tall willow herb and lowered a bunch of corn grains so that they rested alongside the marginal cabbages only a rod's length out from the bank. I did not have long to wait. After a couple of minutes the tip thumped over and I was into a very big barbel indeed. The fish fought tremendously hard and then jammed solid in the mid-stream rushes. I had no intention of losing another so, without hesitation, I slid down the steep bank into what I thought would be four feet of water. As it happened I landed on a sandbank only ankle deep underwater, so did not receive the soaking I was expecting. The different angle of pull made all the difference though and I was very relieved when a rush stem broke away and the barbel came free again. At long last the fish approached the rim of the net and then he was mine.

Once I stood back on the high bank and could examine my prize, I must admit I was slightly disappointed to discover what I did. There was that unmistakable distorted pelvic fin with the double 'V'. There was no doubt that it was the same fish I had caught two years before at 10lb 3oz. I soon confirmed that it now weighed 10lb 1oz, and although I was happy to have caught another double, the edge was taken off slightly by the fact that it was a recapture.

As I stood in the shallows nursing the fish in the well-oxygenated water before releasing it, I suddenly became aware of another angler watching me. He had seemingly materialised out of thin air and his dress and equipment told me that he was a big-fish angler rather than one of the very casual anglers who occasionally fished the stretch. Inwardly I cursed my bad luck. I had so far kept this stretch to myself, or so I thought, and now I had been spotted at the worst possible moment, returning a double-figure barbel. He recognised me and introduced himself as Steve before making a comment that initially irritated me intensely and then had me puzzling for hours over what he actually meant. He said 'I see news travels fast', and left it at that. When I pressed him for an explanation, he clammed up and then disappeared upstream to do some fishing of his own.

The implications of his comment were obvious enough. A very big fish must have been caught recently and Steve had naturally thought that I had heard about it and chased up the news. But what had been caught, how big was it and who was the captor? It was intriguing and I had to get to the bottom of the mystery. I was to do exactly that only a few hours later.

I was sitting in my new swim after dark when Steve came walking past me on the way back to his car. He sat down alongside me for a brief chat and I asked him again what he had meant. There was a short pause, and then he swore me to secrecy before telling me that Simon Lush had taken a barbel of 12lb 1½oz the previous week. That was absolutely amazing to me. Simon and I are old friends and although I knew that he had been fishing the Cherwell for barbel as hard as I had, I was convinced that he was on another stretch several miles away from mine. Until that moment I had no inkling that Simon and I had been fishing the same area. He had similarly been ignorant of my visits and we had obviously been kept apart by the fact that I always fish midweek rather than at weekends.

At home that night it was all buzzing through my mind. Was the twelve-pounder the same fish I had seen and lost? Logic said that it probably was. Also, Steve had apparently foul-hooked a fish that had been weighed at 10lb 10oz, so I now had confirmation that my stretch contained at least three different doubles. It was very exciting and the next morning I was really pent up as I arrived at the fishery once again. I followed my normal procedure of an extensive baiting programme, allowing the barbel plenty of time to get their heads down and did not actually start fishing until after lunch. When I did so I was again rewarded for my patience with instant success in the swim where I had taken the ten-pounder, and soon landed a spirited barbel of 6lb 14oz. That was the only bite I was to get in that area and just at dusk I moved into the bramble hole where I had seen the estimated eight-pounder the previous day. My estimate proved to be accurate as, within five minutes of my first cast, I was weighing an immaculate specimen of 8lb 5oz. I fished on till well after dark with no further response and as I trudged back to the van I was in a very thoughtful mood.

Early the next week I phoned Simon, both to congratulate him on a magnificent capture and to establish the fact that, as we were both fishing the same stretch, it would be common sense to share information for our mutual benefit. Simon saw the logic of that immediately and we agreed that from then on we would keep each other informed of all developments.

That following Thursday was one of the major highlights of my angling career. I baited the usual crop of swims on my arrival and I soon spotted a huge fish in the swim where I had taken the ten-pounder. I knew straight away that it was the twelve-pounder and my plan of action was put into operation. I had no intention of putting a bait anywhere near that fish until just before dark, when it would be at its most receptive and all day I steadily fed the swim with about four pints of hemp, three pints of casters and over half a gallon of maggots. The hours when you are not fishing for small-stream barbel are the most important.

To occupy the time, I spent the day fishing a lovely near-bank run, about forty yards upstream of the hot spot. After I had baited this run first thing in the morning, it had become colonised by a shoal of good bream, two of which looked like samples of 7lb or more. I thought it would be a bit of fun trying to catch one of them, but I never did manage it even though the bream were in and out of the swim all day. I did have one bite, however, that took me completely by surprise. I struck at quite a small deflection of the tip and was amazed when a barbel swirled on the surface and then raced upstream, demolishing a bed of cabbages as he did so. For several minutes that fish dashed around with great enthusiasm, but eventually he succumbed to the relentless pressure from my Tricast 1¼lb rod and slid into the net. He was a lovely barbel, short and deep and took the needle round to 8lb 15oz.

A lovely sunny afternoon was just giving way to a beautiful golden sunset as I carefully lowered a large bunch of casters to rest alongside that near-bank cabbage patch. There was not a breath of wind and I sat there in silent expectation. Five minutes passed and then the line gave a little jerk, followed by the most incredible plunge on the rod. It would certainly have gone in the river had I not been holding it. Perhaps fitting for the size of the fish I had hooked, there followed one of the most memorable battles with a fish I have ever had. Twenty yards of line disappeared on the first run as the fish surged upstream under the dense overhanging alders that lined the bank. I was in imminent danger of becoming snagged and so I once again slid down the bank into the river from where I could impose maximum side-strain, away from the dangerous roots. Very slowly, the barbel yielded, with line singing and I was able to gain a little line. Presently the fish was directly opposite me and then, in the twilight, there was a sight I shall never forget as a huge dorsal broke the surface. Several more minutes of arm-aching stalemate followed before the barbel slowly began to lose ground and was led inexorably towards the waiting net. For what seemed an eternity it refused to come over the net cord, but then suddenly gave up the scrap and sagged heavily in the mesh. I let out a whoop of joy. There was no doubt at all that I had just landed a truly awe-inspiring barbel.

Once it had been unhooked I carefully zeroed my Avon scales and then, with bated breath, lifted the weigh bag on to the hook. Holding the beam of the torch steady, I

My biggest barbel to date – 12lb 5oz from the Cherwell.

waited impatiently for the needle to settle and when it finally did so at 12lb 5oz, I punched the air in delight. It was a truly exceptional barbel and enormously long which suggested that it was nowhere near its maximum potential weight.

It took me quite some time to take it all in, but a little later with the fish safely ensconsed in a capacious carp sack, I telephoned Trefor West with the news to see whether he would be prepared to drive fifty-odd miles to photograph the fish for me. I never had any doubts and, about 1½ hours later we stood on the bank together, admiring that truly magnificent barbel.

The following week it was Simon's turn to congratulate me and during the conversation we exchanged sufficient information about our respective captures to establish that they were in fact the same fish. Probably the volume of feed I had given the barbel to eat before I had caught it accounted for the 3½oz weight gain!

On the following Thursday Simon and I met on the river bank for the first time and discussed the incredible events of the last three weeks. We now knew that there were three different doubles in the stretch and we both said that our target was the fish that Steve had foul-hooked at 10lb 10oz, which was apparently a mint-conditioned and magnificently-proportioned fish. As far as I was concerned, the time when I caught that fish would be the signal for me to move on and search for another area.

The Thursday evening was uneventful, for me at least. While Simon managed a barbel of 7lb 13oz, my sole bite produced a very small chub. The water had been more coloured of late after some very welcome rain and I had persevered with a lump of luncheon meat all night without response. On the Friday morning I noticed that the colour had measureably cleared again and decided to fish with the swimfeeder, using a large hook carrying a big bunch of maggots. I fished all day on my own, Simon having gone to work, and the daylight hours produced one good bite only in the same swim where Simon had taken the seven-pounder the previous evening. It was a good barbel of 7lb 11oz, but the absence of previous hook marks proved it was a different fish.

Just at dusk on a particularly unpleasant evening I moved into the 'doubles' swim. It had become quite windy and the persistent drizzle had now turned into a heavy downpour. For probably half an hour I sat there unmoving, watching the motionless glow-tip as the rain beat down on the hood of my wax jacket. My right index finger was crooked loosely around the line at the reel and my mind was wandering a little. I had not eaten for hours and a local Chinese take-away was becoming a more attractive proposition by the minute. It crossed my mind to pack up early because of the conditions, but I compromised. I would have another fifteen minutes and then I would be off.

That was an inspired decision because, about five minutes later, the pressure on my finger suddenly increased and the rod top arced urgently towards the dark surface of the water. It was like striking into a sand-bag. Unlike the other good barbel I had hooked in the swim, this one showed no inclination to go anywhere in a hurry and simply refused to come off the bottom. I slid into the river once more to be safe with the netting, but it was ages before I had any idea of the size of fish I had hooked. I just knew it was big.

The rain stopped as I entered the river and a bright moon came from behind the black clouds in time to illuminate another very long barbel that was slowly being drawn towards me. I kept quiet and low until the fish was over the net and then watched in triumph as another super fish was safely ensnared. Even in the darkness, I knew it was a double and I took out my small flexible torch while the fish was still in the landing net. A quick scan revealed no distorted pelvic fin and no red scar on the tail root. The barbel was therefore neither of the doubles I had caught so far this season – it had to be the one I was after, the one that had been foul-hooked.

I was exultant as I scrambled up the bank and before long I had my large torch on the job to examine my prize properly. It was then that I started to have doubts. Simon had described the 10lb 10oz barbel as being short and exceptionally deep, whereas this specimen seemed in perfect proportion. I lifted it on to the scales, and could not believe the testimony of my own eyes – it registered 11lb 4oz. I was dumbfounded – what an incredible three weeks it had been, I could hardly believe this was happening to me.

Simon Lush had witnessed the foul-hooked double, so I phoned him at home late that night to see if he would come out and do the honours with the camera. This he readily agreed to do and before long we were walking through the steady rain back to the river. As soon as I lifted the barbel out of the sack, Simon confirmed that it was definitely not the one that we were both after. For a few seconds we were silent and then the realisation dawned that this eleven-pounder had thrown everything back into the melting pot. Here was a fish we had not seen before and which had never before been caught. How many more big barbel could be present that had hitherto avoided detection? Speculation on this is still being investigated.

As I write, we have both just made the decision to move on, for the time being at least. In the last ten days, the twelve-pounder has been recaught by Simon at 11lb 14oz and my 10lb 1oz fish recaught at 9lb 11oz. I have myself recaptured the 11lb 4oz fish at 10lb 12oz, and it is obvious that the fish are now losing weight through stress.

The fact that the last seven fish have all been recaptured suggests that there are very few new fish to be caught, although neither of us has yet seen the short deep one. Even the one recent fish that was not recognisable, a barbel of 9lb 1oz I took on my last trip, did have a clean cut in its tail fin, suggesting that it may have been foul-hooked by one of us. We have both lost several barbel that have picked up the hooks on their large fins.

After four intense seasons I am now starting again, investigating another stretch of the beautiful Cherwell that, as yet, has no known barbel form. It is an exciting, if daunting, prospect and I wonder what the future holds.

9 Royalty Reminiscences

Exactly one week after I had landed the first barbel of my career from the Thames, I fished the famous Royalty fishery for the first time. Again it was my new-found friendship with Merv Wilkinson that was responsible for my presence on this most famous of waters, and as the gates opened we made our way to a swim that was one of Merv's favourites, Harrigans, which is on the opposite bank to the pipe slack. The pressure on the water in the late-sixties was incredible, with anglers actually racing each other for swims and three or more often fishing a swim that really was only big enough for one. Indeed, on that morning, the pipe slack was being fished by no less than three men – Pete Rayment, Terry Eustace and Peter Wheat. Merv and I fished Harrigans together because of the crowds. I had never fished a water before under such intense pressure and I must admit that I was not very impressed with it. I preferred, and still do, a water where I can move freely rather than one where I am forced to stick to one swim. Talking of the crowded banks reminds me of the funniest incident I ever saw on the Royalty.

I had walked down the field from the weir-pool, a little earlier in the morning than I was supposed to, and had just reached

The famous Railway swim on the Royalty.

Harrigans when I saw two anglers on the opposite bank running full pelt towards each other. They both carried little stools and two rod rests and were obviously intent on securing the Pipe swim for themselves. They had entered the fishery from opposite ends, and the race was nearing its climax. Suddenly one of the anglers launched himself in a spectacular dive that would have done credit to Gareth Edwards and triumphantly staked his claim by jabbing the first rod rest in the swim. The second angler stopped, sat down on the wet grass and cried! What a state to get yourself into over fishing!

As we were sharing a swim, Merv and I decided to pool the bait and both fished on the swimfeeder, baiting very heavily with maggots and supplementing the feeder with regular loads from the bait dropper. We used a gallon each and kept the bait barrage up all day. For the first few hours, there were no bites whatsoever and then we started to get the occasional small eel, plus a flounder to Merv. In the early evening, having by then witnessed three barbel – a double to an angler fishing the Trammels, a nine-pounder to Terry Eustace and a seven-pounder to Peter Wheat – I had the first barbel bite from Harrigans. I can still remember the incredible rod-wrenching pull that fish gave me and it took me a long time to get the better of it. A hard-fighting barbel in a powerful river like the Hampshire Avon was a new experience. Eventually, however, Merv swung it ashore and weighed it for me at 7lb 4oz, a new personal best. It was only the second barbel of my career and I was ecstatic with it. Just before dark, Merv finally took a nice barbel himself which weighed about 6½ pounds and then we set off for home.

The journey was interesting. Travelling to the Royalty and back from Coventry in a single day is very tiring and I must have fallen asleep in the passenger seat. I remember being woken up by the wheels bumping over something, and as I opened my eyes I could see that we were driving along the road out of Banbury. The bumping was a result of the near-side wheels going up the verge – Merv was asleep at the wheel! Having rectified that slight problem and having wound the windows down to allow some fresh air into the car, we talked incessantly for the rest of the journey to keep each other awake. Six miles from home, however, we unexpectedly ran out of petrol; the gauge must have been faulty. The car stopped at the top of a very steep hill but we knew that at the bottom of it, about three-quarters of a mile back along the road we had travelled, was an open garage. So Merv and I walked together to the garage, picked up a gallon of petrol and then puffed and wheezed our way back up the hill to the car. It was only when we had regained our breath that the same thing occurred to us

A lovely 8¾-pounder from the Pipe swim.

An 8¼-pounder from the weir-pool.

simultaneously: why had we not turned the car round and free-wheeled down the hill to the garage? What a pair of idiots!

After I had started fishing regularly with Trefor West, we became regular visitors to the Royalty. Throughout the seventies the pressure on the water lessened considerably, although it was still popular, and there was always a choice of available swims. Some tremendous catches of fish came our way, but I have never caught a very big Royalty barbel. The biggest I have ever taken there was an 8¼-pounder and is memorable since it was the first barbel I ever took by legering upstream, a method that has since been developed with such devastating effect.

I was fishing at the tail of the weir-pool on a day when I had already taken a couple of nice fish from the railway pool. I decided to leger upstream in the main flow from the weir, well above the point where the current backs round and flows back towards the weir along the wall. I had never really persevered with the method before, but that day I kept amending the weight of the terminal tackle until I had the balance just right. There was a nice upstream deflection in the rod top and the line was taut – able to withstand buffeting by light surface debris but sensitive enough to drop back immediately if a barbel picked up the bait. After about ten minutes there was a sharp tap on the rod top, and then the tight line collapsed downstream. It was a classic upstream legering bite. Picking up the rod, I wound up a couple of yards of slack and then struck into a strong fish that shot into the white water with almost unbelievable power. For over fifteen minutes I fought that fish, several times having to yield more than ten yards of line to surging runs, before the barbel was eventually wallowing in the relatively quiet water in front of me and I was able to net it. At about the time I caught that fish, there had been discussion in the angling press about the supposed poor fighting qualities of Royalty barbel; that muscular eight-pounder made nonsense of that.

Although I have never caught a double-figure barbel from the Royalty, I have certainly lost one. A few winters ago Trefor and I were fishing side by side in the swim called Engineers, a steady glide above the pipe bridge where the wire compound is. It was a day when conditions were definitely against catching barbel, with the river quite low and clear and the weather cold and frosty. We even had snow flurries on and off throughout the day and an icy wind made it feel positively arctic. The only chance of action lay with maggots fished in conjunction with the feeder and for several hours we fed steadily, without the slightest sign of response. Suddenly Trefor had a good pull and was into a strong fish which gave him a really exciting scrap before the hook quite inexplicably dropped out. It was very frustrating as the barbel looked every ounce of 9lb.

Not long afterwards I was to do almost exactly the same thing. From my only bite of the day I also hooked a big barbel, a fish that Trefor saw more closely than I and swore was easily over 10lb. I did the hard part and successfully held the fish out of the fast flow in mid-stream, but as it came towards me under very little pressure, it also parted company. That would definitely have been a personal best barbel at that time and I was in a bad mood for days after!

10 From Cuttle Mill to Cassien

The first big carp I ever caught (which was without doubt my most undeserved specimen fish) was taken in the early weeks of the 1967 season. That fish remained my personal best for the species for the next seventeen years. An uncle of mine was a keen angler and he had told me about good carp that were being caught from a small local water of about four acres which was situated behind a housing estate. Apparently, the water was very heavily stocked with carp and was utilised as a stock pond by Coventry and District Angling Association.

One Sunday afternoon I drove over to have a look round, and to have a chat to anyone that I saw fishing. I had no difficulty in finding anyone fishing as the water was packed. There were carp everywhere, hundreds of them, and the water was like a giant aquarium. I was ony there for about an hour, but in that short time three carp were taken – two at about five pounds and a thirteen-pounder which was the biggest fish I had ever seen. They all came on huge pieces of floating bread which seemed to be the only method in use. The chap who had the thirteen-pounder told me that he had baited with a whole small bread roll!

I could not wait to have a crack at those carp and the following week found me setting up my Mark IV cane rod, with 10lb line and a size 2 hook. For bait I had brought along a tin loaf and I broke off an enormous chunk, impaled it on the hook and lobbed it out as far as I could – which was not very far as it was totally unaerodynamic! The wind was such that the bait was blown round into the margins of the swim I was fishing (the one where I had seen the double taken) within about five minutes. I twice re-baited and re-cast and the third bait was half-way through its drift when there was an almighty boil on the surface and the bread vanished. Seconds later I was hanging on for dear life as the line streaked off the reel and the cane rod creaked and groaned. I had never been used to fish taking line in this fashion before, and the way I played that fish was amateurish in the extreme. But the tackle was strong, I had a good hook hold and despite my inexperience with fish of this calibre, I eventually managed to land the carp. My landing net, which was more suited to the chub and perch with which I was more familiar, was never the same again.

I did not possess scales adequate enough to weigh the monstrous fish that lay on the net in front of me and an angler fishing a little way along the bank had to do the honours. When he announced that it weighed 19lb exactly, I was dumbstruck. I am not completely sure, but I think that was the biggest carp ever to be taken from that water. I can claim that I have worked hard for most of the big fish in my career and deserved the success that came my way, but that cannot be said for my 19lb carp. I truly possessed the Midas touch that day!

During the early months of the Coventry Specimen Group, we came across a small water that was absolutely heaving with carp although most of the fish grew to about eight pounds only. There were bigger fish present, but we never caught any. At a group meeting one evening, we decided that we would catch a supply of these carp and transfer them to one of our local waters, Napton Reservoir which is near Rugby. In our enthusiasm, we never bothered with irksome trivialities such as asking permission!

I have no idea how many carp we stocked into Napton, but it must have run into several dozens. Most of the stocking took place in the summer of 1969 and then we drifted away to other things. In the mid-seventies the first of these carp started to show up to specialist carp anglers and the weight they had gained was phenomenal. Many doubles were being taken and the best I heard of was a rumoured 27-pounder. Trefor West and I decided to devote one opening day to the reservoir to see if we could join in the fun. That day resulted in a blank, but it was very memorable for a different reason.

Trefor and I arrived well before dark on 15 June and we had the water to ourselves. Naively, we crept into our selected positions along the canal bank, between the tall rush beds – after all, you do have to be quiet and inconspicuous for carp fishing. It soon became obvious that we need not have bothered and by about 2 a.m., we were both wishing we were somewhere else. Well before day-break the water was heaving with anglers. It was more like the Golden Mile at Blackpool than a serene carp lake. There were radios, tilley lamps, torches flashing all over the place, in fact it was total bedlam. Trefor and I were, to say the least, a little disgruntled.

By about mid-morning, with no sign of a bite to anyone, many of the midnight revellers were either asleep or had already called it a day and some semblance of peace descended on the fishery. The sun had come out and was shining strongly, and during a short walk to stretch my legs, I spotted several big carp only a rod's length out in the corner swim where there was a very dense marginal rush bed. I wound in one of my paste bottom baits and crept into position, armed with a chunk of weightless floating bread crust. Carefully inserting myself as unobtrusively as possible in the rushes, I gently swung out the crust so that it landed perfectly over the group of browsing carp. For several minutes it was nail-biting stuff as several fish came to investigate the bread, but they all shied away at the last moment.

Eventually there were no carp in the vicinity, most of them seemingly having taken up a new station some twenty yards away. I went to lift my bait out of the water in order to move down the bank towards the fish, and as I did so a very big carp weighing well over 20lb materialised from nowhere right under the crust. Before I could stop myself, I had literally pulled the bait away from that cavernous mouth – that was fatal. With a tremendous swirl the big mirror rocketed off in panic, taking the others with him. The bow waves never stopped until they reached the middle of the lake. I could not believe what I had just done – what a cock-up!

There was obviously no point in pursuing those lines of enquiry any further for some time and so I returned to my tackle and cast out a bottom bait once again. By mid-afternoon there had still been no action, but we had observed several carp rolling at the surface about thirty yards out, and decided to fish for them with surface crusts, anchored to beat the drift. That was to lead to one of the most amazing sights I have ever witnessed. My two crusts were perhaps twenty yards apart and as there was considerable activity around one of them, I was watching that bait intently. Suddenly, the bite alarm on the other rod screamed and line disappeared from the open spool at an alarming rate of knots. When I struck, I wondered what was going on as at first there was a curious lack of resistance and then, when I tightened up the line led up in the air. It was only when I realised that it was very unusual for crows to fly backwards that it dawned on me what had occurred.

Obviously I had no choice but to bring the bird down as best I could and hopefully release it unharmed. But I had no chance of that. Because the crow fought against the resistance of the line, I had no control over where it came down and it dived into the reservoir like a guided missile. What followed was almost unbelievable – as if from nowhere, scores of water birds of all varieties converged on the crow and attacked it viciously. It never stood a chance and within seconds it was almost unrecognisable. When we eventually retrieved its body, it was little more than a bloody pulp. There is no doubt that the grebes, coots, mallards and pochards knew an egg stealer and a purloiner of small chicks when they saw one.

My serious carp fishing began in 1969 when I first was introduced to Marlborough Pool in Oxfordshire. One of the new Coventry Specimen Group members, Mick Jelfs, was obsessed with catching a big carp and his enthusiasm rubbed off on me. From

An early double from Marlborough Pool.

then on we would conduct an intensive campaign at Marlborough Pool to see if we could get a twenty-pounder. We had been told that the water contained several twenty-pounders, but were to find out later that in fact there was only one fish of this calibre which had been caught at a wide variety of weights. I never did catch it, in fact my biggest carp from the water was only about fifteen pounds. Mick, however, did manage to land it and it weighed in at exactly 21lb.

I will never forget my first Marlborough Pool fish. I was fishing a floating crust alongside the tough Norfolk reeds with which Marlborough Pool abounded. These reeds had formed a closed bay and even on a windy day the water there was calm, making free-lined floating crust a very pleasant method to use. Many carp colonised this area and on my third visit to the water I was very hopeful of catching one and breaking my blank. The crust had been in position for over an hour with no sign of a carp being foolhardy enough to take it when I decided to change my shoes and trousers. Landing a fish could be awkward at the pool because of the reeds and I may have had to wade out, so I decided to put on a tatty old pair of jeans and my waders, just in case.

Sod's law dictated, of course, that at the very moment I stood there in my underpants and stockinged feet, the crust disappeared and the reeds parted as a big carp crashed through them. It was steaming off for the centre of the lake, having gone straight through about eight feet of the tough stems. I thought that I had no chance of landing the fish as my line was caught solidly in the reeds and the fish was more or less going where it liked. I had to go in and so, in my unsuitable attire, I plunged into the lake and waded out to the head-high jungle that separated me from the open water. There is no doubt that I was incredibly lucky with that fish. I only had to break one reed stem away to find myself in direct contact with the carp and when I played it back towards me it very obligingly came straight back through the foliage along its original path so the line did not snag at all. Eventually Mick was on hand to net a very pretty mirror of 12½ pounds – our first Marlborough carp and consequently a fish that meant an awful lot to the both of us.

Mick Jelfs with his 21lb Marlborough Pool mirror carp.

That fish apart, most of our early carp from the water were taken on large pieces of plain legered bread flake. For two seasons this was the standard bait and then we began to experiment more with things like sausage meat and luncheon meat. These were the earliest uses of special baits in our carp fishing experience and it was at the same time that new faces at Marlborough Pool began to appear, armed with exotic concoctions made from various moist cat foods. Many of these newcomers were from the more southerly counties where anglers were ahead of us in carp fishing developments, and almost to a man they were equipped with fast tapered rods capable of throwing baits much further than we could on our plain, orthodox through-action blanks.

Hitherto, we had no cause for complaint, and fished our baits at up to fifty yards from the bank, but our results soon began to dwindle as we continued to fish at this mid-range. Most of the new members were casting their cat-food specials eighty or ninety yards to fish in the proximity of the two small central islands, and after a while it occurred to us that this approach did not entirely add up. In a 25-acre lake most of the baits were landing in a patch of water no more than fifty yards square in the proximity of each island. We reasoned that it would not take long for the carp to wise up to that bombardment and find more comfortable and quieter feeding areas. As we were unable to compete with the long-casting rituals anyway and lacked the cash to do so even if we had been so inclined, we decided to adopt almost the exact opposite approach – we would concentrate on margin fishing after dark and fishing anchored crusts in the dense reed beds during daylight. Results were excellent and most nights saw two or three fish to our margin baits, both floating- and bottom-fished.

On one night that stands out in my mind in particular I was sitting on the bank, totally distracted from the business in hand by a family of badgers cavorting in the hedge behind me, the only time I have ever seen badgers in the wild. I snapped out of it when something smashed into my right knee – it was my nearer rod which was gambolling down the bank! An 11lb mirror had taken off at such speed with my margin-fished sausage that it had tripped the bale-arm and yanked the rod clean off the rests.

Mick and I did have one quite frightening experience at Marlborough Pool. Throughout one Friday night we sat out an incredible thunderstorm and I have never known thunder and lightning to be quite so persistent. As the night wore on the storm grew more intense and at about 3 a.m. its centre was right above us. There was an almighty bang which made the earth shake and then we both saw a ball of fire which seemed to be heading straight for us – it was obviously a thunderbolt. Seconds later there was another immense crash from the other side of the hedge at our backs. That bolt cannot have passed far above our heads because, when we investigated the field the next morning, there was a large circle of scorched grass no more than fifty yards behind our fishing position. We had been very lucky.

When Marlborough began to get impossibly crowded in the early-seventies, it lost much of its appeal to me and for about four years I did very little carp fishing. It was the emergence of Cuttle Mill that regenerated my interest and, although that was also a water that always had its full complement of anglers, it was controlled. Overcrowding was impossible as there was a strict booking system. I suppose in many ways the choice of swim was artificial as it initially involved a race along the bank with a first come, first served regime and later a lot-drawing system. However, the fishery was, and still is, very pleasant and one that provides a valuable amenity in these days of ever-increasing demand for carp fishing.

Trefor and I enjoyed many relaxing days at Cuttle Mill with plenty of hard-fighting carp to provide occasional explosive bursts of activity. It was a lot of fun because, as it is such a shallow water with a good head of fish, the carp show themselves well and are reliable surface feeders. We never did catch any of the twenty-pounders for which the venue was famous, but plenty of double-figure fish came our way.

My own best from the pool weighed 16lb 4oz and was caught on by far my best day in terms of the numbers of fish I caught. All day long runs came regularly and at the end of it I had taken eleven carp weighing from

Trefor with a pretty Cuttle Mill common carp.

5lb to the sixteen-pounder and including five other doubles, and I had also lost three others and missed two runs. They were caught on a variety of baits and I think they would have picked up anything that day. I had one on corn, five on anchored floating crust, four on legered cheese and one on legered sausage meat. The total weight of fish was just over 112lb, which gave an average weight of 10lb plus. These days that will obviously sound like chicken-feed, but in the mid-seventies eleven fish averaging over 10lb was a hell of a catch to an angler who was still waiting for his first twenty-pounder, and I still remember it with great affection.

After about three years of quite contented fishing at Cuttle Mill, however, the lottery system started to prove very irksome and I hankered after more freedom of expression and more solitude in my carp fishing. I was

The biggest I took from Cuttle Mill – 16lb 4oz.

looking for competition between me and big carp rather than between me and other anglers. For several more years my interest in carp fishing once again waned, but then a neighbour mentioned that he was heavily into carp fishing and belonged to quite an exclusive Midlands carp syndicate. Two waters were involved, both of them not too far from my Coventry home and I asked John to investigate the possibility of my joining. This he did, and I was invited down to one of the lakes on the following Sunday afternoon to talk to the man who headed the syndicate. After an hour's conversation I was offered my place and I went away quite happily. The cheque was in the post that same evening.

While we talked on the bank, I saw many giant carp cruising around the shallow water in the strong sunlight and was informed that at the last count the pool contained at least twenty different twenty-pounders, with one fish that could be scraping 30lb. While I was there two high doubles were landed after accepting floaters, and my appetite was well and truly whetted.

For what remained of the summer of 1983, I fished the new water, taking several nice fish up to 16lb, but I still never managed that elusive twenty-pounder. That was all to change on opening day, 1984.

One thing I had certainly noticed in the time that had elapsed since my last trip to Cuttle Mill in the late-seventies, was how

Margin-fished luncheon meat accounted for this Cuttle Mill leather carp.

carp fishing had changed, particularly in relation to baits and bait presentation. In the close season of 1984, I endeavoured to learn as much as possible about the relatively new boiled-bait scene and the family of terminal rigs that had grown alongside these new baits. At a NASA conference I remember spending hours with Clive Diedrich and Malcolm Winkworth, who at that time were taking phenomenal catches of big carp from the southern pits, and in that time learned a lot about the new methods.

One thing I had gleaned from my new syndicate water was that, although there had been fish caught on floaters in my presence that first day, that particular presentation was becoming more and more ineffective. For one thing, the enormous population of water birds made using floaters an exercise in total frustration. The bulk of the fish over the previous two seasons had been taken on hard boilies and almost all the members had been using sweet fruit flavours, particularly strawberry. I admit that I would have done the same, had not Clive pointed out to me that a totally new flavour could be very successful. He also advised me to bait very heavily if I were to use a new flavour. I found this very interesting since the consensus of opinion among the members was that very light, free feeding was the best approach. Most of them put out no more than a dozen loose offerings in the vicinity of each hookbait.

There was no more successful carp angler from whom to take advice than Clive and so in the three weeks leading up to opening day, I pre-baited very heavily every evening, with a home-made boilie based on Richworth ready-mixed base, flavoured with peanut and sweetened. The swim I had earmarked as my favourite was vacant when I arrived on the afternoon of 15 June and I waited for midnight with great impatience. No matter how many years pass, I am still as excited on the night of the 15th as I ever was.

The swim I was fishing is still my favourite at the fishery – a prominent point about forty yards from a substantial bed of potamogeton, close to a small island and separated from my position by a very narrow strip of water. My pre-baiting had been concentrated around the fringes of the weed bed and the point of the island and during the dark hours, one bait was positioned in each of these areas.

Soon it was midnight, and all over the pool splashes could be heard as baits landed in prepared pitches, to be followed by the bedlam of Optonics being set. After a frenzied ten minutes of activity, silence reigned again and the warm breathless night closed around me. I had intended to stay awake all night, but my drooping eyelids got the better of me and I slept until a little after 3 a.m., when I was startled back into wakefulness by the complaining of a grebe that had fouled one of my lines in the darkness. After I had sorted that out and had taken up the slack line, I put the kettle on for a cup of tea; I would sit and watch the dawn. At that moment, there was a short shrill from the

Pop-up strawberry cream boilies were used to catch this 22½lb beauty.

other alarm, and then a high-pitched scream as line disappeared rapidly from the open spool. That carp never stopped for about thirty yards, luckily running straight out into open water. It was then a case of my winning the line back a little at a time. The fish never actually took any more line off me, but put up a dogged and stubborn resistance for all that. When I eventually landed a superb looking mirror, I knew I had been in a battle – my right arm really ached. As soon as the net was lifted from the water, I knew that I had caught my first ever twenty-pounder and the scales soon confirmed 22lb 12oz. After seventeen years, I had finally caught a deserved personal best, to overshadow that streaky nineteen-pounder of the late-sixties.

One of my biggest regrets is not having any photographs of that fish. There is a strict rule against carp sacks at the water, and as it was still only the dawn half-light, I set up my flash and enlisted the help of another angler fishing nearby, Barry Jones. Barry took several shots for me, but after the fish had been put back, I noticed that I had incorrectly set the aperture. My worst fears were realised when I picked up the photographs. They were all so badly under-exposed as to be totally useless. That was bitterly disappointing as I had waited many long years for that fish.

The lack of photographs made me determined to return and put another twenty-pounder on the bank, but for many weeks I was destined to lose every candidate I hooked. By early October, I had pulled out of no fewer than four definite twenty-pounders at or near the net cord and was starting to have doubts as to whether I was ever destined to land another. One particular session was especially frustrating.

In early evening, I hooked a very big fish which promptly snagged me in a distant weed bed and then stuck solid. I was convinced that the fish had gone, as for over ten minutes, I pulled and heaved from every angle without anything moving. Eventually however, direct hand-lining did the trick. I had decided to pull for a break, but that did not happen and instead a great ball of weed started moving slowly towards me. It never occurred to me that the carp might still be there, and when the mass of vegetation lay in the margins I climbed down into the water to free my tackle.

The first big clump I removed revealed the presence of a great golden tail and the carp promptly took off into another weed bed, only about ten yards away. I wish I had stopped and thought out the situation before taking the action I did. It would obviously have been common sense to have left the carp in the sanctuary of its new refuge and taken advantage of its docility to clear the great raft of weed in the margins. That would have given me more than a sporting chance of landing the fish. As it was, I got overexcited. Without thinking, I made a grab for the rod and played the carp back towards me, with half a weed bed still draped over the line. The result was predictable. Within minutes, everything was jammed solid and there was so much weed clogging the rod rings that I could neither give nor gain line. Heaven knows how the carp stayed attached so long. For a good twenty minutes, I patiently hand-lined the carp to the near bank and tried to net it, weed and all. It was a job requiring two hands because of the weight involved and each time I stopped to pick up the landing net, the carp swam back out of reach. I was nearly screaming with frustration and eventually the carp must also have realised that he was getting a little bored with this game. With an angry flick of that big tail, he shot away with great purpose. I was powerless to stop him and the line parted with a crack like a pistol shot.

Later that night I hooked another very big carp adjacent to the same weed bed at long range. This time there were no mistakes and I do not think that I could have controlled that carp any better than I did. I was able to counter its every move, even though I was being buffeted by a very strong wind in the darkness and soaked by heavy rain, and when I reached for my landing net I was congratulating myself on catching one of the lake's largest known inhabitants, an Italian mirror. I had twice had a good look at it with my small shaded torch and was therefore absolutely gutted when the hook dropped out just as it approached the net cord. Unbelievable as it may sound, I actually swore!

One of my most fascinating days at the water in 1984 resulted in my second twenty-pounder as well as several doubles, but it was not just for that reason that the session was so memorable. That weekend was probably the most extreme example in my career of following an instinct to fish somewhere other than the planned venue. The session had started out as a Queenford bream expedition, but all morning the constant nagging in my skull that I ought to be carp fishing simply would not allow me to relax. In the end I had to give way to it and return to my syndicate carp water. When I tell you that this decision entailed travelling unnecessarily for over 100 miles, you will perhaps be able to appreciate quite how strong the instinct was.

I can still remember clearly how certain I was that another twenty-pounder would be the outcome, and sure enough the Sunday morning found me on my feet, playing a big fish that had ploughed straight through that potamogeton bed. That muscular mirror gave me a memorable scrap and it was some considerable time before it slid agonisingly slowly towards the waiting net. This time there were no last minute disasters and my second twenty-pounder was recorded, a chunky specimen of 20lb 10oz.

In the years that have elapsed since 1984 I have fished the pool a lot, and have taken several more twenties, but not one to better 22lb 12oz. That remained true until opening weekend 1989 when, not only did I increase my personal best, but I had the best carp fishing I have ever experienced.

I had actually decided to start at the carp water at the last moment and had to shelve other plans at short notice. Consequently, I did not arrive until early evening on the 15th and all the swims on the main lake were occupied. I was in a real quandry. The only vacant water was the narrow strip round the small island where one position looked possible. At this point, the lake did open into a slightly larger bay, which I decided might prove to be a holding area for a carp or two. In fact the more I looked at the swim, the more excited I became about the possibilities. There was an almost total lack of weed in the main body of the lake and therefore no cover under which the carp could take refuge in the very hot, strong sunlight. In the bay in front of me, however, although there was no bottom weed, there were extensive mats of surface algae which had been blown in and then trapped by the steady breeze. Those algae could prove to be a magnet for all the carp in the lake in the conditions that were upon us. With this thought in mind, I baited very heavily with Streamselect strawberry cream boilies, and set up two heavy bolt rigs. I would plunge the baits through the algae and fish in the midst of that sea of green.

On the evening of the 15th many fish could be spotted quite easily, cruising around the main lake, but the clearer areas in front of me appeared barren and I thought perhaps my theory was mistaken after all. My solitary sighting came just before dark and even that was only a small common, but I need not have worried.

At only about half past midnight I had my first run of the new season, a real butt ringer, and a big fish scorched down the

My first fish from Cassien – a beautiful 32lb 4oz sample.

lake towards the small overflow. Its intention was to go round the back of the island, but maximum side-strain just prevented that manoeuvre being successful and the carp turned back towards me, heading fast for the open water of the main lake. Again he was successfully frustrated in his intentions and I now had the upper hand. Before long, he was wallowing in the margins, completely obscured by algae and I netted a carp and a mass of weed together. I still had no idea of its size, but when I had pulled the weed away, I could see that I had again opened a new campaign with a 20lb carp – 22lb 8oz to be exact.

That was exciting enough, but I was on

cloud nine at exactly 2 a.m. when the needle on my Avon scales registered 20lb 4oz. The season was two hours old, I had had two runs and caught two twenties – what a start!

Before day-break, incredibly, I had another two runs which were both from common carp of about fourteen pounds. One was successfully landed, but the other eventually pulled free after towing a branch around for ages. As I prepared breakfast and another steaming mug of tea, I looked back on a truly memorable few hours.

The excitement, however, was only just beginning. At exactly 9 a.m. on opening morning, I was away again and there followed a truly marathon battle with a worthy adversary. The steadily thickening algae made playing the fish extremely difficult, and in fact it became impossible to land a carp from my fishing position, so dense had the weed become. After a long and dogged fight, the net mesh eventually closed around a very fat mirror carp, about fifty yards away from where I had first hooked it. As soon as I lifted it I knew that it was extra special. I had hoped to break my personal best with a fish of 25lb or more and the scales confirmed that I had surpassed my target. 26lb 2oz it weighed, and as I watched it glide away into the depths, my mind was in a daze; three twenties in a morning, could this really be happening to me?

In the late afternoon of opening day, two more double-figure commons were landed and then it was time once again to prepare for the second night. The events of that night were not quite so happy. I had but the one run, undoubtedly from another very big fish indeed. For ages I played that carp, never getting it closer than within about thirty yards of me. It just did not want to yield, and with the interference from the thick algae there was no way I could bully it. Before long, the build-up of weed on the line became so heavy that it was difficult to keep a tight enough line to the fish and the

The swim that produced three twenty-pounders on 16 June 1989.

hook dropped out. Sadly, exactly the same thing happened with an equally big fish on the third night.

I did have some little consolation after dawn, however. I was just cooking my breakfast when a fast run had me tumbling off my bedchair to grab the rod before it flew into the lake. I fish with the bale-arm open and a loose loop of line must have caught behind it, making it snap shut. Another tremendous scrap was terminated when a very fat carp sagged in the net, and for a while I thought that I had managed a fourth twenty. But the scales would have none of that, and my diary received an entry of 18lb 14oz.

Before I left on the third afternoon, I took two more double-figure commons, and I drove home reflecting on the most incredible carp action I havee ever experienced in this country.

In April 1986, I made my one and only trip to date to the water that has become a Mecca for carp anglers in recent seasons – Lake Cassien in the South of France. Andy

Barker and I had been planning the trip for quite a while and had selected mid-April as the otpimum time for an extra big fish, as they packed on weight prior to spawning.

In a normal year, mid-April could be relied upon to give at least pleasant weather in the South of France, but as the date of our trip neared it seemed that this was far from a normal year. Weather reports coming out of the area were very depressing, mentioning torrential rain, storm-force winds and even highly unseasonal frost and snow in late-March. More importantly, the fishing was apparently at a dead stop and only one week before our departure there were reports that very few carp had been caught since before Christmas. The week before we were to leave, Neville Fickling returned from the venue and was able to give us an up-to-date report. Despite fishing very hard for two weeks, Neville had only managed one solitary run and had to wear his one-piece fishing suit for much of the time to keep out the cold and rain. We had been anticipating ten leisurely days soaking up the Riviera sunshine!

All anglers are, however, eternal optimists and Andy and I were no exception. The weather had to break soon and when it did there was every chance of the carp turning on in earnest. Full of hope, we set off from my house in mid-afternoon on Sunday, 20 April. Fourteen hours' hard driving and 1,000 miles later, we were buying our tickets at the restaurant Chez Pierre. It was a lovely warm, sunny day, if a trifle windy and as we set off on a tour of the lake, we felt that we had timed our arrival perfectly. Our first reconnaissance was around the south arm of the water. This had been very little fished during the previous fortnight as there had apparently been no sign of fish activity there, whereas several fish had been seen rolling in the west arm. The handful of fish that had been caught in the preceding weeks had come from the west arm.

With the possibility of a change in weather conditions now upon us, both Andy and I thought it likely that the south arm bars could start to fish, and this belief was soon excitingly reinforced. Within ten minutes of starting to look around, we met Don Smith and his son Jason who were there with a couple of friends, Eamonn and Andy. They had been there for several days and confirmed that the weather had indeed been diabolical for most of the time, but on the one fair day Don had caught a carp of 53lb. On the same day Andy had lost two fish and Eamonn had landed a 41-pounder and so, with this cheering news, Andy Barker and I were straining at the leash.

After a good look around both the south and west arms, during which time I was appalled at seeing the disgraceful amount of litter left by visiting English anglers, Andy and I retired to our caravan to organise our gear. After our long overnight drive we were both badly in need of sleep so we decided to bait up our intended opening swims, find a decent restaurant for a good meal and then get our heads down for an early night. We would start fishing at dawn the next morning.

We had talked at length on which groundbaiting technique we should use. Other anglers had taken catches by fishing boilies over large beds of peanuts or sweetcorn, but in the end we decided to concentrate solely on heavy baiting with boilies. One variation from the norm was that we had decided that our hookbaits would be of a different flavour to the loose feed and that these would be fished on stringers. The idea behind this thinking was that the loose offerings would be used primarily to attract large numbers of crayfish, which in turn would attract the carp to feed on these crustacea. Drawing on my chub fishing experiences and after years of catching crays on a drop net, I know that there is no better attractor for crays than rotten fish. The boilies for loose feeding, therefore, were Richworth neutrals very heavily atomised with fish flavour, the amount of flavour used being totally over the top for normal hookbaits. Believe me, those baits were rank. Unfortunately we made the mistake of atomising them in the caravan, with the result that everything stank of fish for the duration of our stay. The first evening 2,000 of these fishy boilies went into the swim.

The next morning we were disappointed to find that it was overcast, windy and very cold, and it was then that I discovered that I had left all my waterproof clothing hanging in my garage at home. I was missing both my one-piece suit and my wax jacket and trousers. Luckily Andy had a spare set, but at the time I did not realise how much I would need them in the days ahead. Just after first light we commenced fishing using three rods apiece. We used three different baits for the first few days. On two rods we baited with neutrals atomised with salmon and seafood respectively, and on the third we used the ever reliable tutti frutti. About 100 tutti frutti boilies had also been baked to make them buoyant – this would give us the option of fishing a pop-up bait. Three boilies were fished on each hair and each bait was fished in conjunction with a ten-bait stringer to give a local concentration of the given flavour.

Within a very short while of commencing fishing the rain started and it was perhaps as well for our peace of mind that we did not know at the time that the rain was to continue virtually non-stop for almost five days. We fished that first swim for two days without the slightest sign of a fish, and in the incessant, torrential rain it was cold, wet misery. When we eventually packed it in on the third afternoon (which was a Wednesday) all our gear was completely soaked and we were in a disconsolate mood. That night we thanked our foresight in booking a big caravan for the trip. At least we were able to dry the gear in time to re-start operations in a fresh swim on Thursday morning. That night we cheered ourselves up by having a welcome break and driving into Cannes for a civilised meal.

The next morning I awoke early to the most incredible noise. Rain and giant hailstones were hitting the caravan with such force that it sounded as though it were being bombarded with rocks. When I looked out of the window, the rain was falling with such ferocity that I could barely see my car which was parked only a few feet away. There was no way I was going fishing in that lot and so I climbed back into bed to wait for the storm to clear.

Two hours later the rain had slowed to a steady drizzle, and after a leisurely breakfast, we drove back down to the lake. The new swim we had selected was a lot further down the south arm and it took quite a while to ferry our gear into position. The car was left in the compound of Chez Pierre for security. It took about an hour and a half to set up our camp, and during that time the rain intensity began to build up once more. We just about had time to get our baits out before the heavens opened again, and for hour after miserable hour Andy and I were trapped in the bivvy as torrential rain lashed the lake, driven by gale-force winds. An air of deep depression had settled over us both, and at that moment we were both resigned to the fact that our trip was turning out to be an unmitigated disaster. As the evening wore on and the rain became even heavier, we were able to watch the level of the lake rising before our eyes and by midday on Friday, I estimated that the lake had risen about three feet in four days. At lunchtime we packed up and it was then that we discovered that only one of our six Optonics was still working; the others were too sodden to function.

It was a thoroughly brassed off collection of anglers who gathered in Chez Pierre restaurant that wet and windy Friday afternoon. None of us had had the slightest sign of a fish and, which was even more depressing, none of us had expected to. Over a few beers, Don, Jason, Andy and Eamonn decided to call it a day and return home early. They had been sleeping in the back of their vans and as they had no dry clothes between them, remaining would have been both foolhardy and miserable. As the weather forecast for the next week promised more of the same, Andy Barker and I were only a whisker away from making the same decision. After the optimism at the start of the trip, we had now reached an all-time low.

That evening, with all our gear drying in front of the gas fire again, and our Optonics in bits for the same reason, Andy and I discussed the options. At that moment, with the rain still hammering on the caravan roof, it would have been easy to have packed up the car and gone home, especially as the weather forecast gave no real prospect of improvement until at least the following weekend. It was then that the vital decision was taken that it would be silly to go home. After spending the money on the caravan, ferry, petrol and road tolls, we decided that we would stick it out until the bitter end. After all, while there was a bait in the water there was always a chance. I still had an unshakable feeling that one of us would land a monster, but somehow Andy did not appear convinced.

We did not go out for a drink or meal that night, but ate in the van while discussing the situation for hours. Finally we decided that we would switch our attention to the west arm the next morning, a decision that was to prove crucial – we would search this arm, rain or no rain, in a last effort to find some fish.

I was awake at dawn and as I came round there was a strange and unfamiliar sound – total silence! The rain had stopped and there was even blue sky overhead. We spent the first few hours of the day exploring and, although there had been one or two light showers, conditions were definitely improving – it was much warmer for one thing. At mid-morning we finally found what we had been looking for. As we stood alongside yet another west-arm bay, a very large carp obligingly rolled about eighty yards away. Even at that distance, the big golden tail was impressive. We both said the same thing simultaneously: 'We are going to catch from this bay'.

The first job was to get my float rod out and I used it to carefully plumb the depths. After about an hour, I had etablished the essential features before us. We were on a spit of land and directly in front of us, and to the right, the bay was quite narrow – it was perhaps only seventy yards to the opposite, tree-lined bank. To the left, the bay widened out so that it was perhaps 150 yards to the opposite bank which was a steep, boulder-strewn cliff. Further left still was the entrance to the bay and the main body of the west arm. Directly in front of us, there was a wide gravel bar which was a uniform 15ft deep, gradually tailing off to the right to 22ft. The fall away to deeper water to the right was far steeper, dropping to 30ft very quickly. There was a deep channel under the opposite bank at the narrowest point. All in all it looked a perfect place to intercept fish as they moved in and out of the bay.

We set up our rods so that we each fished one bait on the top of this bar and fished the other four where the bottom dropped off on either side. Initially Andy had his two to the right of the bar, with mine positioned to the left. Once again, we had baited heavily with our fish-flavoured boilies, using the other flavoured baits on the hairs in conjunction with ten-bait stringers. By early afternoon we were sitting behind the rods, contentedly enjoying a well-earned beer. There had been one or two showers around midday, but now the sky was blue, the sun hot and the lake flat and calm. This was more like it.

As the evening approached, carp began moving regularly, with one noisy roll only a few yards out from Andy's right-hand rod. We were fully alert and, at long last, one of the Optonics burst into life. It had been a long time in coming. Something had picked up three pop-up tutti frutti boilies which were presented on top of the bar on my right-hand rod. The line was a blur as it left the spool, and as I dropped in the pick up, the rod slammed over to the impact of a big fish moving very fast. Despite the clutch being set very tightly (with the security of 18lb Sylcast) it still screamed out as several yards of line were wrenched away from me. Andy reminded me of the snags with which the bed of Cassien is littered and of the need to get the fish off the bottom as soon as possible. I flipped off the anti-reverse, tightened the stern drag as far as it would go and decided to stop the fish in its tracks if possible, to bring it higher in the water. If I was still forced to give line, then I would yield as little as possible by back-winding. Holding the fish hard and heaving was the order of the day while playing the fish on a properly set clutch, as I like to do, was a luxury I could not afford. Every foot of line lost to the carp increased its chances of finding a snag.

For about ten minutes a really dogged fight continued, with me refusing to give line, and the fish refusing to yield. My arm was aching. Eventually, the pressure had to tell and slowly the fish came towards us. This was the danger time because the margins were a mass of sharp boulders, which even the strong line would not have withstood. I crammed on pressure to the limit to keep the fish on top and Andy waded out beyond the worst of the rocks with the net. There were no mistakes – Andy netted the fish sweetly at the first attempt and a lovely leather carp swung ashore. When he confirmed a weight of 32lb 4oz, I was obviously over the moon. All we needed now was at least one fish to Andy's rods and we could relax. The nightmare was coming to an end.

Andy Barker sets one of his 'monkey climbers'.

We were fishing again well before dawn and it was not long before were were in action again. This time it was Andy's bait on top of the bar that did the trick – three salmon-flavoured Richworth neutrals. The fight this carp put up was a little disappointing, although Andy did the right thing in piling on the pressure straight away. The fish was never given any opportunity to get its head down, and I soon netted a very chunky mirror. It weighed exactly 26lb and was consigned to a carp sack alongside my thirty-pounder to await better light for a photographic session.

After the early morning mist had cleared, it turned into a hot day and one of the perils of fishing at Lake Cassien soon became apparent. Being sunny, warm and a Sunday, lots of French anglers and picnickers made their way down to the lakeside. When Andy and I took the photographs of the two fish at about 11 a.m., we had a crowd of interested French people around us, many with knives and forks at the ready!

We had just returned the fish to the sacks so that I could give Andy a little tuition on how to use my video camera, when I had a slow run on one of my deep-water rods, again on three pop-up tutti fruttis. I had had a small bream earlier on an identical slow run and we were both convinced that this was another of the same. I was soon to discover my error, as my strike was the prelude to the most incredible battle I have ever had with a fish in my entire angling career. Despite the clutch being apparently screwed down as tight as it would go, and the anti-reverse turned off, ready to back-wind if necessary, a fish of unbelievable power and speed took line against the clutch! For a few seconds I was out of control and the scream from the clutch rose to a high-pitched whine. An incredible bow wave headed straight for the boulders on the opposite bank. Knowing that if the fish swam only a few more yards certain disaster would occur, I jammed the rod butt into my groin, clamped the reel face tightly with my hand and leaned into the fish as hard as I dare. It was more like big-game fishing. The rod was nearly ripped out of my hands as the line tightened to singing pitch, and it took all the strength at my command to keep the rod up and to avoid being pointed. I hung on grimly, the rod bending far past its test curve; I could feel the curvature under the reel seat.

Full frontal of my 58-pounder.

For a few seconds, all was stalemate and then, with a thunderous roar of water, an enormous fish surfaced and turned over on its back, the huge tail lashing the water. What an unforgettable sight that was! Foiled in its first attempt to gain sanctuary, the fish now rocketed to my left, heading for some more boulders about 150 yards away. The problem now was that I had so much line out that it was difficult to prevent the fish kiting. Applying the heaviest amount of side-strain possible I only just managed to turn the fish in time, and with every sinew straining I hauled the carp out of the danger area, gaining a few precious yards of line in the process. With the fish now swimming towards me for the first time, I crammed on the pressure to keep it in the upper layers of water. About thirty yards out the carp rolled. A huge golden flank and massive yellow tail made me catch my breath. 'Please don't let me lose this' I said out loud. There were excited shouts from behind me and for the first time I realised that we had an audience. It seemed that every Frenchman within miles was gathered around me! At that moment Andy was a calming influence. 'Just take your time and keep the fish in mid-water and he's ours!' he said, 'he's well over forty.' About ten minutes after I had first hooked it, a tremendous carp rolled into the landing net. With an almighty heave, Andy hoisted it ashore and we were greeted by an appreciative round of applause from the crowd behind us. Only then did we realise the carp's incredible thickness. Even before we weighed it, Andy reached over and shook my hand. We both knew that this fish was not just big, it was gigantic. I still could not believe it when Andy declared exactly 58lb – surely I was dreaming. For the record, the dimensions of that fish were: length, from nose to fork of tail, 38in and maximum girth, 36½in.

I will never forget that Sunday afternoon. For several hours we sat there in the sun, drinking beer and re-living the scrap over and over again. It was hard to take it all in. At about 5 p.m. we re-baited all our tackles and topped up the groundbait. Keeping our faith in the hookbait/stringer arrangement, we catapulted about sixty fish-flavoured free offerings in the vicinity of each hookbait.

Not long after the rain returned, and I do mean rain. For two hours we sheltered under the umbrellas as rain and hail pelted down. The last thing either of us wanted at that moment was a run! Just as it became dark the rain stopped suddenly, although there was still a heavy cloud cover, and there was a decided increase in temperature. It was very warm and humid. In early evening fish began to roll everywhere and then I was away again. Three salmon and trout boilies this time proved the fatal attraction. This was on my deepest rod, and although I had another pulsating and arm-aching scrap, the fish never gained an inch of line. Once again Andy only needed one chance with the net, and we were soon admiring another cracking Cassien carp. Coincidentally, it weighed exactly the same as my first, being 32lb 4oz. I had now taken two thirties and a 58-pounder in twenty-four hours – quite a way to end a lean spell.

The following morning, despite the early promise of a carp fisher's dawn – a glorious sunrise over a calm misty lake – the weather deteriorated rapidly and we were soon back to conditions equalling the worst we had during our first week. The rain started at about 9 a.m. and quickly became torrential. Again we were consigned to hours of sitting under our umbrellas. After I had caught my second thirty, it became clear that the fish, in the main, were feeding in the deeper water. Andy's one fish had come to the top of the bar and his rods to the right had not produced a single run. The water level was now dropping rapidly as the French authorities pulled off the excess. The one thing we did not want was for one of us to get all the action and so we decided to move two of Andy's rods to my left where he could also place baits in deeper water. The priority now was for Andy to get a big fish and he was certainly due one.

The rain finally stopped in late afternoon and the carp activity became intense. It was as if someone had thrown a switch as they were rolling regularly. As dusk approached, a big carp rolled to our right, exactly where one of Andy's rods had been. Every few minutes that fish rolled, each time further left and it was only a matter of time before it found one of our baits. Sure enough, just as it became dark, one of Andy's deep-water rods was away – salmon and trout boilies had scored again. A tremendous battle followed. Early on, the fish

Andy Barker prepares a stringer.

The 'business end' of Andy's 66lb fish.

took one of my lines and this complicated the issue somewhat. This was where the break-away leads we were using proved their worth. Only a few minutes into the fight, my lead was dragged into a snag and for a second or two the fish went solid before the lead link snapped. This was a small price to pay for landing the carp safely and there were no more anxious moments, although it was a further ten minutes before I was able to net the fish. As the carp was layed in the weigh sling, we both estimated it at about thirty-eight pounds, but I was as delighted as Andy when the needle eventually settled on 42lb 8oz. That evening, the beers were on me.

At last, Andy had caught a very big carp, but the next morning he was to catch another fish that was absolutely mind blowing. In the half-light of dawn, old faithful tutti fruttis were taken by a slow-moving fish that fought deep and stubbornly for about twenty minutes. It never made any long surging runs, but a succession of heavy lunges on the rod were irresistible and Andy was often forced to back-wind. There was no doubt that this was an especially big fish; it was sulking deep and just would not come up. Eventually though, I had the fish in my sights, and my first estimate of its weight was way out. The fish seemed about the same length as my 58-pounder but lacked the depth of body, and I thought that it would be a high forty. However, when it eventually slid into the landing net and rolled on its side, I realised that it was much bigger. The width of its belly was amazing. This was confirmed when I tried to lift the net – it was an absolute dead weight.

It was then that I knew that the fish would be close to 60lb. Andy still had not felt the full weight of the carp and his estimate was between forty-eight to fifty pounds. 'Do you want the good news or the bad news?' I said, as I read off the dial. 'Is it a fifty?' he asked. 'No' I said, 'I'm afraid it's not, it's a bloody sixty! Sixty-six and a half, to be exact.' To be honest, neither of us believed it at first, but when we had re-zeroed the scales and re-checked the weight, there it was again – 66lb 8oz. The dimensions were: length, 40in and girth, 38½in.

With the sun rapidly climbing in the sky and the prospect of a hot day to come, Andy's two fish were videoed early and released safely. Understandably we were not really that bothered, after the fish we had caught, whether we had another run or not. In the event we did have one more fish, to Andy's rod the following morning – a beautifully shaped mirror of 35lb 12oz. Of all the fish we had this one gave us the most trouble to land, mainly because a storming initial run to the right took every other line with it. For the last few hours' fishing, we had to re-tackle every rod from scratch. When we eventually had retrieved all the snagged tackles, we had an unbelievable tangle of line, leads, balsa paternoster floats and beads about two feet high. When you have had a few good fish you can laugh more easily at such mishaps, as we did later that morning over a few more beers. A

Andy's unbelievable 66lb carp.

French angler who had been there most days and who was keenly interested in the English carp fishing scene, donated a bottle of very powerful Beaujolais from his father's vineyard to help the party along.

So there you have it. What began as an absolute disaster finished on a high note, culminating in the capture of seven carp for an aggregate weight of 293lb, or an average of about forty-two pounds. When Andy found out later that for the duration of our stay not one single carp was landed by anyone other than the seven we had, you will perhaps appreciate why we both felt so privileged to have enjoyed such a memorable occasion together.

11 Thirty Years on the Leam

The Warwickshire Leam, near my home town of Coventry, will always hold a special place in my affections as it was to its banks that I travelled with my friend Dave on the first day I ever went fishing, aged thirteen. We were on our school holidays and when Dave suggested the trip I was not at all keen, but I went along for something to do. I would have been quite content to sit and watch, but Dave insisted I have a go and borrowed an uncle's tackle for me to fish with.

I still recall the events of that day as clear as if it were yesterday. After a few hours I had mastered the rudiments and started to enjoy myself, trotting down the shallows with a great bulbous float and catching a gudgeon now and again, despite the horrendous presentation! And then I hooked a roach, not a big fish, but at 8oz, one big enough to put a bend in the rod and dash around a bit. From that moment I was hooked and within a few short weeks I had become an angler for life.

For about two years Dave and I fished the Leam regularly, still catching mainly gudgeon and small perch, but occasionally picking up roach weighing a few ounces and small dace and chub. The method was always the same – running a large buoyant float through the streamy water with a tiny hook carrying a single maggot. In October 1959, however, a significant step forward was made. When I arrived at my intended swim just after first light, one of the first things I discovered was that I had left all the maggots at home and as I had taken care of the bait supply, Dave was similarly baitless. We decided to dig up some worms and fished quite happily until mid-afternoon, taking a few small perch. Just after I had lost my last worm, I saw a large swirl in mid-river about twenty yards away and went to investigate. The only thing I had to use as bait were my sandwiches, or what was left of them. So one was vandalised and a lump of cheddar cheese moulded round the hook. The bait had not been in the water ten seconds when the float socked away and I found myself attached to a monster. Actually, it was a chub weighing 1lb 8oz, the biggest fish we had ever seen. Although the presentation was crude in the extreme, I managed a second fish of the same weight and then Dave joined in the fun, taking a bigger one of just over 2lb. In many ways, with the benefit of the wonderment of childhood, those chub gave me more of a thrill than do the comparative leviathans I catch today.

An early encounter with a big Leam perch was to take place only two weeks after that chub catch. I was fishing the same swim, but this time with a big lobworm and played the fish for ages before it came close to the net, where it subsequently came adrift just before the mesh could close around it. After so many years, I know that estimating the weights of lost fish is notoriously unreliable, but I can still clearly picture that gigantic perch slowly sinking into the depths after my tiny hook had pulled out. Even today, I am convinced that perch may well have weighed three pounds.

On Boxing Day 1961, I caught a fish that remains a personal best to this day. Dave and I had arrived at the river to find it frozen over in all but the fastest runs and our favourite swims were all out of bounds. In the end we decided to smash two holes under a line of willows where we knew there was deep steady water and fish through them, Eskimo style. About two hours later, after having created enough commotion to scare every self-respecting chub within five miles, we were ready and we each lowered a big piece of flake under the ice. Incredibly we both had bites within a few minutes, Dave taking a 1½lb chub and me netting a superb dace of exactly 1lb, still the only dace of that size I have ever seen.

My worst ever angling experience took place on the banks of the Leam in the summer of 1960. Dave and I were fishing the Leamington town stretch where we had been taking lots of nice roach to just over a pound on stewed wheat. We were float legering in the very sluggish deep water when Dave went to the public toilets about thirty yards away, leaving me watching both floats. I was relaxing in the sun when Dave's float shot under, to be followed by the rod slowly bending round and being pulled off the rest. I dashed over to pick the rod off the grass and whatever I hooked felt like a sack of potatoes. As I bent the rod more and more, I felt something start to rise and then a jacket cuff broke the surface, along with a bluish-white hand. I dropped the rod in fright. Once my composure had been regained, I jabbered out my story to a passer-by, who dashed off to call the police. Before long, both they and an ambulance were in attendance and the body of an old man was subsequently removed from the water. Although we were told to keep back, curiosity got the better of me and I sneaked a look at the corpse as it was lifted clear of the water. I was to regret that for years. The body had apparently been in the water for some time and was partly eaten away by eels, not a very pleasant sight. Until that day I had thought that the life of a police frogman sounded quite glamourous – I rapidly changed my mind!

As the years passed and I gained more experience of catching big fish, I gradually drifted away from the Leam. I had become involved with the exceptional chub of the Claydon Brook and the Leam fish were now small fry. A three-pounder was still an exceptional chub from the river and this was further confirmed after I had started the Coventry Specimen Group in 1967. Our first target was chub and we all decided to put in an effort to see if we could catch a big Leam fish, but we never did. Although a couple of fish just scraping four pounds were eventually taken, a three-pounder was still a rarity and we all switched our efforts to the Cherwell and Ouse system, where there were much bigger fish to fry.

My re-acquaintance with the Leam was somewhat accidental. In 1975 my son Christopher, who was then seven years old, was pestering me to take him fishing and I thought that the Leam would be the ideal venue. It was close to home and although the chub were not very big, there were plenty of them and they would be quite big enough for a seven-year-old. What is more they had always bitten freely, which would prevent a youngster from becoming bored. However, in the four years since I had last fished the river, something had altered drastically. After two hours on a day when fishing conditions were perfect, I still had not had a bite from a normally prolific stretch and Chris had long since decided that chasing cows and climbing trees were more worthwhile and meaningful pursuits. And then, at long last, I had a bite – a good solid pull that heralded a stirring scrap with a chub only an ounce short of my biggest from the river. That fish weighed 4lb 1oz, a cracking chub in every respect – short,

Chris Miles with a 4lb 14oz chub taken on New Year's Day.

stocky and totally unmarked, certainly having the appearance of a fish in its prime.

That was the only bite I had that day but Chris was delighted with it and I drove home reflecting on the odds of catching one of the biggest chub in the river on a one-off session like that. As the days passed, however, I thought about the events of that day more and more intently. The fact that I had only the one bite nagged at me continually and I had to return the following week to see if that session really had been a fluke, or whether there was anything more to it. That next trip proved to be extremely exciting. I fished hard from dawn till dusk, covering a great deal of water again in perfect fishing conditions, and this time had a total of five good bites. One was missed, but the others yielded chub of 3lb 10oz, 3lb 12oz, 4lb 4oz and 4lb 6oz. After more than fifteen years on the Leam, during which time I had only caught one four-pounder, I had now taken three over that weight in two weeks, including two in one session that beat my previous best. There was now no doubt that the pattern of chub fishing on the river had changed dramatically in a few short years, for reasons that I have never been able to ascertain.

The following weekend I returned once more, to a different stretch and the two fish I caught that day convinced me that I had stumbled across an untapped gold-mine. Within a few minutes of my first cast, I had a 4¼-pounder in the net and then there were many hours of inactivity, despite my fishing many perfect looking swims. About an hour before dark I settled into a swim opposite thick alders and, after putting out four handfuls of mashed bread, I tossed a nice piece of crust under the far-bank branches. A few minutes later the bow in the line lifted and then the rod top bent round as a big fish ploughed off downstream, straight into a mat of fallen branches. Although I eventually managed to haul it clear, the size of the fish was temporarily obscured by the large branch it was towing round, and I thought I had hooked an average chub only. But when I netted it I was dumbfounded. There in the mesh lay a chub in mint condition that looked every ounce of five pounds, and although the scales were actually to confirm 4lb 14oz, the day was yet another confirmation of the exciting possibilites the river offered. A brace of four-pounders two weeks running, with all four fish beating my previous best, could be no coincidence.

When I had relayed my findings to Trefor and he had confirmed them with several fours on his first few trips, we agreed that we had to keep the information to ourselves for as long as possible. The average weight of the fish made it certain that there were five-pounders waiting to be caught and we wanted the first crack at fish of that calibre.

It was actually several seasons before we were to achieve that ambition. In February

An old friend. This 4lb 5oz fish was caught several times.

1980 it still remained unfulfilled, both Trefor and I having come as close as 4lb 15oz. We trudged across the fields on a bitterly cold morning, with thick lying snow and a heavy hoar frost in the air making our ears tingle. As is our normal procedure, we selected a central point with Trefor working the river upstream and me down. That way neither of us impedes the other nor disturbs whatever baiting programme is initiated.

My first swim was one of those classic looking, but frequently barren raft swims. Experience had taught us that a lot of these swims were useless on the Leam. Nevertheless, I would give it half an hour before moving on. Looking back on it, that was quite a surprising decision because I must have fished that swim thirty times over the previous five seasons without a single bite. Something kept calling me back despite the blanks and that February morning was to provide the reward for my perseverance. Only minutes after a piece of crust had been introduced under the rubbish, the tip bent round and I was firmly fastened to a big fish that chugged slowly along the bottom without showing any inclination to go anywhere in particular. The sheer weight on the rod top told me it was a big fish, despite its fairly spiritless performance and that was soon confirmed when I knelt beside a chub that was obviously our first Leam five-pounder. I was in a state of euphoria when I confirmed 5lb 3oz and raced over the fields to Trefor to impart the glad tidings. Incidentally, I have probably fished that swim another thirty times since the capture of that chub, and am still waiting for my second bite from it!

One thing that characterised the Leam

My first Leam five-pounder – 5lb 3oz to be exact.

chub in those days was the incredible condition of the fish. Almost without exception, they were small headed and short for their weight, being very stocky and thick shouldered. But there was one fish that I took from the river that was exceptional, even by those high standards. It was my misfortune that I should catch the fish on a day when I had no colour film with me, as its unusual pigmentation made it the most beautiful chub I have ever seen, either before or since.

The length of alders from where I had taken my 4lb 14oz fish had proved to be a reliable holding spot for several big chub, but there was one section that was very difficult for access. For about six yards the trees hung right down to the river, creating a tunnel about two yards wide. It was impossible to position a bait under that tunnel from the opposite bank and it occurred to me that a big chub could quite possibly have made its home under there, safe from our attentions.

One morning I took along secateurs and a small saw, and spent about an hour making a hole in the alders which were intertwined with clinging brambles. At the end of that hour my hands were covered in cuts, but I had created an access just about big enough to sit in and get a bait in the water. The only problem was that the overhead trees made it impossible to raise the rod very high. Also the bank was quite steep, which would make fishing quite uncomfortable. Once the work had been completed, the swim was pre-baited with four large handfuls of mashed bread and then was left alone for a couple of hours to settle.

At about midday I eased my way into the tiny hole I had created and lobbed out a large piece of crust by hand, three yards downstream and only about three feet from the near bank. Making myself as comfortable as possible in such a cramped little space I waited expectantly, but I was not to wait long. Instead of the downstream pull I was expecting, all the tension fell out of the tackle as the line shot upstream at speed. The chub hooked itself, which was just as well as striking was next to impossible because of the lack of headroom. The restrictions of the swim then became painfully obvious and within seconds of hooking the fish – a chub I could see was clearly approaching five pounds in weight – I was hopelessly tangled. The line was wrapped around a dozen separate alder twigs, while the rod itself was caught fast in the brambles. I was able neither to give nor retrieve line and the chub plunged around on the surface on a short line. How the hook did not pull out or the line break I do not know. In the end I had to put down the rod and apply both hands to the job of freeing the tackle, which took at least ten minutes. My hands were sore and bleeding from being torn by the alders and brambles, but eventually I could resume playing the chub which was by some miracle still attached. Even then I had very little control over the proceedings as I had to hold the rod in the middle to exert any pressure.

With the fish lying docilely in front of me, I reached for the net only to discover the next problem. If the line had been badly tangled, it was as nothing compared to the net mesh. Again I had to put the rod down and let the chub do as it liked while I freed the net, and I soon assembled a further crop of cuts and scratches to add to my collection. Incredibly the chub still lay obligingly in clear water after all that confusion, and at long last I was able to net it. Once I had crawled out of that torture chamber, I could better examine my prize and that is when the profuse bleeding from my hands was forgotten. I had never seen a chub like it. Instead of the normal pale fins they were of the most striking scarlet, and the tail was a very rich royal blue as was the back. While

What an immaculate fish this 4lb 14oz beauty is.

most of the big Leam fish had silvery-grey flanks, this one had a belly which was a much brighter silver and above the lateral line it displayed the same kind of brassy gold as a common carp. The chub obviously lacked much of the normal black pigmentation and because of that it had grown into the most beautiful creature. Not only did its colouration make it special, it was also in tremendous condition and I am as sure as I can be that the fish had never been caught before. With such a lovely specimen, the weight was almost incidental. It did not quite make my estimate of five pounds, being 4lb 14oz, but it still remains one of the most memorable chub I have ever caught.

Apart from my 5lb 3oz chub and one of 5lb 4oz that Trefor had taken the following summer, we did not know of another confirmed five-pounder from the river. There had been the inevitable rumours, but none of them substantiated. One of the rumours was more persistent than most and that concerned a supposed six-pounder that had been taken by a pleasure angler. Trefor and I were a little sceptical to say the least. Although we did not discount the possibility, we had caught so many big chub from the Leam by the winter of 1982 that we felt that had there been any fish of that calibre to be caught, we would have had one by now. Four days before the end of the season, we were proved wrong.

We had arrived well before dawn on one of the stretches we knew best of all, a stretch where the average size of fish was highest but where neither of the fives had been taken. The best we had managed was 4lb 15oz, both of us taking the same fish on successive weekends. The conditions that day were a dream for winter chubbing – calm, mild and with a nice colour slowly fining down. As soon as I saw the river I knew that we would be on to a few fish. The first job was to walk the first length I had designated and bait all the swims I intended fishing in the morning. About ten swims received four handfuls of mashed bread apiece and about an hour and a half after my arrival, I was ready to begin fishing swim number one.

About two hours later with two nice chub already in the bag, I was strolling down the long meadow to the third pre-baited pitch when I stopped quite suddenly alongside a non-descript looking glide under a big willow. I had often fished the swim in the past but with no success and I had not intended fishing it today – it was not one of the pre-baited pitches. Something, however, told me I had to fish it and as I never ignore such impulses, I decided to give it half an hour while I ate a leisurely lunch. I did not even cast for fifteen minutes, but sat on my box flicking in small pieces of bread flake as I devoured my sandwiches. Finally, I baited with the normal crust and flicked it out to the faster current under the far bank, holding the rod high for a little while to allow the bait to bump around naturally and to come to rest on the crease between the fast and slow water, opposite the old willow. I remember how tensed up I was. Suddenly, I knew without doubt that I was going to catch a very big fish and sure enough a few minutes later the tip slowly bent round and the clutch screamed as a powerful adversary shot into the far-bank fast current. For quite a while it was a stalemate, but slowly the fish was drawn into the slacker water where it rolled, giving me my first clear sight of it.

I noticed two things immediately. Firstly the fish was huge, possibly six pounds and secondly my size 6 Au Lion l'Or was holding on by the tiniest sliver of skin imaginable. The next few minutes were agonising as I played that chub with kid gloves, but much to my relief everything held and the fish was soon swung safely ashore. As I unhooked it I was still sure it would go six

Trefor's first Leam 'five' – 5lb 2oz to be exact – which was taken on free-lined lob.

pounds; it really was a very big chub indeed. So my emotions were very mixed when I confirmed 5lb 10oz; I had been way out in my estimation. Upon closer examination, I could see why I had been so badly misled. Although the flanks were very deep, the fish was empty. The belly was so flabby it looked as though it had not eaten for days and I have no hesitation in stating that, in its prime, that chub could well exceed 6½ pounds. Was this the six-pounder that had been reported recently, having lost a few ounces through the stress of capture? It was interesting to speculate.

The next time I saw that fish it was leaner still. It was after dark on, of all evenings, Christmas Eve when the phone rang. It was Trefor. 'I'm down the Leam' he said, 'can you come out and take some photographs for me?' It transpired that he had taken my big fish again, weighing only 5lb 2oz this time and his flash-gun had failed. To the sound of my wife's dire warnings about being late ringing in my ears, I set off for the river after having had to disturb another friend for his flash-gun. Luckily, I had checked mine before I set out and found that that too refused to co-operate.

Not long after, and to the accompaniment of Trefor's apologies for dragging me out at such an inconvenient time, I set up the equipment, checked that the flash-gun was working properly and went to wind the film on. After half a turn, the film jammed. It was the end of the roll and Trefor had no spare! I have never let him forget that and he always carries spare films these days.

Over recent seasons I have devoted a lot

An absolute cracker of a chub. It was taken from the Leam and weighed 5lb 5oz.

less time to chub fishing than I used to, spending much of my winter seeking pike, barbel and roach. So when I do go chubbing, it is with the intention of sorting out the bigger fish. When I gave thought to how that could be achieved on a regular basis, I came to the conclusion that the answer could revolve around the pre-baiting process. This book is not the place to expound the theories I came up with, but suffice it to say that the hub of my plan involved walking the banks and baiting swims for more hours than I actually spent fishing. The first time I took this new approach to a stretch of

A 1lb 15oz Leam roach for Trefor.

the Leam, I was to have quite startling results.

For at least four hours I walked backwards and forwards over about four hundred yards of bank, carefully baiting six selected swims and by about midday I felt that it was time to put my plan into action. Minutes after my first cast, the technique proved gloriously effective. A savage wrench on the tip was the prelude to a good scrap which eventually led to the landing of my second best Leam chub – a short, deep specimen of 5lb 5oz. That was a fish I had not seen before and I took several photographs with the aid of my tripod and bulb release before I slipped back the chub and moved down to the second swim. Ten minutes later, I was regretting not retaining that fish for a little while. The reason was that I found myself weighing a second of 5lb 2oz. I was dumbfounded – never in my wildest dreams did I expect my theoretical solution to be so immediately successful, and to catch two Leam fives in a matter of thirty minutes was tremendously exciting and, I believe, unique. A tremendous trio was completed when a third fish of 4lb 4oz came to net in mid-afternoon.

During our many years of Leam chubbing, Trefor and I came to look upon the multitude of roach bites we experienced on most days as nothing more than an irritating nuisance. Even the odd one that we did pick up on our chub gear did not encourage us to fish for them deliberately, despite the fact that they often went to 1¾ pounds. One

Seven Leam roach in mint condition that were taken on lobs.

February day, when the river was very highly coloured and the chub remained very tight lipped, all that changed. I was fishing lobworms, but the usual chub swims were so fast and full of floating rubbish that fishing was hopeless. On impulse, I decided to go downstream and fish a little backwater that was of steady flow even in high flood. I thought perhaps some chub might have moved into there. In the event it was not chub that found my lobworms to their liking, but roach; and what roach they were. I had bite after bite on the biggest lobs I had and after an hour had landed seven roach, all over a pound with the best a specimen weighing 1lb 14oz, as well as missing other bites. I went and found Trefor and he joined in the fun. Before it was time to go, we both had several more good fish.

After that day, I decided that I would never again struggle to catch chub in high, coloured water. Those conditions obviously favoured roach and they would be my target from now on. The following September (in 1981) was to lead to the first 2lb roach of my career.

I had arrived at the river to find it up 18in (46cm) and a rich brown colour with the first autumn flood. I knew where to fish and before long stood on the banks of the little backwater. All day long I caught roach steadily on both lobs and large pieces of flake and by late afternoon I had taken about a dozen fish, with three between 1lb 12oz and 1lb 14oz. Then followed the highlight of the day. I had just moved into a new swim, one that I had pre-baited with mashed bread about an hour previously, and the first cast with flake met with a firm jab on the quivertip. I thought I had hooked a chub at first, so hard did that roach fight, but when it rolled in the landing net I knew it was over 2lb. I made a quick examination of the anal fin to confirm that it was not a roach/bream hybrid as there are some of those in the Leam, and then I weighed a new personal best of 2lb 2oz which I have yet to beat.

The best catch I have ever taken from the river came on the most unlikely of days. I was fishing for the first time after a prolonged and enforced lay off because of a severe freeze. The weather had broken quite suddenly and I set off for the river on a very mild, pleasant morning. The sight that greeted me was not encouraging – the river was raging with melted snow and was the colour of oxtail soup. I resigned myself to a relaxing blank in the winter sunshine, but I was to be pleasantly surprised.

Within a minute of my first lobworm

My first ever 2lb roach – it weighed 2lb 2oz and was taken from the Leam.

Portrait of a big Leam roach.

settling under the fallen branch of my favourite roach swim, it was taken by a magnificent fish of 1lb 15oz, and this was quickly followed by a brace of fish, each only an ounce less than the first. What a start! After that hectic opening, the fishing steadied down to about one fish every half-hour throughout the rest of the day. I landed about twenty all together, which included several small ones. At home later that night, I worked out that the biggest twelve roach I had caught had an aggregate weight of exactly 21lb, which is one hell of an average.

Ever since my earliest experiences on the river, I had known that it contained big perch. Not only had I lost a huge fish at the net myself, but had once been present when another angler had taken two fish which he claimed were over 3lb. I doubt whether they were quite that big, but they were certainly good fish. They were taken on float fished minnows and I adopted the same tactics for a while, catching a few perch weighing up to just over 1½ pounds. I also caught a few weighing up to a pound on a red-tasselled spinner.

A lovely perch swim on the Leam.

When I moved off the river to fish the Claydon Brook in the early sixties, those Leam perch were forgotten about and it was not until I started seriously to fish the river again in the mid-seventies that I decided to have another go for them. I had learned an awful lot about small stream perch during my years fishing the Ouse system and took this knowledge with me to the Leam. In particular, I had learned that the best time to find perch was at first light in the summer and my very first trip in July 1976 led to the capture of my first Leam two-pounder, a fat and immaculate specimen weighing 2lb 2oz. There were never any big catches of fish – two or three perch being the average – but they were always of a good size. As with the Claydon Brook a few years earlier, it was noticeable that the biggest perch of a session was usually the first.

A very fond memory is of a fortnight in July 1977 when I had a further four two-pounders over two successive short morning sessions. My son Chris, who was eight at the time, was with me on both occasions and on the first morning we had a lot of fun together. We were in position well before dawn, fishing side by side in a deep pool from where I had already taken many good perch to just under 2lb. Chris was laying on with a small redworm alongside some rushes that had produced mainly small fish, but plenty of bites, while I legered the much deeper water alongside a fallen tree about ten yards downstream. Very few fish came from there, but they were invariably of good size. I was to lose a very good fish in that swim on my very first cast. At the time I was engaged in sorting out Chris's hundredth tangle of the first ten minutes when my quivertip plunged round and the rod nearly left the rest. Whatever I had hooked shot into that tree and I eventually had to pull for a break. That was not a good start, but the next bite which was about ten minutes later, made up for it. A typical

Portrait of a big perch specimen

Rushey Weir on the Thames in 1968.

A fat Cherwell chub, weighing in at exactly 5lb.

(Left) *A lovely barbel taken from the Cherwell. It weighed 10lb 12oz.*

(Below) *Jacqueline Miles with an 8½-pounder from the Cherwell.*

Trefor West with a Royalty nine-pounder.

(Opposite) *A lovely double-figure common carp.*

The author's biggest English carp yet which weighed 26lb 2oz.

The incredible 58lb carp taken at Cassien in France.

Two lovely Leam roach.

A 2lb 6oz perch taken from the Leam.

The author's biggest chub from the Leam – it weighed in at 5lb 10oz.

A 25lb reservoir pike.

Another specimen taken from a reservoir, and which weighed 20lb.

Two eight-pounders and a six-pounder from Dean's Farm.

Four crucian carp weighing from 2lb 9oz up to 3lb.

(Left) *A 7lb 12oz TC Pit tench.*

(Below) *A bream from TC weighing 11lb 2oz.*

(Above) *Trefor's first twelve-pounder from the Wensum.*

(Right) *A Wensum five-pounder caught on a winter's night.*

A 20lb common carp caught at Redmire.

(Above) *Dawn over Queenford.*

(Right) *The author's first big bream taken from Queenford.*

Another magnificent Leam perch.

jagging fight resulted in the landing of a perch weighing exactly 2lb. Chris was extremely pleased and so was I. I was to take a small jack pike on the very next cast and by now Chris was getting a little restive. He had yet to have a bite and so I told him that he could strike the next bite to my rod.

Perhaps half an hour later, my quivertip again indicated the attentions of a fish and Chris struck into it like a veteran. I will never forget his face at that moment. In an instant his expression turned from one of joy to one of terror. Whatever he was attached to almost dragged him in, but luckily the clutch slipped before that could happen. He could not hand the rod to me fast enough and for the first time I felt the power of a fish I thought must be the daddy of all perch. The fight was very similar to that of a perch, but I soon had it under control and then could see that it was a big eel. Although I cannot stand eels at the best of times, the size of this one compensated somewhat and I weighed my best eel ever at 3lb 12oz. Chris was anxious to have his photograph taken with it and I could hardly hold the camera still for laughing. One of the funniest things I have ever seen is Chris wrestling with that eel and I managed about three decent shots. The rest of the film were like stills from a Tarzan snake-fighting sequence.

The following weekend, I increased my personal best Leam perch to 2lb 6oz on a day which also saw my best Leam perch catch in terms of numbers. From a near-bank steady glide alongside high marginal rushes and hemmed in on all sides by thick cabbages, I took nine perch in three hours. Of those, seven were over a pound and three were over two pounds; a memorable session indeed.

Years later in August 1983, that same swim produced my best Leam perch to date. I was fishing a good hour before dawn, with a small torch on the porcupine

My son Chris with the eel that nearly pulled him in.

Chris with one of my first big Leam perch – it weighed in at 2lb 6oz.

float and in the half-light of day-break had a lovely lift and run away bite. Almost as soon as the fish was hooked it had me hung up in the cabbages. Usually, becoming snagged by a perch results in a lost fish as the hook soon pulls out of the soft tissue, but that morning I was lucky. After a few minutes of applying steady pressure, the fish came free and was successfully netted. It looked huge in the gloomy conditions and weighed 2lb 10oz. The only other bite that morning followed about an hour later, from another good fish of 2lb 4oz to complete a lovely brace.

A still unfulfilled ambition is a Leam three-pounder and I have fished the river

Another beauty, weighing in at 2lb 10oz.

hard this season for such a specimen. The best I have had this season was 2lb 3oz, but as I had confirmation of a definite 3lb 4oz fish in September, I will continue my search with renewed confidence. I know it is only a matter of time.

12 Stillwater Piking

MEMORIES OF BLACK HORSE

During our years of gravel pit piking, Trefor and I devoted much of our attention to the Black Horse pit, which was part of the Linford Fisheries and which is now, of course, part of the very popular and successful Linear Fisheries complex. Black Horse was always the best of the pits in terms of the numbers of big fish caught, although we also had some good pike from another one of the pits in the complex called the Red House.

A 14lb fish taken from Black Horse at dawn.

In all my years of fishing at Black Horse I never caught a really big pike, the best reaching only about sixteen pounds, but I was present when Trefor caught several twenties – it became very frustrating at the time. Week after week, Trefor and I sat alongside each other and enjoyed roughly the same number of runs, but you could bet your life that if there was a really big fish on the prowl, it would be one of Trefor's baits it would pick up. Despite that, I can look back on my years of fishing the water with a great deal of pleasure. It was never crowded; hard fighting, double-figure pike picked up deadbaits with pleasing regularity and we had a lot of fun.

Because of my lack of action with very big pike, most of my outstanding memories of the water concern unusual or amusing events – one of the most bizarre involved my old friend Merv Wilkinson. Trefor and I were fishing our usual spot, directly opposite the first car park and Merv was fishing the car park bank itself – facing us, but a good three hundred yards away. At about midday, we saw Merv jump to his feet and strike into a fish. Almost immediately, he threw the rod down in disgust and it was obvious that he had lost the pike. Shortly afterwards, he wound in his other rod and started to walk round the bank to us so that we could share his annoyance. We had all been talking for about ten minutes when one of Trefor's bite indicators dropped off and line began paying out steadily. He

Another twenty-pounder for Trefor – this one weighed 22lb 8oz.

struck into the pike and then began the most peculiar fight. Although the fish was obviously not that big, Trefor seemed to have hardly any control over it. Every time he pulled one way, the pike seemed to turn in a full circle before he regained direct contact. It was really weird, but when the fish was eventually netted all was revealed. Trefor's trace was not in the pike's mouth at all, the one that was present being recognised immediately by Merv as his and the one he had lost only minutes earlier. One of the barbs of the bottom treble of Trefor's trace had passed through the eye of the swivel on Merv's trace! I have no idea of the odds against that happening on a water the size of Black Horse, but they must be immense.

One of my most irritating trips to the water was one day when I went on my own, a day that started badly and steadily deteriorated. About half-way down the motorway, my car suddenly stalled in the middle lane and all I could do was roll to a stop on the hard shoulder. I was very lucky that there was only light traffic at the time. I checked everything I knew, which took very little time as my knowledge of car engines is sketchy to the extreme and there was nothing for it but to phone for help. Of course, I had to break down exactly at the mid-point between two motorway phones and it was a good half-hour before I was back with my car, awaiting the arrival of a breakdown truck. I was not in the AA at the time. Eventually, I was towed into a garage in Northampton, where they soon located the problem. Then the next problem manifested itself. I had neglected to bring either any money or my cheque book and had no way of paying the garage bill, which was horrendous after having been towed for several miles. Promising to send them a cheque the next day was to no avail – they wanted the bill settled there and then. They did, however, allow me to drive home and pick up a cheque, provided that they could keep my fishing rods as security until my return. I had no choice but to agree, even though it meant about a sixty-five mile round trip to get back and I set off with my temper at about boiling point.

By the time the garage had been sorted out and I had completed my interrupted journey, it was almost midday. After having set off well before dawn, I was actually sitting behind two rods for the first time at 12.30 p.m. I was not in a good mood and things got no better. I had my first run after about an hour and when I jumped up from my chair, I somehow managed to lose my footing on the gravel. This caused me to fall back across the chair, breaking the legs off it and ensuring that I spent the rest of the afternoon perched on a rock, like some gigantic gnome. I missed the run into the bargain.

About an hour before it became dark, I had my other two runs of the day, both on the same rod and about twenty minutes apart. Both pike accepted half mackerel and they both looked as if they could go twenty pounds. The distinctive markings of the second pike confirmed that they were certainly different fish, but I was never to weigh either of them. In each case the hooks pulled out as the fish was close to the net! At home that night I was not good company!

Returning a gravel pit twenty-pounder.

Trefor and I met one very strange character when we were fishing Black Horse with Alan Lane one winter's day. The fishing was very slow (in fact none of us had had a run) and we were standing talking when this Irishman came down the bank with his young son in tow. He introduced himself as Pat and expressed a great interest in our pike fishing tackle. He soon confided in us that in his home town in southern Ireland he was known as 'King Pike', on the strength of two pike weighing 23lb and 17lb he had caught one day from a local water. The manner of the capture will not be found included in any Pike Anglers' Club publication, although I have no doubt that some of the idiots who call themselves carp anglers will be able to relate to it. Apparently, the method was to arrive at the lake early in the morning and bait two rods with a herring mounted on two size 2 trebles, using 30lb wire and mainline. Once the baits were in position, the rods were left to fish for themselves, while the 'anglers' retired to the nearest pub.

They stayed there until closing time when, well lubricated with Guinness, they returned to the lake, wound in and went home: shades of Savay, perhaps? Anyway, on the day in question, Pat had the two pike on the end – both neatly hooked in the vent!

During the course of the conversation, Pat mentioned that he was shortly to appear in court on a charge of grievous bodily harm and criminal damage. We were intrigued by this and pressed him for more details. Apparently he lived in a caravan near to the

A lovely brace. These ones weighed 17lb 8oz and 14lb.

building site he was working on, and one night he was playing his radio at a volume which his neighbours considered excessive. So they did the neighbourly thing and dragged him out of his van and gave him a good kicking. Understandably, Pat felt a trifle aggrieved at this treatment and vowed revenge. In a flash of inspiration, a novel form of retribution occurred to him and in the middle of the night he borrowed a steamroller from the site and proceeded to demolish his assailant's caravan with it. That effectively ended the argument!

Although this was a marvellous story, we never for one moment thought that there was a grain of truth in it. But we were to be proved wrong. There in the Sunday newspaper, two weeks later, was the story exactly as Pat had relayed it to us. He was fined heavily, given a suspended prison sentence and warned to keep a tighter control over his temper in future!

A TAIL-WALKING FIRST TWENTY

One of the very first gravel pits I ever fished was Hardwick on Oxfordshire, the water that eventually became famous for the monstrous chub that fell to Peter Stone and others. The water also held a good head of double-figure pike, as well as several twentiesand one confirmed thirty. In the late seventies, Trefor and I spent a lot of our time on its banks – surely this water offered me a very good chance of catching my first twenty-pounder?

For two seasons my results were much the same as they were at Black Horse with plenty of pike but the biggest being only 16lb. Trefor fared about the same, but we kept plugging away, knowing our luck had to change eventually. Mine did in the winter of 1978 in spectacular fashion. Over the previous few weeks, we had noticed that the pike were confirmed night feeders and instead of packing up at dusk as we had been doing, we began staying on for a couple of hours. Those first two dark hours were very reliable. This particular night, we were fishing side by side off the beach near the culvert joining the two halves of the pit. We were fishing into the larger area and my baits were being fished in the vicinity of a sunken tree, a feature that had produced several good pike.

A little after dark, Trefor was away and a

brief flurry of excitement ended when he landed a fish of around eleven pounds. All went quiet again for an hour and then line streaked off my open reel and the rod shook in its rests as something made off with my whole herring at break-neck speed. I will always remember the heart-stopping sight as I set the hooks – a large pike flying angrily clear of the water, shaking his head viciously – a drama that was clearly visible in the still water under that bright winter moon. After that initial surge the fight continued on the surface, that superb predator making many strong runs, tail-walking across the surface in breath-taking fashion. Trefor did not help to soothe my nerves. 'It's a definite twenty' he said, 'you don't want to lose this.' I was well aware of that! There were no mistakes, however, the hookhold was secure and soon I was kneeling beside a fish I had been hunting for so long – a twenty-pounder. It was only just there, at 20lb 4oz, but it really was a magnificent and superbly marked specimen. Needless to say, I was overjoyed with it and, if anything, Trefor was more pleased than I was. He had caught several twenties while we had been fishing together and it was becoming slightly embarrassing for him with my continual failure. This fish helped to redress the balance a little and the lifting of my pike hoodoo, which that magnificent Hardwick capture achieved, has led on to me catching many more big ones

My first twenty at 20lb 4oz.

since. Whenever I go over my angling experiences in my mind, I can still see the silvery sparkling water, cascading off those beautifully speckled flanks in the moonlight. Such memories are precious.

THE PIKE THAT COULD TELL THE TIME

Hardwick pit was also the scene of a very amusing day that Trefor and I shared when it really was bitterly cold. One of the beautiful things about the water was that much of its perimeter was accessible by car which avoided the necessity for long, tiring hikes. Also, it was handy to be able to sit in the warmth of a car and watch the indicators without having to endure the biting easterly wind.

On our arrival that particular morning and after casting out his baits, Trefor performed his normal beachcombing stint, searching along the gravel margins for any discarded tackle. The number of leads and other assorted items he had collected in this way was quite staggering. His haul was to be quite special – several leger weights, a perfectly good bait box and a travel alarm clock, still ticking and apparently in perfect working order. We could only assume that a match angler had been using it to time himself the previous day and had forgotten it. 'This will save us a bit of trouble' he said, 'we will be able to set the alarm for when we want the runs today, which means that we will be able to relax for the rest of the time. What time shall I set it for our first run?' Proving conclusively that I can be quite as crazy as he is, I said '10.15' and then we both retired to the car for a welcome brew up.

A couple of hours had passed pleasantly when the alarm bell from the clock startled the pair of us. No sooner had it finished than one of my bobbins dropped off! We looked at one another and burst out laughing. Before long, I had landed and returned a plump ten-pounder and then I turned to Trefor. 'It's your turn next mate' I said, 'what time do you reckon?' '12.30 will do fine' he replied, and I set the clock accordingly. For it to happen once was coincidental, but to happen a second time really was remarkable for, as the bell was still ringing, one of Trefor's lines was whirring through the rings, resulting this time in a scrappy thirteen-pounder.

Believe it or not it was to happen a third time. After Trefor's fish had been returned, I stipulated 2.30 p.m. as the next run. Astonishingly, only about a minute after the alarm had gone off I had my second and last run, from a seven-pounder. 'You got it wrong this time Milesy' Trefor said, 'you were at least a minute out.' I glanced at my watch. 'Actually, I was spot on' I replied, 'the alarm clock has gained about sixty seconds since this morning!'

Trefor and I often laugh about that remarkable day at Hardwick, but our one big regret is not having had a novice angler with us – it would have blown his mind!

THE SKIERS OF THE LAGOON

Many years ago I was fishing a large brick pit which was famous for its big pike as well as good rudd. The pike were my target and for the first couple of hours I enjoyed solitary peace and quiet on that misty winter morning. At about mid-morning the peace was shattered as the water-skiers arrived. Within a few minutes, the calm surface was a distant memory as those power boats howled around. I was prepared to tolerate the skiers, although they certainly spoil my enjoyment of angling, but since it was a very big water there should have been

A good rudd from the brick pit where the water skier had his come-uppance.

plenty of room for all of us. To be fair, most of them were considerate and stayed well out in the middle, which was not difficult in over two hundred acres. However, there was one exception. One boat, which was full of young ladies was towing a particularly objectionable chinless wonder, who frequently came within ten yards of the bank. He was totally ruining my fishing. The skier (on hire from Rent-a-Prat) was obviously playing to the gallery and trying to impress the women with his skill. He had gone through his repertoire, which had included a couple of ski jumps and he approached the ramp at high speed for a third, which he obviously intended to be the most spectacular yet. Holding on with one hand, he waved to me in a most superior fashion and then veered to the side suddenly, having been knocked off course by a wave. The result was that he missed the ramp itself but went full tilt into one of the upright ramp supports, hitting it with his legs wide apart and one on either side of it. It was just like a Tom and Jerry cartoon. After the impact, our hero just slithered down the timber into the water and stayed there until his companions unceremoniously dragged him into the boat and roared back to the boathouse. I bet that brought tears to his eyes – it certainly did to mine!

RESERVOIR PIKING

Over recent seasons, dead-baiting at the Midland reservoirs has rapidly become one of my favourite forms of piking. For one thing, the big pike take dead sea fish quite freely and this avoids the necessity for livebaits. Although I am not a hypocrite and will use livebaits where I feel they are necessary, I am becoming increasingly uneasy about their use. There is no doubt that livebaiting is probably the most indefensible facet of our sport. If anything, I have found livebaits at reservoirs counter-productive as they certainly attract hordes of jacks. The average sized pike I catch on the waters I fish are dramatically higher when deadbaits are used. Some days also, they produce more runs. Three years ago on my favourite reservoir and the last time I used livebaits there, I used three rods. One was baited with mackerel tail, one with paternostered live roach and the other with a lively free-swimming dace. Many times the dace, swimming only about a foot from the bottom, swam over the mackerel, but I never had a take on it. Neither for that matter did the paternostered bait elicit any response and all five of the pike I caught that day picked up the mackerel tail. Others had the same experience and these days I never bother to take livebaits to my reservoirs. I am happier and it is certainly much more convenient.

I have been experimenting with colouring baits and injecting them with various fish oils, and the latter resulted in one of the most interesting takes I have had from a pike, a lovely specimen of just over 20lb in March 1988. On one rod I was using a small whole herring that had been very heavily impregnated with pilchard oil and I sat behind the rods on a very cold, clear and frosty morning. It was the sort of winter morning I love so much – blue sky, flat calm water and air crisp enough to make your ears tingle. I was looking idly across the shimmering water when I suddenly became aware of several large bubbles bursting to the surface above where my herring lay. There was a corresponding 1in (2.5cm) drop on the indicator and then a circular oil slick spread out from the bubbles, becoming very rapidly bigger. I could picture what was going on. A pike had picked up the herring and the crushing action of its teeth had released the quantity of oil which was now making its presence so obvious at the surface. Sure enough, within a few seconds, line was peeling off steadily and I was soon admiring my prize – a pike of 20lb 1oz.

That same March, I took two catches of pike from the same water on successive Fridays to static dead-baiting techniques. These pike are the best of my career. The first week saw the best catch for numbers, with twelve fish landed weighing between eight and nineteen pounds, but the quality of the fish on the second trip really was outstanding. Not long after dawn, the first of ten pike came to net weighing 13lb 2oz. Another thing that was quite remarkable was that each pike was bigger than the one caught previously and with over ten fish in total, the odds against that must be quite high. The fish I had that day came to either mackerel or smelt with one to a sardine, the exact weights being 13lb 2oz, 13lb 14oz, 14lb 4oz, 14lb 9oz, 15lb 8oz, 15lb 10oz, 16lb 6oz, 17lb 6oz, 18lb 14oz and 20lb 12oz. In anyone's language, that is piking of the highest calibre.

One of the problems that I had to contend with at that reservoir was a loud-mouthed old buffoon of a bailiff, who has thankfully been replaced now. I was fishing one morning using three rods, as did the handful of other keen pike men who patronised the fishery when the bailiff arrived. In a most unpleasant manner, he ranted on about how damaging it was to pike stocks to use three rods and so on. Experienced pike men know that this is garbage, but he was within his rights and so I dutifully wound in the third rod. He went off, muttering about how it was still impossible to fish two rods properly and how he had only ever used one pike rod at a time in his life. That had caught him plenty of big pike, he said, including one that he had not been able to weigh but that he knew was enormous because it measured a foot between the eyes! Now that is what I call a pike!

He went about a hundred yards down to my left and commenced to fish himself using very small roach livebaits, which I could see were only being fished about two feet deep beneath a bulbous monstrosity of a float. After an hour, I had seen him lose three pike and the time it had taken him to cast out again led me to believe that he was being bitten off. After the third such incident I could stand it no longer and walked down to see what he was doing. I arrived just in time to see him prepare to cast another roach, mounted on a wire trace no more than 4in (10cm) in length. I pointed out to him quite sarcastically that he was a much greater threat to the pike stocks with his woefully short traces than I ever was with three rods and suggested strongly that he use one of my 2ft traces, before attempting to cast out again. I went and fetched one for him and then returned to my own fishing. Two hours later, I saw him land a fish that looked as if it weighed about seven pounds and when it had been on the bank about ten minutes without any sign of it being returned, I went walkies again. The sight that greeted me horrified me. Believe it or not, that bailiff had no means of unhooking the pike and was trying to remove the trebles by the simple expedient of holding the fish still with his left hand while he pulled on the trace as hard as he could with his right in an attempt to tear the hooks out. I went absolutely balmy and snatched the fish off him. Within a minute, it had been properly unhooked and returned, hopefully to survive and fight another day.

At about mid-afternoon and having used or cast off all the livebaits he had brought, the bailiff left and just after he had pulled away, something in the margins where he had been fishing caught my eye and I walked back down to investigate. There I found two empty beer cans and a discarded wire trace. That old idiot was the bailiff at the water! Honestly, there are times when I really despair.

On a similar vein and two weeks after that incident, two of the bailiff's old cronies were fishing in the same swim he had and the chain of events was very similar. Again, they had mouthed off about my using two rods and this time I discovered one of them using two treble hooks mounted on nylon. Not only that, they had no landing net between them. Every pike that took their baits was potentially a dead one. This time I lost my temper in a big way and the driver shot off to get some wire. Naturally, I assumed that he had gone to a tackle shop, but when he had returned and they recommenced fishing, I just did not believe what I saw. This time they were equipped with 4ft traces of bright red electrical flex! It was enough to make a sane man scream!

The weekend before the twelve-fish catch mentioned earlier, I was to take my second biggest pike ever and the manner of its capture was quite amusing. At the back end of the season this particular reservoir fishes very well near to the access road, where a culvert under the road links a small stream with the reservoir itself. The stream bed leading out into the main body of the lake is a hot spot at this time of the season and the best place to fish it is from right alongside the road itself. You can literally fish feet away from the car which is a great boon for convenience or bad weather conditions. This culvert is in the left-hand corner of the water and good swims are also located down the left-hand bank from it. On the morning in question, my daughter Jacquiline had begged a trip with me and so I went very early, the plan being to park my caravanette near to that culvert. That way Jacqui, being only ten years old, would be close to the van if she got cold or needed to go to the toilet. When I arrived, therefore, I was annoyed to see that I had been beaten to it. There was a car parked where I had intended on being. However, it transpired that the angler concerned was Darryl Wilkinson, Merv's son, whom I knew well. Normally I have the courtesy to give any other angler a wide berth but, as I knew Darryl, I asked if he minded my fishing close to him for Jacqui's benefit. He had no objection whatever and that in any event his baits were angled slightly to the right. I could fish about twenty yards down the left-hand bank, have baits in the culvert and stream-bed areas and still be close to the van. I thanked him for his consideration and moved my gear round to my fishing position.

At that time Darryl was going through a spell that I had undergone earlier in my piking career. Try as he might, he could not catch a twenty-pounder and this reservoir was particularly unkind. He had been fishing very hard all winter and still had to beat thirteen pounds. So what was to follow must have been particularly hard to bear. I set up my first rod, attached a mackerel head and lobbed it underhand only a few feet from the bank into the culvert. After taking in the slack and attaching the drop off indicator, I set up the second rod, moved down the bank a little and then heard a click. I looked back and could see that the indicator had dropped off. The bait had been in the water all of thirty seconds. When I got back to the rod, the line was lying very slack and I re-attached the indicator, thinking that perhaps I had set it too finely initially. Hardly had I released it when the line lifted sharply and then rocketed across the culvert, heading straight across Darryl's lines. As I struck, there was an almighty swirl and then a gigantic pike tail-walked in most spectacular fashion. It must have surfaced only a few feet under Darryl's nose and what he said at that moment is totally unprintable!

That was a spectacular battle, the best I have had with a stillwater pike and as it fought entirely on or just under the surface, I could clearly see how big it was. It was Jacqui's first ever fishing trip with me and she was jumping up and down with excitement as I slipped the net under it at last. Darryl came down the bank to join in the fun and he witnessed an absolutely cracking pike of 25lb 1oz. His face was a picture and

My best reservoir pike to date at 25lb 1oz.

of course he took some unmerciful ribbing from the rest of the lads for ages. No one was more pleased than I when he took a very well-deserved fish of over 26lb last season, just reward for many long hours of determined effort.

13 Down on the Farm

During my first telephone conversation with Alastair Nicholson, he mentioned that he had been fishing regularly with the man who held the tench record at the time, Eric Edwards and had been present when that fish had been landed. The location of the water which had produced that gigantic tench had always been kept secret and so it was quite natural that I should want to find out as much as possible about it. In fact, Alastair was very open and said that although he and his friends had kept their results very strictly to themselves over the previous few seasons, they would be quite happy for Trefor and myself to come down and have a go. It seemed that a very big water was involved and that only a handful of anglers were fishing it regularly. As Alastair had already got wind of a possible marina development on the pit, which would probably destroy the fishing in the next season anyway, I think that he felt that he might as well share the information with a few more people he could trust.

When I met Alastair for the first time a fortnight later in his Oxfordshire cottage, he showed me many slides of fish he and his friends had taken from the pit, which I soon discovered was Deans Farm, near Reading. The average size of the tench was amazing, being over 7lb and there had been several nine-pounders as well as Eric's double. Alastair also made my mouth water with stories of the huge bream the water contained. They had all taken double-figure fish to over 11lb, but there had also been several witnesses to a fish Alastair had lost one night which was estimated at sixteen pounds.

It was the tench that particularly interested Trefor and myself. Although TC held fish much bigger than my best of 7lb 13oz, it was a water that was coming under more and more intense pressure every season and I was looking around for pastures new. Also the average size of TC tench was definitely dropping. As the average fish from Deans was so large, it seemed very likely that it would produce a truly exceptional tench before long. Apart from that, it was obviously a water where there would be plenty of peace and quiet. Although it was widely known that it contained big fish, it was also a very hard water and therefore not very popular. Trefor and I were not worried how difficult it was so long as it held the fish we were after and we made plans for our first assault on those massive tench in June 1984.

Our close season reconnaissance in May was daunting. The pit was very extensive, at about eighty acres, but the main problem appeared to be the hundreds of gravel bars that were easily visible through the crystal-clear water in the strong sunlight. Feature fishing in gravel pits is possibly my favourite form of stillwater angling, but this water contained so many features that finding the right one would largely be a lottery. It would not have been so bad if there had been a large head of tench to colonise all these features, but apparently that was not the case. The tench were so big because their numbers were severly limited.

Our information was that large areas of the pit could be barren for weeks. Despite all this, we were itching to get cracking and 16 June could not arrive fast enough.

Trefor had to begin our campaign on his own as I had to attend a company conference in Athens for the first week of the new season, but I joined him in the middle of the second week. On the drive down to the pit in the early hours of that Wednesday morning, I was really pent up through wondering what exciting news Trefor had to tell me and it was bitterly disappointing when he confirmed that he had yet to have his first tench bite. Despite fishing very hard, all that had rewarded his efforts had been the occasional jack pike, but he had the small encouragement of seeing an occasional big fish being landed by one of the other anglers in the handful on the bank – Eric had managed a nine-pounder by stalking one morning.

After ten days of intense effort, Trefor was naturally a little dejected although as determined as ever. After my arrival, he took time off from his fishing to look around the water with me and it did seem to me that his choice of swim should have been the right one. The tench had so far shown no signs of spawning activity and the bank where he was camped had to attract the large females. So convinced was I that he was in the correct area that I moved into a swim about thirty yards to his right.

It was midday and very hot by the time I had my temporary home to my satisfaction, and as serious fishing would not commence until the cool of the evening, I took the opportunity to search the water in front of me from my inflatable boat. I discovered two bars that I would fish – one very close in, no more than twenty yards offshore and the other at about fifty yards. There was a total lack of weed in the gullies between the bars, although the tops of the bars themselves were covered with fine silkweed, the only exception being the deep marginal channel under the rod points. There there was a very thick weed growth, which would prove hazardous to the safe landing of any big fish. The most interesting area I found was an oval clear patch of gravel at the shallowest point of the nearer bar which was so uniform and marked that it had obviously been formed by browsing fish. There may well have been a bloodworm colony in that vicinity and so that was one obvious area to present a bait. The other area I decided to fish was where the bed of the pit commenced to shelve up to the further bar.

Having selected the two fishing positions, I baited them both in early evening and settled down for my first night's fishing at Deans Farm. The groundbait consisted of half a bucketful of fine breadcrumb in each area, coloured yellow and laced with maple

A lovely Deans Farm specimen weighing 6lb 15oz.

8lb 14oz of tench.

cream flavour. It also contained a few chopped lobs, which were to be the hookbaits.

My arrival at the water improved Trefor's luck at least a fraction because the next morning he was to take his first two tench from the water at last, certainly no more than he deserved. They weighed just over 5lb and 6lb 15oz and, if nothing else, they increased our confidence. Despite that there were no further bites to either of us and when dawn broke on the Friday morning, I had been fishing for about forty hours without a single twitch on either indicator. I had also not seen a single fish of any species break the flat calm surface of the water since my arrival, other than the two Trefor had landed.

I remember that I was just pondering this point as I sat in my chair with the first cup of tea of the day, when a large tench dorsal silently cut through the surface film close to my nearer swim marker. I was instantly alert. Moments later, I put my cup down as there was a single bleep from the Optonic and then the bobbin slowly rose to the butt. A firm strike met with a spirited resistance and a satisfyingly heavy fish surged to my right, making the clutch whine. For several arm-aching minutes, it pulled and bored, fighting every inch of the way as most tench do, and before I caught my first glimpse of the fish I knew it was big. It was as well for my peace of mind that I was unaware of quite how big and even when I landed it, my estimate was way off the mark. It looked as if it weighed about 7½ pounds, but when the needle shot past the 8lb mark I knew that my first bite at Deans had yielded a new personal best. When Trefor joined me he witnessed the weighing – a weight of 8lb 4oz was recorded. Trefor was full of congratulations, although he must have been contemplating the injustice of it all. He had fished hard for twelve days and undoubtedly deserved a fish of that calibre before I did. But that is the way fishing of course and the roles had often been reversed in the past.

Not long after that super tench had been consigned to a sack to await a photograph I was away again, and this time I was destined to lose a tench that gave me nightmares for weeks. I had it close in twice and had a good look at it as it rolled – I know that it cannot have been less than about 9½ pounds and it may even have been a double. I managed to free it from becoming snagged in the marginal weeds, but in the end the hook simply pulled out and I was left to reflect on what might have been. I was not allowed to mope about that lost monster for long though, because I was soon into a third tench – one that came into the landing net without causing any anxious moments at all. So easily did I land it that I was fooled into thinking that it was only an average fish until it was on its side and approaching the net. I could see then that it was huge, possibly 9lb. Again Trefor's presence was requested and we confirmed this second specimen as 8lb 14oz. To quote Ritchie

Macdonald: 'A brace of eight-pounders in a few hours is a right result.'

The flurry of activity in front of me resulted in my third and last tench of 6lb 1oz, which took a bait off the far bar as Trefor and I were still admiring the second eight-pounder. After the biteless hours since Wednesday, the last few had been hectic. They were followed however, by another fishless twenty-four hours for both of us, although I did somehow manage to lose another two good tench before I left late on Saturday morning.

I have often said that I felt the reason for my early success at the water, where there was a small head of big tench, lay in the decision I had taken to flavour the feed. Flavourings undoubtedly carry far and wide in shallow waters and cannot be ignored by the fish. The top carp men had proved conclusively what tremendous attractors maple and maple cream were and on my second trip to Deans Farm the following week, I decided on some small modifications to my feeding technique to attain the maximum advantage from this principle. I decided to incorporate fine rusk in the breadcrumb groundbait. This has the effect of breaking away from the heavier feed when soaked and rises in the water to give a cloud bait effect. It occurred to me that if this clouding effect was coupled with heavier flavouring, the dispersal of the rusk would automatically disperse the flavour at the same time. The further the attractive powers of the flavour, the more chance I had of pulling a decent head of fish into the swim. The only worry was that very heavy flavouring carried with it the risk of making the actual feed bitter to the taste, and to counteract this I added sweetener to the feed.

I am convinced that my reasoning was entirely sound. There had always been very little evidence of rolling tench at Deans Farm, yet within an hour of baiting the swims on the first evening of my second trip, tench were rolling regularly. Despite that, there were to be no bites that first evening – in fact the sun was high in the sky the next morning before I was on my feet, rod well bent, as another big tench fought for its freedom. That was a lovely clean female of 7lb 2oz, followed shortly afterwards by a 5lb male, and I was now thinking in terms of a big catch of fish. A really big bag of tench had never been achieved at Deans.

What a trio – 8lb 14oz, 8lb 4oz and 6lb 1oz.

After the male, however, the lake went dead again and it was not until after the evening baiting that things livened up again. The rolling told me that the swim was full of fish and I paid the penalty for that in the multitude of line bites I experienced over the next few hours. They were not all liners though, and during the dark hours another 7lb female and 5lb male found the lobs irresistible. The last fish I ever caught from Deans Farm came just after dawn in the shape of another 5lb male, and I could cry when I think that I never went back to the water for another session after those successful first two. It was not intentional, but just the way things worked out somehow.

I know that I threw away a tremendous opportunity to land an exceptional tench and one that no longer exists. Although Deans Farm still has a very limited amount of water available to anglers, a great many of its big fish are either trapped in the marina or have escaped down the cutting to the adjacent River Thames. Deans is a pale shadow of what it once was and the access is so limited that an extended campaign on its banks is no longer viable – and that is very sad.

14 Days on the Upper Great Ouse

During my formative years on the Claydon Brook, I was unaware of quite how close I was to Dick Walker's famous Ouse fishery at Beachampton. I had read of his exploits on the river and was just coming to grips with the fishing at Padbury as Dick was building his palatial fishing hut. By about 1970, the quality of the Claydon Brook fishing was declining rapidly as a result of water abstraction, dredging and the infamous perch disease, and I decided to give some attention to the Ouse itself.

One week in an edition of *Angling Times*, I happened to spot a small advert placed by Ian Howcroft who was (as well as being Fred J Taylor's son-in-law) Dick's fishery manager. The gist of the advert was that if any anglers were interested in fishing that stretch of the Ouse, could they contact Ian for details. Dick was anxious that other keen anglers should be given the opportunity to sample the superb fishing that was available. I wasted no time in penning a reply and was gratified to receive an answer

Trefor fishes the stretch above Dick Walker's at Beachampton.

by return of post. There were several weekends available and I could select whichever I required.

On a pleasant Friday evening in August 1972, I arrived at the river in the company of Ray Brown and his brother Derek, who were to share the hut with me. We made our way through the pig farm, over the little canal bridge and finally stood on the threshold of the famous fishing hut I had heard so much about. When I went inside I was taken aback. Dick Walker never did anything other than perfectly and this hut was no exception. It was positively luxurious with every comfort you could want and positioned only yards from the river bank. Once organised, I had a few hours' fishing, managing three nice roach before turning in for the night. A crack-of-dawn start was on the agenda the following morning.

Just as the early mist was lifting from the water in the half-light, I was crossing the short stretch of field to the swim known as the Small Cabbage Patch. The plan was to fish for perch for the early hours and then switch to roach fishing under the pads for the rest of the day. The evening and first hour of darkness would be spent trying to catch one of the large chub for which the river was so renowned.

I had been fishing for several hours and had failed completely with the perch. I had long since reverted to stewed wheat alongside the lilies and had managed only one average sized roach when I was disturbed by a voice behind me. 'Good morning, my name's Walker' he said, and I jumped up to shake the hand of the man who had done so much, both to make me an angler and for angling in general. We were soon joined by Peter Thomas and Fred J Taylor, and it transpired that Dick and Pete were to make a film for television on the Monday following our trip. It was to feature roach fishing and Dick had come down to the river to request that we leave one good roach swim unfished, so that it would be undisturbed and give them the best chance of producing fish for the cameras. Obviously, we were more than happy to oblige and Dick also asked me if I would mind keeping any roach I caught in a keep net, just in case they were uncooperative on the day of filming.

For the rest of that day we all talked together, and I gained an insight into Dick's sense of humour as well as his generosity. He told us the tale of the wooden chub which he and Fred had positioned in a swim called Whitebottom, and which they fooled Peter Stone with – he thought it was a monster for hours. Pete Thomas also told me the tale of Dick's 30lb Redmire carp which had always been reported at 31lb 4oz. It was, Pete confirmed, actually weighed by him at 34lb, but Dick did not allow Pete to tell Bob Richards that. Dick had already beaten Bob's record fish of 31lb 4oz with his 44lb monster, but Bob's fish still remained the largest mirror carp ever caught. Dick did not have the heart to overshadow that capture as well, so instructed Pete to say that his fish was exactly the same weight as Bob's. That little story sums up the man more adequately than a thousand words. The conversation lasted well into the evening, over endless cups of tea, and with Dick smoking a non-stop chain of Consulate cigarettes. It is an evening I cherish in my memory.

The following morning I was on the river at the crack of dawn again, trying for one of the big perch to no avail. Like the Claydon Brook they had been ravaged by the disease. At about mid-morning I was still fishing the Small Cabbage Patch when I spotted a very big chub at the far-bank extremity of the lilies, and so I went grubbing around in the bank-side burdocks, looking for slugs. I quickly found three and amended my gear to a weightless line and size 4 hook. The first cast met with a crashing take and the chub ploughed through the pads for about ten yards before the hook pulled out. That was the end of that and I never saw the chub again.

At lunchtime, I was laying on stewed wheat once more in the tiny clearing in the lilies, and by mid-afternoon was taking roach quite regularly. I had eight or nine fish weighing up to 1lb 14oz – superbly conditioned specimens. Dick joined us again in early evening and before starting to fish himself, he donned waders and went paddling in the swim known as Two Willows. He was searching for crayfish for use in the film the next day, and showed me the way of catching them he had often written about – that of putting his hand into all the bankside holes he came to where the crayfish lived. He showed me the difference between a crayfish hole and a rat hole, but I still remained unconvinced. I was, I said, very impressed with the technique but would continue to search for crayfish under stones. It struck me as being much safer!

Dick and I fished together for a couple of hours that evening, with me still in the Small Cabbage Patch and Dick trotting a little swim known as Rook Run. As it started to get dark it was time for Ray, Derek and I to leave for home. Before doing so, the roach in my net were transferred to Dick's and we said our goodbyes. I never did see the film which appeared, I believe, on a programme called the *Philpott File*, and have often wondered whether my roach were needed. That weekend was the only occasion I ever met Dick Walker, although we spoke on the phone and corresponded by letter. He was, without doubt, a truly unique man and I doubt whether anyone will ever replace him.

So enthralled was I with the fishing at Beachampton that I had to go again and so a second weekend was booked with Ian Howcroft, in the remarkable summer of 1976. This time I took with me an angling

A catch of early morning bream from the Large Cabbage Patch swim.

friend from work, Fred, who was a good match angler but had done little big fish work. We were again fishing from Friday until Sunday, and on the first evening I had a definite plan in mind. Dick Walker had written several articles about the good bream that inhabited some swims on his stretch and I had decided to have a crack for them. Apparently, the early hours of the morning were the best and so I pre-baited a swim known as the Large Cabbage Patch on that Friday night in readiness for a dawn assault the following morning. I spent the rest of the evening chubbing, taking two average fish, while Fred managed a string of decent roach on his light float tackle.

Long before light, Fred and I made our way to the Large Cabbage Patch swim with our tackle already set up. We would be fishing adjacent swims, both laying on with a porcupine float cocked by one large shot and using large lobworms as bait. As soon as it was light enough to see, my float was riding steadily in the mid-river clearing and then my heart missed a beat as a large bronze back broke the surface and slowly rolled, almost submerging the float. Minutes later, the float tilted and lay flat, before lazily moving away to my left. It was just like a perch bite, but when I struck I knew this was no perch. I had been mentally unprepared for quite how hard the bream would fight, as the ones I had been in contact with previously had given a very unconvincing account of themselves. This one, however, which I now know is typical of a small river bream, was the equal of a chub of the same weight and gave me a stirring scrap in the confines of that little swim before its broad flanks nestled at last in the mesh of my landing net. I could see straight away that it was the biggest bream I had ever caught and the scales confirmed that. It weighed 5lb 2oz and I slipped it into my keep net to await better light for a photograph.

That bream was not destined to remain a personal best for long. Within half an hour I had taken two more, weighing 5lb 10oz and 6lb 4oz and Fred managed a five-pounder as well. An hour after we had started fishing, it was all over. All evidence of feeding bream – the clouded water and disturbances in the weed beds – stopped and there were no further bites. At about 9 a.m., Fred and I were enjoying bacon and eggs back in the hut.

After a much appreciated rest, we were back on the gravel shallows where I showed Fred how to catch crayfish under the stones. With a few baits in a bucket, we wandered down the river looking for chub. The first fish I cast to was an object lesson for Fred on how not to do it. The cast itself was perfect, with the cray dropping just ahead of the biggest fish of a group of three. The chub intercepted the bait savagely. Whether it was because I was tense because Fred was watching I do not know, but I had the line far too tight and before I could strike, the chub had bitten the cray clean in half and discarded the half carrying the hook. Pretending that I meant to demonstrate that, I tied on a new hook and cast a second cray. This time there were no mistakes and I soon landed a fish of just over 4lb. I could see that Fred was very impressed and he was itching to have a go. The next swim we came to it was his turn and although the fish he cast to was not very big (barely three pounds) he did everything perfectly. He was delighted with the first chub he had ever caught on a natural bait fished in that manner.

The second swim Fred fished resulted in an occurrence that I have never seen repeated. In a small clearing between the branches of a fallen tree, he spotted a big chub over the gravel in about three feet of quite fast water. A crayfish was dropped upstream of the chub and could not have sunk more than a few inches when there was a sudden flash from under the near bank and the cray was seized by an eel of about two pounds. When on the bank, it was quite comical how the shape of the crayfish bulged out of the eel's throat, and it was unhooked and returned to the water to finish its meal in peace.

A few weeks after that trip I stayed in the hut for the third and last time, this time in the company of Trefor West. By now, the drought conditions were really starting to bite and much of the river was covered in a thick algal scum. The only swims where we could get a bite were the few areas where there was oxygenation below shallows and several average chub fell to loose-lined slugs and crayfish. Many of the known chub swims were impossible to fish with naturals because of the thick algae and we had to resort to plunging baits like cheese through the weed, attached to heavy leads. The presentation was unnatural in the extreme, but several chub were caught this way. Despite the initial alarm when the bait was introduced, the fact that the algae quickly closed around the line meant that the chub had the confidence of feeding under cover and were more responsive than they otherwise might have been.

Trefor had by far the best catch that weekend. He wandered upstream of Dick's stretch and came to a lovely little pool which was clear of algae on account of the lively current that fed into it from a very narrow stretch of river. I believe he had seven chub in consecutive casts with floating crust – as fine a piece of angling as you could wish to see. Sadly, within two weeks of that catch, a lot of the big chub were dead. A silage pollution resulted in thousands of fatalities along the river and at least one confirmed six-pounder was among the casualties. Dick's stretch was never the same again.

As well as myself, other members of the Coventry Specimen Group turned their attention to the Ouse in the seventies, and one of the earliest captures was a superb chub of exactly 6lb to Merv Wilkinson from a slow, deep stretch. This was a stretch of totally different character from the norm, being of uniform depth and flow for several hundred yards. It looked remarkably similar to a stretch on the Cherwell that had produced many big chub to us all. The opposite bank was a mass of trees and bushes, and fallen timber littered the margins. It soon became apparent that the big chub lived in or near those snags and to catch them the hookbait obviously had to be positioned in the danger areas. The closeness of all the snags to each other meant that the normal downstream-and-across presentation resulted in fish being lost in the timber. As most fish naturally move downstream with a bait, the chub were often snagged before the bite was seen. So we

Fred Starkey with his surprise eel.

developed an upstream-and-across presentation, fishing baits behind snags rather than above them. The reasoning was that this should give us a fraction more time to get the fish out of the obstructions. To make the set-up as sensitive as possible, we used heavy bobbins that would drop as soon as the bait was lifted and a little slack introduced into the line. Because it was a tight line technique, we would get the earliest possible warning of a bite.

The new approach brought immediate success, with several big fish coming to the group members. The most memorable were two more six-pounders to Trefor and Keith Walton, and Trefor's 6¼-pounder was the biggest ever caught in the group's life. Two weeks after its capture I had one of my first sessions there, which resulted in the biggest chub I have ever taken from the Ouse. I was fishing opposite a jungle of fallen branches where there was a little bay in the bank. It was the next swim down to

Trefor admires a 3½-pounder from Dick Walker's stretch on a bitterly cold day.

where Trefor's fish had been taken. I arrived at the swim a little before dusk, having spent the day fishing Dick Walker's stretch, and amended my tackle to fish upstream into the snags. The river was extremely sluggish and a single swan shot was all that was required to keep a small piece of crust nicely anchored. In the first half-hour I struck and missed two false bites, a common irritation when fishing a very sensitive upstream presentation, but about an hour after dark (with it by now bitterly cold and frosty) the bobbin fell 6in (15cm) very sharply. This time, solid resistance met my sweeping strike and a big fish was hauled out of the immediate danger area of the tangle of branches, below which he had been hooked. The problem was that one of the branches came with him – I must have cast over it in the near twilight. Luckily, the branch was not attached to any others and, although it hampered me when playing the fish and prevented me making an accurate assessment of its size, it never gave me any fear that it would cause me to lose the chub. In spite of the anchor he was towing around, the fish fought well – he had to be turned several times to prevent him from gaining the sanctuary of the opposite bank and I was relieved when I eventually netted him. Only then did I appreciate how big the chub was and in the torch beam it looked massive, so deep were its flanks. It weighed 5lb 6oz and was a typical small-headed and stocky Ouse specimen.

Despite the fact that Dick Walker's stretch produced so many big chub over the years, I was destined only ever to catch one five-pounder from it. I had arrived at the river one winter's day. The weather had deteriorated from the moment I set off from home, well before day-break – the early drizzle turned to heavy rain during the journey and it remained with us all day. I was not encouraged when I saw the river which was running high and very brown after all the heavy rain and snow we had had during the week. In these days I would not bother fishing for chub in such conditions but switch to roach, or barbel if the river contained any. But that day I was determined to fish for big chub no matter what and after donning all my waterproof gear, I ventured out into that inhospitable and bleak landscape. My years of experience with chub told me that the conditions were terrible and I was soon proved correct. After several hours, I was still biteless and the most sensible decision I could have made would have been to pack up early and go home. But I am stubborn when it comes to fishing and so I decided to stay put in a known big chub swim, in the hope that one fish could be encouraged to pick up a bait.

The most famous chub swim on the stretch was Two Willows, which was also a good bet under the prevailing conditions as the high floodwater meant that a very inviting crease had been formed alongside the high bank. I was fishing off the opposite bank to Dick Walker's stretch that day and at about midday dropped my bait in the very steady water close to the near bank, just above the more downstream of the two big willows. The line was looped over the index finger of my right hand and because of the unfavourable conditions, I had decided to strike at anything vaguely resembling a bite; I had nothing to lose.

The heavy cold rain made touch legering very unpleasant, but after an hour it was to pay dividends. There was a sudden pluck, a momentary slackening of tension and then a slow draw on the line. It was very like the sensation when a clump of submerged weed fouls the line, but weed does not shoot upstream on its own! The chub fought like a tiger, kiting across to the far bank and using the very heavy mid-stream current to maximum advantage. The appalling weather was momentarily forgotten as I enjoyed a momentous battle with the fish and when it was landed I could see that I had been very lucky. The hookhold was at the extreme edge of the top lip; a few more minutes and we would have parted company. That chub weighed 5lb 2oz. I was not so lucky with a second big chub that I hooked shortly afterwards. This time the hookhold did give way and I was left to reflect that I could have banked a brace of five-pounders on a day when I had dismissed the conditions as hopeless.

It was an abortive trip to the same stretch of the Ouse that could so easily have led to Trefor and I losing our lives. We had arrived to find the river impossibly high and coloured, still rising fast and choked with rafts of drifting debris. After an hour of attempting to fish, we knew that we were wasting our time so we packed Trefor's car and set off home. We had not been travelling long when heavy snow commenced and the road became axle deep in slush. We were heading down a fairly steep hill when the car went out of control and, even though Trefor was certainly not going fast, there was nothing he could do to stop the car. His brakes were useless and we went into an uncontrollable skid. We bumped over the grass verge and headed at speed towards a fence that overlooked a steep drop to the valley beyond and then a railway line below that. The fence support posts were spaced only about every ten yards and by sheer chance we crashed into one of those. That prevented the car from going straight through the fence and toppling over the drop and although Trefor's car was written off, we escaped virtually unscathed.

15 Hawk Lake Crucians

It was one of the Queenford syndicate members who first put me on to Hawk Lake Fishery which is alongside Hawkstone Park Golf Course in Shropshire. We had been talking about big fish in general and I mentioned that it had been about twenty years since I had caught a big crucian. Hawk Lake was apparently well known for its large stock of good crucians as well as mirror and common carp, and so I wasted no time in contacting the club that controlled the fishery and getting my name down on the waiting list. It took some while for me to be invited into the club and I eventually made my first visit in September 1988.

I was immediately impressed with everything about this beautiful water, apart from the never-ending walk from the car park to get to the swims. The banks are immaculately kept, completely free of litter and heavily populated with mature shrubs and trees. The lake itself which is only fishable from one bank as the golf course is on the other, is long and narrow and is itself very well looked after. With its thick rushes and beds of water lilies it is a pleasure to fish.

Hawk Lake – home of some giant crucians.

My conversations with a few anglers on the bank revealed that some areas were better known for crucians than others and I settled into a swim I fancied about half-way along the water from the car park. My plan was to fish one rod for the crucians all day and into the dark hours, while I would set the other up for big carp. I tackled up a second carp rod but did not use it. When I was ready to get my head down for the night, the crucian rod would be put away and a second carp bait cast out. That first session at the lake was unproductive for no other reason than I was simply not used to the delicacy of presentation required for successful crucian fishing. I was laying on with flake, using a float that would be suitable for tench and in retrospect I am convinced that I simply did not see the bites I had. Several times I wound in a bare hook.

The following week I thought about those crucians a lot and came to the decision that I would scale right down to fish for these most shy biting of big fish. I obtained a two AAA Drennan Betalight float and decided that I would fish it on a 4lb mainline with a 2lb hooklink, using a single grain of sweetcorn as bait. I had also given the groundbaiting some thought and had de-

A rotund three-pounder – best out of a catch of ten fish.

cided to opt for a very light, slow sinking feed rather than the more stodgy mixture I had used on my first trip. Instead of baiting at the start of the session, it would be introduced on the little and often principle through the day.

By the time I had myself organised, it was late afternoon on the first day of a two-day session and my first job was to fire out several hundred mini boilies and a few dozen standard tutti frutti boilies for the carp fishing. With one carp bait in position and the second carp rod on standby, it was time to set up the crucian tackle. I intended to float fish well after dark. It was a warm and flat calm evening, so the Betafloat would provide some entertaining after dark fishing. The float was shotted exactly as I had planned so that the Betalight rode within ⅛in of the water surface, with the bottom AAA shot exactly on the bottom. This arrangement meant that after dark the light would appear as two halves separated by a ¼in dark band. Even the smallest lift or

Kevin Lumley with a lovely mirror carp.

dip of the float would be immediately apparent, especially as I would only be fishing at a rod's length out, alongside the marginal rushes.

In the early evening my first cast was made and two small balls of feed were placed near the float as were about twenty free grains of corn. For about an hour I sat there, periodically flicking in half a dozen corn grains and then there was a slow ½in lift. I struck immediately and an energetic fish shot to my right. On the light hooklink, I played that chubby little carp with respect, but soon was netting the biggest crucian I had seen for many years. It weighed in at 2lb 10oz – an excellent start.

I missed two other fractional indications before it became completely dark and then I sat in rapt concentration, staring intently at that greenish-white glow. It was positioned nicely in the dark shadow of a tree and that is how I knew that it was moving very slowly to the left. When the narrow dark band separating the two halves of the light disappeared, I struck into another good crucian that led me a merry dance before he joined his companion in the large sack. This second fish was only 3oz lighter than the first. Apart from a 3lb bream, there were no further bites after dark and I settled down in my sleeping bag at a little before midnight, having first cast out my second carp bait.

The night passed totally without incident and I was crucian fishing again a little after dawn, but there was no action whatever for the first few hours. Kevin Lumley from Carlisle was fishing the next swim for carp and he kindly photographed my two crucians for me so that they could be returned. He then decided to move swims and as he knew the water well, I went for a walk with him to the new pitch he had selected. On the way he pointed out to me all the areas that had produced big carp most consistently and it was a most informative morning. I suppose I spent an hour chatting to Kevin as he set up his gear and then I returned to my own tackle. Having recast the carp bait, I put out two balls of my light feed, a few corn grains and settled down once more to my crucian fishing. After the biteless previous few hours, it was quite a surprise when the first bite came only a minute after the float had settled. Again, a very delicate lift was followed by a slow run to the right and I struck into what turned out to be the biggest fish of the session, exactly 3lb and my second biggest crucian ever. Having just walked perhaps half a mile from Kevin's swim, it was time to walk back again to ask him to photograph this latest capture for me.

I was to take crucians steadily throughout this second day and by the time I was ready to leave late in the evening, I had caught a further seven weighing between 2lb 1oz and 2lb 13oz. That gave me a total catch of ten crucians over 2lb with one three-pounder, plus a 3lb bream and several smaller bream. After the heavier tackle that much of my specimen hunting demands, such delicate float work is a very pleasant change and for big crucians it is undoubtedly an extremely deadly method.

There was only one disappointment with the session. During the day I had been privileged to witness and photograph a superb 24lb mirror carp for Kevin and thought to myself that all I needed was a big carp to make the session complete. Half an hour before I was due to leave, I had not had a single bleep on my carp outfit Optonic, despite it being in the water all but an hour since my arrival. Sod's law again was to prevail. The last two crucians I caught, fish of 2lb 12oz and 2lb 13oz, were taken quite late on in the evening and I decided to photograph them in self-portrait style, using my tripod and bulb release. All the equipment was set up and then I took the two fish from the sack, sat on my bedchair and grinned at the camera, foot hovering over the air bulb. Just at that moment, the Optonic screamed. Something was making off at a great rate of knots with three mini boilies. Obviously the welfare of the crucians had to be the first priority and I quickly popped them back in the sack before striking at the run. That delay, however, cost me the carp. By the time I had set the hook, the fish was deep in the rushes on the far bank and I eventually retrieved a bare hook. In over forty hours, the carp had to choose exactly the wrong minute to pick up my bait.

16 TC Pit

TC TENCHING

In the summer of 1976, Trefor West and I were engrossed in trying to catch our first ever 6lb tench, both having a personal best of 5lb 10oz. Our efforts were being concentrated at Sywell Reservoir near Northampton, the water where Phil Smith had set the Coventry Specimen Group buzzing with a fish of 6lb 10oz several years earlier. It will perhaps seem incomprehensible to big fish anglers who have come into the sport in the last decade, but in the mid-seventies a 6lb tench was a very big fish indeed. Very few anglers had caught one and the national record of 8lb 8oz seemed an impossibly unattainable target. Only a handful of 7lb fish had ever been recorded.

You can therefore imagine our excitement when a close friend contacted Trefor, with news that he had taken a gigantic fish of 7lb 14oz from a little fished gravel pit in Oxfordshire and that he had heard confirmed reports of one weighing over 8lb. Our first reaction was one of incredulity, but examination of the photograph of the fish was proof enough; here was one mammoth tench.

As it was late autumn when that news broke and as neither Trefor nor myself wanted to chase the fishing straight away, we decided to give the pit a look at the start of the following season. We already knew of the water. During our days in the late sixties fishing Marlborough Pool, we had to drive past it and had often meant to investigate the fishing. It had already produced some good bream, but as neither of us was the slightest bit interested in bream at the time, it was always someting we put off until another day. Big tench were, however, a different matter entirely and consequently 16 June 1977 saw us settling into a swim on the canal bank for our first session at TC Pit.

The origin of the name TC has aroused quite considerable speculation since the water had become famous. It has been suggested that it was conjured up as some sort of code to disguise the water's location. Nothing could be further from the truth. During our initial investigations into obtaining permits to fish the water, it transpired that fishing was not actually allowed. The water was controlled by the Thames Conservancy who turned a benevolent blind eye to fishing, although never having given official permission. Bailiffs would come along the bank on occasions to check Thames River licences and to make sure that cars were not causing any obstruction, but we were never asked to leave the fishery. The water therefore became known as the Thames Conservancy Pit or, as that was a bit of a mouthful, the TC Pit for short.

The water was not fished very much in those days which was confirmed by the fact that on our first visit there were just four other anglers on the water besides ourselves. Trefor and I were instantly captivated by this beautiful lake. It had not been despoiled as it has been now and the banks were attractively overhung with trees and bushes almost around the entire perimeter.

A fat 7lb 11oz fish for Trefor.

There were very few swims as such and it was a matter of making a small hole in the rushes to fish through. Even now I cannot understand the obsession many anglers have of creating enormous open swims which totally destroy the atmosphere of an overgrown water.

That first trip lasted four days and we caught very few fish, in fact the first one I had was the smallest tench I had ever seen! At the end of the session we had caught one fair tench apiece – fish weighing about four pounds – but we had seen enough to convince us that TC was a very special water indeed. Every dawn enormous tench would roll in front of us, and those were a very exciting few days. There was also one very amusing incident which I shall never forget.

Those were the days before bivvies or brolly camps and we used to sleep in the open air, with the top half of our bodies covered by a 36in umbrella, the biggest you could buy at the time. We had those folding supermarket-type bedchairs, which were very prone to collapsing if you moved violently while asleep. Just as dawn was breaking, I was awake and was just putting the kettle on when I heard a noise from my right, where Trefor was fishing about ten yards away. He was still fast asleep, tightly wrapped in his sleeping bag. A creaking noise had alerted me and as I watched, the front legs of his bedchair suddenly gave way, turning the bedchair into a very efficient water chute. Gracefully he slid down into the lake, just like a burial at sea! 'Oh dear!'

Our first big TC tench which weighed 7lb 2oz.

he said (or words to that effect) as he awoke with a start, writhing in the cold margins like some gigantic maggot. I would have gone to his assistance, but I was aching so much with laughter that I could not move!

The following weekend I had to work and Trefor went to TC on his own. In fact, he went straight to the Cherwell directly from a night-shift on the Friday morning for a day's summer chubbing, arriving at TC in late evening. As he had had no sleep since the previous afternoon, his intention was to sleep until day-break the following morning. With this in mind, Trefor set up in one of the closest swims to the access point and got his head down for the night. He was up early the following morning, put little bait out and soon he was into his one and only tench of the session, but what a tench. It weighed 7lb 2oz and Trefor called round to my house on Sunday morning to bring me the news.

Returning a seven-pounder.

I had already made plans to fish TC for three days beginning on the following Wednesday, and Trefor's fantastic news meant that I was champing at the bit until I could get down there. It also meant that my choice of swim was made for me. Trefor would not be there, so I would obviously fish the same swim. In the event, when I arrived early on Wednesday morning, the swim was already occupied by two teenagers who were there for a couple of days. That was naturally very disappointing, but I pushed my way through the undergrowth to the next available opening, about forty yards away. I was encouraged immediately by the sight of several tench rolling about thirty yards out and hurriedly set up my gear. Although events were not to prove so dramatic as they had for Trefor I had an interesting three days' fishing, landing five tench weighing up to just over 5lb, and pulling out of another in the weed that looked a good six-pounder. I also experienced what is still perhaps the most incredible tench bite I have ever had. These were the days before Optonics and bite indication was via swingtips. I was just filling the kettle when one of the tips shot out straight with no prior warning whatsoever, and then the rod rocketed forward, dragging the front rest out of the ground as it did so. I hurled myself off my seat and caught the rod butt in mid-air, just before it was going to vanish into the lake, and then held on for grim death as about thirty yards of line whistled off the spool against the clutch. The culprit was a male of no more than 4lb, and whenever I read about twitchy tench bites, I think of that fish.

Those two sessions were to have an unpleasant side-effect. It transpired that the

Two 'fives' and two 'sixes' for my son Chris.

two swims that Trefor and I had fished albeit quite innocently, had been pre-baited by two other anglers. As the swims were not marked, however, we had no way of knowing this. We were then accused in the angling press of spying on the anglers concerned to see where they were pre-baiting and then fishing their swims deliberately! As we lived almost sixty miles from the fishery, this was arrant nonsense. This accusation was followed up by a letter to us from one of the men concerned, laying down his requirements for the following season. He and his friend, we were informed, would be pre-baiting a swim ready for the opening of the season and Trefor and I would be expected not to fish there for the rest of the summer! This was of course totally unacceptable, and as one other local angler had already made it clear that his swim was not to be fished by anyone else whether he was there or not, Trefor wrote to the angling press himself, highlighting the situation. Hence began the famous Oxford Debate which went on for months. Our stance was, as it always has been, that pre-baited swims will be respected for the first session of a new season, but thereafter it is first come, first served. In practice we would both leave a swim vacant if we knew another angler was conducting a campaign there, but we certainly would not be dictated to about where we could and could not fish. Mervyn Wilkinson summed it up more succinctly than anyone else: 'Bums reserve swims' was his contribution to the

My first big one at 6lb 15oz.

debate and those three words say it all. The overwhelming weight of public opinion was in our favour and when the dust had settled, we were able to enjoy many years of terrific fishing at TC without any further problems.

For the rest of that first summer I fished TC very hard and as often as possible, and although I had lots of tench, I never achieved my dream of a fish over 6lb. On 16 June 1978, that was to change. I had arrived early the previous day and had cut myself a brand new swim in the middle of a thicket. Let anyone dare accuse me of swim jumping! About thirty yards out was a very interesting bar and shelf and that is where I concentrated the bulk of my feed, consisting of fine breadcrumbs containing about 200 chopped lobworms, flake samples and two tins of corn. I was going to fish two rods with lob on one and a large piece of flake on the other. I started fishing at dawn on the 16th and by 11 a.m. I had not had the slightest indication of a bite. At about that time, I wound in the flake rod and re-baited with two grains of sweetcorn. Only a couple of minutes after casting, this rod was away with the tip shooting up in very determined fashion. A pulsating scrap followed and after about five minutes a very big tench slipped over the rim of the net. I was very excited indeed. I could see that the tench was easily over 6lb and could even be up to 7lb. In fact it was 1oz short at 6lb 15oz – a magnificent fish. That was my only fish in that first session, but I was not bothered by the lack of further action. I had achieved an ambition I had held for very many years.

Once again that early success was the biggest fish either of us landed that season, and it was not until the following June that I was to catch a fish beyond our wildest dreams. I opened the season at TC on my own as Trefor had been side-tracked by some big barbel on the Middle Severn. Opening day was very successful and I had a

TC tench weighing 7lb 1oz, 5lb 12oz and 5lb 14oz

good catch of tench, all over 5lb with a top fish of 5lb 10oz. It was now June 1979 and the water was still very little fished. In fact, when I returned the following week there was only one other angler on the water, Rolf Wobbeking of Oxford. It had been my intention to fish the same swim in which I had achieved my opening day success, but there was a very tricky wind blowing directly into the pitch, carrying a great deal of heavy algae and floating weed with it. Fishing would have been very uncomfortable, so I broke out my binoculars and scanned around the lake for an alternative. Almost immediately I spotted intense fish activity about forty yards offshore in the far corner along my bank where it was also nicely sheltered and calm and, more importantly, free of algae. I decided that would do

My 7lb 12oz TC catch.

A lovely 9lb 7oz to Alan Rauden which was unfortunately foul-hooked.

and I humped my gear round to the new area. Rolf had obviously spotted the activity as well and come to the same decision, and so it was that we met, intending to fish the same spot. Rolf had been dragged into the Oxford Debate, and this was an ideal opportunity to show that there were no hard feelings on either side. We therefore came to the civilised conclusion to fish adjacent swims. As well as giving us both a chance at the big tench in front of us, it would also give us a good opportunity to spend three days in clearing the air through discussions. In the event, we fished very well together as a team with absolutely no animosity and both succeeded in catching a few lovely tench. I am still indebted to Rolf for the superb photographs he took of a fantastic fish I was to land on the second afternoon.

I was fishing two distinct areas. On the closer swim, at about forty yards and where the first rolling tench had been observed, I was fishing lobworm over a heavy cereal baiting, and had taken several fish weighing up to just under 6lb. I was fishing my second rod at about sixty yards with maggots and a swimfeeder, where I had seen a very big fish turn over at dawn. I had twice had sharp lifts on the tip that I had missed on that tackle and so I re-cast with a large piece of flake on the hook in place of the bunch of maggots I had been offering. The response was immediate, the tip straightening almost as soon as the flake had settled. I will never forget the memorable fight that followed. Twice that fish weeded me and I was convinced that the line would fall slack at any moment. But everything held firm, and eventually a monstrous tench rose from the depths and folded into the net. Rolf's first estimate was 8lb. I was absolutely dumbstruck and when the needle finally settled on 7lb 12oz, I had difficulty in convincing myself that this was really true.

When we had first started to fish TC, one fact that neither Trefor nor I could reconcile ourselves with was that the few other anglers on the water invariably fished light tackle, with maggots and the feeder. The standard approach seemed to consist of one or two maggots on a 16 or 18 hook to 3lb line. This made little sense to us as we felt it highly unlikely that the tench could be tackle-shy, with such limited fishing pressure. It was true that a few very big fish had come out, but they were usually isolated captures. Right from the off we had decided to approach the fishing in a more traditional style, baiting heavily with cereal feed and loads of particles, and fishing over this feed with large baits such as flake and lobs. Almost straight away we began to make multiple catches when the occasional fish had been the norm previously. By the end of the summer of 1979, it was common for us to have catches of between six and a dozen fish, but as yet few other anglers were copying our approach. We knew that eventually we would be in the right swim at the right time and accumulate an exceptional bag of fish, and that time would be when the tench potential of TC might be exposed far and wide. That was to happen in opening week, 1980.

After my heady success in 1979, Trefor and I decided to give the same swim a concerted attack during the first week of the season. Our preparations would be the most intensive we had ever undertaken,

A perfectly proportioned 7¼-pounder for Trefor.

and included groundbaiting with over a hudredweight of pure fine breadcrumbs and hundreds of lobworms. The swims were carefully dragged, and the baiting accuracy was maintained by the simple expedient of Trefor swimming to the respective fishing areas, towing a baby bath full of groundbait behind him while I directed operations from the bank. There were several new faces at TC that summer, our catches having begun to leak out and they watched our antics, initially with tolerant amusement.

Fishing began at first light on opening day and Trefor and I made a tremendous catch of big tench during the next seven days. The first fish came to my rod about three minutes after my first cast – a male of over 5lb and the highlight of the catch was a new personal best for Trefor – a beautiful tench of 7lb 13oz. There were other tench of over 7lb, several over 6lb and I believe only about one fish under 5lb. That week changed the face of TC tenching for ever in two ways. Firstly, we would never have the water to ourselves again as the secret was well and truly out. Also, heavy pre-baiting and fishing with bigger baits became a standard approach for a while until the tench wised up and began to give much more twitchy bites. At this stage, even Trefor and I had to switch to feeder tactics to keep catching consistently. Within two years, everyone on the lake fished feeders with maggots exclusively once more and that is when I switched back to fishing large lobs. I again had several large catches of very confidently biting tench in a few weeks, but this time I kept what I was doing very strictly to myself! Other anglers had also taken the baiting accuracy idea one stage further, equipping themselves with inflatable boats – a ploy that is now a standard tactic on many gravel pits.

The famous 8lb 12oz fish for Dave Boulstridge.

A few weeks after our epic opening week catch, a week that had also seen the TC record pushed up by Dave Boulstridge on his first visit to 8lb 12oz, I was also to beat my personal best, with a fish the same weight as Trefor's at 7lb 13oz. I actually caught that tench twice in the same day and the manner of its capture makes an interesting story.

I had settled into a weedy corner of the lake, where a lot of intense fish activity was apparent, and had spent some considerable time searching around with an empty feeder to try and find clear patches of gravel on which to present my hookbaits. I had decided not to drag out any weed as the water at that point was very shallow and the weed probably the factor why the tench felt secure there. Apart from a deep clear run under the bank to my right, there were very few clear spots, but eventually I found an interesting feature – a clear gravel hump barely eighteen inches deep, at about fifty yards range. It was several yards wide and after a few attempts I had one bait positioned at each extremity. The left-hand rod was baited with flake, the right with two maggots on a size 12 hook. Both were feeder rigs.

At about 11 a.m. I had a screaming run on the maggots and after an exhilarating and tense battle through the weed, a very big tench lay in the net at my feet. The first thing I noticed, apart from its size, were the two very distinctive parallel scars on the flank just behind the dorsal. I shouted to Trefor who was fishing about a hundred yards away, and he came and did the honours with the camera. After it had been admired again and Trefor had offered his congratulations, the tench was put back into the water, where it swam away strongly.

About four hours later after no further action, I wound in the flake rod and rebaited with a large, lively lobworm. On impulse I decided to fish in the deepish marginal run to my right. After adjusting the rests, I put the kettle on. Only a few minutes later the rod top hammered round, just like a barbel bite and I was playing a very big tench again. I had another tremendous scrap, but eventually the fish came obediently towards the waiting net. The first thing I saw were those parallel scars. There cannot be many anglers who have caught the same personal best fish twice in one day.

A BREAM CAMPAIGN

On the Thursday night of that fabulous opening week at TC in 1980, an event took place that was to redirect our angling efforts at the water thereafter. In the early hours of the morning Trefor had a very different type of bite from those we had been experiencing from the tench. Instead of the usual smash-and-grab take, his swingtip rose very slowly. When it was horizontal he struck into a very slow and ponderous weight that kited slowly and purposefully across the swim, before the hook pulled out. Very obviously, Trefor had just hooked and lost one of the water's big bream.

My best TC tench which tipped the scales at 7lb 13oz.

Until now, catching one of those had been a long way down our list of priorities, but that incident at last stirred in us a passion to put one on the bank. The following week, we returned to the water with a different approach to the fishing in mind; to fish for bream. We planned to fish the same swim but it was occupied, which was only to be expected after the tremendous number of tench it had produced for us. So we switched our attention to a swim on the main-road bank, the bank where Tony Charlett had taken one or two good bream, weighing up to an incredible 12lb plus. The problem that season with this area was that the bottom was carpeted with incredibly dense weed and we had to spend the best part of a day clearing a a small area where we could place our baits. Even then they became snagged as often as not and, as it would be as bad as ever the next time we could fish, after trying for about four weeks we gave it up for that season. We had already made up our minds that, from the start of the following season, we would put in a concerted effort for a double-figure bream.

A fat nine-pounder from TC to Terry Jones on one of his first trips.

During the close season plans were laid and we decided that we would be more single-minded in the pursuit of our objective than we had ever been before. From 16 June we would fish as often as possible and round the clock until we had achieved our goal. When we took that decision, we knew that we would possibly be sacrificing some excellent tench fishing in that our baiting programme would be designed deliberately to discourage tench from coming into the swim.

We had two swims in mind: our original tench swim, which we preferred, and another one on the far bank which had deeper and more weed-free water within forty yards of the bank. We discussed in great detail our plans for the approach to each swim in case one of the swims should be occupied on our arrival and we had to switch to the other. Whatever swim we fished, we agreed that the success of our plans hinged around attracting the fish into our swim and holding them there for a sufficient length of time. Correct groundbaiting would be vital and there were four factors we needed to get right to maximise our chances of success. Firstly, we had to decide on the composition of the loose feed and, going on from that, how much of it we should use. The accuracy of the introduction of the bait was also a factor, as was the correct time of introduction.

As far as the composition was concerned, we were agreed that the traditional approach of heavy cereal feed in conjunction with a large volume of particles was the one we would adopt. We would start with pure breadcrumbs containing gallons of maggots. The quantity of bait to use took many hours of discussion and in the end we decided to bait very heavily. The general consensus of opinion among the anglers on the water who had caught the bream was that very light feeding was the order of the day, and although we obviously respected these opinions, they did seem to us to be illogical. We could not see how a shoal of huge bream could be held in an area for any length of time by half a pint of maggots. We were convinced that the bream that had been caught so far from the water had come despite and not because of the light feeding.

Introducing the bait accurately would be vital and we would adopt the same procedure as that we had used for our tench catch. Trefor, being a very strong swimmer, would swim out to the fishing area with baths full of bait and would bait by hand. Beforehand, and in the same way, he towed out one terminal tackle with the bait and when he had reached the correct position, I marked the line at the reel. Each of the rods was then marked on the bank at the same range, so that we now knew that each tackle could be cast in the dark and had the certain knowledge that we would be able to fish in the correct area.

The time to introduce the bait was also extremely important. Regular introductions of feed during the session had worked effectively with the tench – as the tench activity had slowed down, another couple of balls of bait had livened them up again. We did not think that this disturbance would be tolerated by the bream, plus the fact that that would be doing exactly what we did not want to do, which was to attract tench into the swim. As far as possible, we wanted the swim devoid of any fish but bream. Another factor to consider was that we expected the bulk of the bream activity to be in the dark hours. Men who had caught a lot of big bream, such as my old friend Phil Smith, had confirmed that they were very nocturnal in habit. In the end, we decided to bait very heavily once a day in the early evening.

On 13 June Trefor arrived at TC early to both secure the swim we wanted and to do some advance baiting. Our previous year's success had, however, rebounded on us. The new TC era had begun. Three days before the start of the season, there were several anglers already in attendance and the swim where we had intended to start, from where our tench catch had come, had been occupied by Des Taylor and Pete McMurray for four days. Obviously, those lads had been determined to beat us to it! Undaunted and recognising the fact that they had as much right to be there as we had, Trefor set up shop in our second choice swim, which thankfully was vacant. I joined him on the 15th and as midnight slowly approached, our feelings of mounting excitement were difficult to contain. Our bream hunt had begun and to give an idea of the intensity of the campaign, we fished at least four days every week until the end of September. Very rarely were we able to be together for all that time because of work commitments, but our jobs allowed at least one of us to fish from Thursday morning until Monday morning.

Right from the outset, we knew that the tempo of the fishing would be extremely slow and so it was important not to make any mistakes with the chances we did get. For this reason, we had given a lot of thought to our bite detection arrangements. Other anglers had told us how difficult the bream bites were to connect with, with a frustratingly high percentage of missed bites. Also, problems had been experienced with hooks pulling out of fish after a few seconds. It occurred to us that there was a strong possibility that bites were being struck far too early and also that line bites may not have been recognised for what they were. What we wanted to avoid was striking at liners and possibly spooking feeding bream. Our bite detection methods were therefore geared so that when we did strike, we could be reasonably certain that it was at a bream with the bait well in its mouth.

Trefor and I adopted different bite detection methods in that I employed a butt-mounted bobbin on a 3ft drop, while Trefor used a shorter drop of 18in, but also used a swingtip as his line-bite indicator. My bobbins were sufficiently heavy to register liners as they would drop back as the line came free. We were both agreed that no attempt would be made to strike until the line was tight with the bobbin in the butt ring, and to ensure that we would not be tempted into a premature strike in the excitement of the moment, we sat at least four yards behind the rods. As we had to get out of our seats to get to the rods, sufficient time would have elapsed to show up the majority of line bites. Realistically, we knew that we could not expect more than a handful of bream bites during the summer and we had to make the most of those that did come our way. Self-control was therefore vital.

One terminal tackle was quite orthodox, each rod carrying a loaded Drennan feeder stopped by a swivel 2ft from a size 14 or 16 hook. The main line was 6lb, the hooklink 4lb and the bait either maggot, or a maggot and flake cocktail. Later we used bigger hooks carrying full-sized lobworms on one rod.

During the first week of the season our fishing was very slow indeed, with only a handful of tench weighing up to 5lb 9oz to show for our efforts, and no sign of bream whatsoever. The first night of the season, however, did see a little bit of history created as Pete McMurray landed a bream of 13lb exactly from the spot where I would have been sitting in our first choice swim! Trefor and I were among the first to congratulate Pete, and the sight of that massive slab only increased our determination to land one ourselves. There was also an interesting occurrence on the second night of the season, when I had an incredibly fast run that nearly emptied one of my spools in the thirty seconds or so it took me to get to the rod. The strike met with absolutely no resistance and I retrieved a limp line minus the terminal tackle. It seems likely that a big pike or one of the water's few big carp had fouled the line and bolted off with it.

The next four weekends were very uneventful, with a few tench being landed, topped by a nice 6lb 6oz fish to myself at dawn one day. During this period it was difficult to maintain our determination as on the shallower bank the tench were feeding well, with several seven-pounders and one eight-pounder having come out. Topping that was an incredible fish that was caught while we were there, the first authenticated TC nine-pounder to my friend Terry Jones, from the same swim where I had taken my 7lb 13oz fish the previous season. During this period big bream were observed spawning on the shallows hundreds of yards from our baited area and in retrospect we were a bit blinkered carrying on fishing for them over that period. We would have lost nothing in having one weekend after the tench. Anyway, during that spawning ritual one angler was observed fishing for the bream with float tackle off the bottom. It was deliberately designed to foulhook fish and that is exactly what happened, with two doubles being landed – one hooked in the back and one in the belly. That 'angler' was left in no doubt as to my opinion of him. I wanted to catch a big bream very badly, but certainly not that badly.

In the late evening of 17 July 1981, our usual thorough and accurate baiting programme completed, we settled down for another night session in the Oxfordshire countryside. It was a lovely breathless evening and the water surface was mirror-smooth. We were full of anticipation as usual, as indeed we had been during the previous twenty-four nights we had spent in the swim. We sat talking and drinking endless cups of tea. The light gradually faded and in the gathering dusk everything was quiet and peaceful. And then, a little after ten, there was a short shrill from an Optonic and one of my bobbins leapt up a few inches and then dropped immediately back again. Seconds later one of Trefor's bobbins did the same – liners! And so began nearly two hours of non-stop line bites, which was something we had not experienced before. The swim was obviously full of fish, but were they bream? The one thing we had to do was exercise all the restraint at our command.

A little before midnight, the swingtip on Trefor's right-hand rod twitched again and lifted half-way. But this time the bobbin rose slowly and steadily to the butt ring and held there. As Trefor moved to the rod, the tip straightened and a firm, controlled strike set the hook into a fish that we knew straight away was not a tench. It was too slow and ponderous. So unspectacular was the fight that Trefor was convinced at first that he had hooked a modest-sized pike, but he played it very carefully just in case. It was as well that he did, because when the fish came in close we could see clearly that it was a huge bream. I was able to net it at the first attempt, much to Trefor's relief and at long last we had our first double. The feeling of elation as we looked at the fish in the torchlight is difficult to describe. All our efforts and sacrifices over the last few weeks had been rewarded. The scales confirmed 10lb 10oz, and we shook hands in triumph.

What was to follow was almost unbelievable. I had only just put the bream in our mammoth net to await the morning when another Optonic sounded. The bobbin on Trefor's second rod rose straight to the butt and as the tip again locked into the horizontal, Trefor set the hook into another fish we knew to be a big bream. A third indicator had risen at the same time and it was a little difficult initially to tell exactly what was going on, but it soon became apparent that two tackles were tangled together. As Trefor pumped the bream towards us in the darkness, line was disappearing off the second reel at an alarming rate, and I was not certain at that moment on which tackle the bream was actually hooked. With the bream clearly visible in the moonlight about twenty yards from the bank, an incredible bird's nest of line jammed solid in the tip ring of the rod Trefor was holding, and he could then neither give nor retrieve line.

Something had to be done quickly to avoid the fish being lost. The decision was taken to bite off the line on the second rod, which I did, but not before wrapping the line securely round my left arm for retrieval later, or in case that was in fact the line the bream was on. I then crouched low with the net, while Trefor walked slowly backwards, towing the bream behind him. Luckily the bream did not have much fight left in him, or there would have been no way we would have been able to handline a double-figure fish on 4lb line. There were no hiccups however, and the bream was led docilely over the net and lifted out of the water.

For the first time we could see exactly how big the fish was and, when the scales confirmed 12lb 10oz, we could hardly believe it. It had been an unbelievable twenty minutes. That second fish signalled the end of the action for that night, but the following evening Trefor had a third double of 10lb 8oz in the same feeding period – a fish that was to be our last for several more weeks.

The heady success of that July weekend was not to be repeated until early September even though we fished very hard. I was more determined than ever after seeing the magnificent fish Trefor had caught. Throughout August the conditions were far from ideal for bream fishing, with little or no wind. The bream had responded best in the past in rougher conditions, and what we were really looking for was a steady and sustained headwind to stir them up a bit. During that period, plenty of tench were landed and I had one memorable morning's catch of three six-pounders. Another problem during that time was the increasing numbers of small perch we were landing. In fact they became an absolute menace, so much so that we were forced to amend our baiting programme. The maggots in the feed were an obvious attractant and we started to substitute them for casters and hemp and bait much later in the evening when perch activity was almost nil. Whatever the baiting programme, however, perch were very active at dawn. We just had to live with that.

The fourth bream came on the first weekend in September. I had fished three very gruelling days and nights without a single bite to show for my efforts and packed up at mid-morning on Saturday when Trefor took over from me. It had been flat calm the entire time, with cold foggy nights – poor conditions indeed for bream. With no change in the conditions, Trefor had but one bite in the early hours of Sunday morning, and duly landed another great fish of 10lb 5oz. That was immensely encouraging, but also puzzling. Why had that fish been caught when we had fished for weeks in similar conditions with no signs of bream? I also began to wonder for the first time whether I was actually destined to catch one that season. I knew it was only a matter of time, but felt that time may be running out. The weather conditions suggested that we were not very far away from the first frosts when the chances would diminish even further.

The next week I again pinched an extra day from work and arrived on Thursday to fish three more days and nights. I would give it everything I had for the remaining time. As I set up the gear, I was more confident than I had been for some time. Conditions were a lot more promising, with a strong wind blowing offshore. I sat expectantly in my bivvy after dark with one small tench to show for my efforts, and at about 11 p.m. the heavens opened as a tremendous thunderstorm broke. For over three hours that storm raged, with the rain falling so hard that it was difficult to see the Betalights on my bobbins. The howling wind made it difficult to sleep and then, above the wind, I could hear an Optonic screaming. Within seconds, a reel handle was spinning crazily and I scrambled out into the elements and struck into something that was going like a train. To start with I thought a very big tench was responsible, but it quickly became apparent that I had hooked one of the numerous tufted ducks which had become more and more persistent over the weeks. That night I was fishing with three rods, and by the time the duck had been brought to the bank, it had taken the other two lines as well. You may be able to picture the scene – it was the middle of the night, blowing a gale and hammering down with rain. In my haste to get to the rod, I had rushed out in my trainers without having time for my waterproof coat, so I was now drenched and plastered in mud. A demented tufted duck had clambered up the bank and was now dashing around in a frenzy, taking three lines with it and causing all three Optonics to scream at once. I was in a state of total chaos. In addition to that lot, I had pulled two bivvy pegs out as well, so that my sleeping bag and bedchair were also soaked, as were my spare clothes. I was not happy!

Trefor with a superb 11lb 4oz specimen.

After I had released the duck I simply could not face unravelling the mess in the dark. I was totally demoralised and settled down as best I could in my wet gear to get a little sleep.

The next morning dawned bright and sunny, and I was mentally prepared to attempt fishing again. It took some time to sort the mess out, but after about an hour's daylight, I was relaxing with a cup of tea and with three baits out in position. That morning the perch were even more persistent than usual and I had several small ones on both maggots and lobs. And then I had a sudden impulse. Thinking that there might be a bigger perch on the fringes of the shoal, I put on the biggest lobworm I could find in my box and cast it a good ten yards past the actual baited area. A sizzling run resulted almost immediately, with the bobbin literally slamming up into the butt ring. The culprit was an extremely hard-fighting perch of 3lb 1oz, a superb consolation for the bitter disappointment of the previous night.

During the afternoon, the wind veered right round and was now blowing just as strongly inshore. I was now more keyed up than ever, but despite having a very strong intuition that something was about to happen any minute, there were no bites whatsoever. Despite that, I knew that I had the best chance of the season and my intuition was as strong as ever on the Saturday night, the last night of the session.

At 8 p.m., with the baiting programme completed and the light fading rapidly, the wind dropped to nothing and there was intense fish activity in the swim. I was reminded immediately of that night in July when Trefor had the first catch. Line bites were now coming to all rods in rapid succession, and I was hopping from one foot to the other, chain-smoking. I just could not relax, I knew I was going to catch something. At 9 p.m., the bobbin on the right-hand rod began to creep up agonisingly slowly. Some 9in (23cm) before the butt ring, it stopped. My hand hovered over the butt while I resisted the almost overpowering temptation to strike. And then the bobbin moved again, rising the rest of the way to the butt. As the reel began to backwind, I struck and felt the satisfying thump of a big fish. The slow, heavy and sluggish fight told me that it was indeed a bream that I had hooked and I told myself very firmly to keep calm. Because of an intervening bank

A surprise perch of 3lb 1oz.

of Canadian pondweed some thirty yards out, I had decided that I would bully any bream I hooked to the surface if possible and bring it over the top of that weed; I did not fancy trying to pull a fish through it. In that aim I was successful, and on that bright moonlit night I could quite clearly see a massive silver shape break surface some forty yards out and come towards me across the top. I was very pleased that the fight from my first double-figure bream was pathetic – I do not think I could have handled losing it after all those weeks of effort.

It went into the net at the first attempt, and as I fumbled in my tackle bag for my forceps and scales, I was so excited I could feel myself trembling. I will never forget that evening. Eventually, the fish lay suspended on the scales and the needle gave a magical reading of 11lb 2oz. I did a victory jig around the bivvy – I am just glad nobody was watching!

The activity in the swim had continued unabated during the proceedings and at midnight I was in again, this time banking a much smaller bream of exactly 7lb. Shortly

My first double at 11lb 2oz.

Returning an eleven-pounder.

after this the sky clouded over, the wind picked up again and all activity ceased for the night. The following morning I was able to get the two bream witnessed by Dick Matthews, one of the TC regulars, and then the seven-pounder was returned while Dick took the photographs of one of the most memorable specimen fish I have ever taken.

The last fish of that campaign was taken the following weekend when Trefor had one bite over a two-day session and landed another magnificent specimen of 11lb 4oz – a tremendous finale. We are both agreed that, of all the memorable fishing we have enjoyed together, that TC bream campaign was one of the most stimulating and rewarding of our entire careers.

NIGHT OF THE THIRTEENS

In the early eighties, as a result of the string of big bream to Tony Charlett and the publicity surrounding our campaign, big bream and TC became synonymous and anglers travelled from all over the country to fish it. One such angler was Alan Wilson from Blackpool. I first met Alan on the banks of TC Pit and he has since become a good friend. He first arrived on the water in the summer of 1982 to fish for the tench, and that summer is memorable for being the poorest for bream in my association with the water. Very few indeed were caught and not one of my friends had a bite.

Turning this over in my mind in the close season of 1983, it occurred to me that perhaps we were all becoming a little stereotyped in our approach to the bream fishing. During the previous four seasons, almost all the bream had been taken from the main-road bank, and so during 1982 we had all fished those same few swims without success. I therefore decided that on 16 June 1983 I would start at the other end of the lake. During a close season reconnaissance, the decision was made to fish a very attractive little swim towards the bottom of the left-hand bank. Plumbing had revealed a very interesting topography up to sixty yards out from the bank. At only about twenty yards and to the left of the swim was a very shallow, small gravel hump only about two feet deep which I felt would be a natural feeding area after dark. Straight out from the bank there were two very interesting bars, one at about forty yards and one at about sixty. In both cases, the water rose quite sharply from thirteen feet to about seven and these were also natural ambush points.

On the first trip of the season, I was to take a good catch of tench from that swim and although I never caught a bream, I saw two roll over the further bar. Over the next few weeks I fished the swim as often as possible, although I was often beaten to it. A friend of mine and a superb angler, Alan Smith from Northampton, had also discovered the same swim and had come to the same conclusions I had about its potential. Which one of us fished it depended on who got there first. That summer, I believe that I was very unlucky not to catch a bream. Whenever I was first to the swim it appeared that the tench were active, but I never had one bream bite. I did catch many big tench, with several over 7lb. Alan Smith on the other hand took several bream, culminating in a new British record of 13lb 12oz. I was a definite jinx to the big bream that summer. Three times Alan and I actually fished the swim together, and on those occasions Alan did not have a bream bite either!

In early September 1983, both Alan Wilson and Phil Smith were off work for an extended period because of ill health, and both decided on an extended autumn campaign at TC. Understandably, the swim was the place to be as it had produced the record and Phil moved in for a two-week session. His second morning in the swim provided the forerunner to what was to prove a few days of unbelievable bream fishing. I just wish that I had got there first! At about 10.30 a.m. during a rainstorm, his first bream proved to be a new personal best of 12lb 14oz.

On the Wednesday Phil was joined by Alan Wilson who moved in on the left-hand side of the swim. That night Alan was biteless, but Phil added a second big fish to his tally – 12lb 8oz this time. Thursday night was quite remarkable – while Alan again had no action, Phil scored heavily, taking no fewer than four more bream during the dark hours and several tench. As three of those bream were over 10lb, Phil had now taken five doubles and quite a few nice tench, while Alan had yet to have his first indication even though they were fishing the same gravel bar only a few yards apart. I arrived just after dawn on the Friday morning and was delighted to assist in the photographic session and to shoot some film of Phil's catch on my video. After a long chat with Phil and Alan and a couple of cups of tea, I moved in to the swim to Alan's left, some thirty yards away where I could fish one rod on the same bar and the other on a very close bar from which Cliff Dean had taken a thirteen-pounder a few weeks previously. Later in the day Alan Smith arrived, moving in to a swim about forty yards to Phil's right. As darkness began to close around us, little did we anticipate the historic events that were to transpire during the next few hours.

Even the weather seemed to be holding its breath. Up until that Friday night the week had been very blustery, but as soon as darkness had fallen a complete calm descended. A light drizzle commenced and everywhere was eerily silent on that very black night. It remained that way until about 11.30 p.m. I was relaxing in my bivvy when I heard rustling as someone walked up to me. Phil appeared in the doorway holding a plastic carrier bag. I can still picture it now, with that big black tail hanging out of the top. 'We need another witness, Tony', he said, 'Alan's cracked it.' That was an understatement. Alan Wilson's first ever double-figure bream was confirmed by us all at an incredible 13lb 8oz. Naturally there was considerable euphoria and we all shared a cup of tea before settling back to our own fishing at around midnight. Shortly afterwards Phil and Alan, who were very short of bait, went off for an hour's worming.

The next thing I remember is excited voices being raised at about 2 a.m., and just as I was coming to my senses, Phil appeared in my doorway again and there was another tail hanging out of his weigh bag. An action replay! Unbelievably, the scales confirmed that Alan had achieved something unique – two 13lb bream in a session. This one was even bigger than the first. More than that, it was potentially a new record at 13lb 13oz.

Again, there were two quiet hours and then two fish came in quick succession – a 12lb 13oz fish to Phil and incredibly yet another thirteen-pounder to Alan, 13lb 2oz to be exact. By this time we were all slightly numb at the events that were occurring. Alan Wilson just kept repeating over and over again 'I don't believe this is happening to me.' Not long after I had witnessed Alan's third fish, I had my one and only bite of the night, on my right-hand rod. What I hooked was heavy and slow-moving and was almost certainly a big bream, but I was not destined to see it. I had it about half-way back to the bank when it stuck solid in submerged weed. As I applied pressure I felt the fish come free, but just after it started to come towards me again, the hook pulled out. What a sickener that was.

After I had recast, and with all the others now asleep, I also slid down in my sleeping bag and closed my eyes. When I awoke just on day-break, everywhere was silent and I put the kettle on for the first cup of tea on that chilly September morning. I had drunk half a mug when I heard an Optonic. Within a couple of minutes I was walking slowly down to Alan and Phil's swim, arriving just in time to watch Alan slip the net under another huge bream. 'It's probably another thirteen' I said almost flippantly. Alan weighed the fish, apparently in a daze, and when he announced 13lb 6oz neither of us said a word at first. It was all too much to take in.

Later that morning I had the extreme pleasure of videoing that memorable catch for Alan, who is without doubt one of the real gentlemen of angling. We were also able to establish a quite remarkable fact about the big bream potential of TC from that catch. When we studied the fish we realised that two known thirteen-pounders were not among them: a two-tone fish that Andy Barker had first caught at 13lb 4oz and Alan Smith's record fish. We therefore had the most positive proof that TC held at least six different fish of over 13lb, quite a remarkable statistic. Both Alan Smith and I blanked on that momentous Friday night, but we both agree that we would not have missed that experience for the world. It must still rank as one of the greatest catches of specimen fish ever known.

TC TODAY

A predictable result of the incredible summer of 1983 was that TC, which was already popular, became more and more overcrowded in the seasons that followed. Inevitably this situation brought with it many undesirable side-effects. During the summer of 1984, I fished the pit only a handful of times and made prophecies which were to become true even faster than I had imagined to my intense sorrow. Many of the newcomers to the water did not adhere to the standards that we have a right to expect from anglers. Litter became a problem and a water that was always immaculate quickly became a disgrace. Several friends and I filled bin liners with rubbish whenever we went to the water, but it was an uphill struggle. Within two weeks it would be as bad as ever. It was not only the youngsters either. Several times middle-aged anglers were equally guilty. On one occasion that stands out in my memory, two men who were in their late fifties at least enjoyed three days of good tench fishing on the opposite bank to myself. When they packed up I was initially gratified to see them gather up all their litter which included empty cans, bottles and mounds of used packets and papers, and deposit it all in a very large cardboard box in which they had carried their provisions down to the lake. My gratification quickly turned to horror when I saw them heave the box into the lake on their departure. I hurried round to their swim as fast as I could, but the distance meant that they had disappeared when I arrived. I was very angry indeed that morning. I hate to say this, but within the ranks of coarse anglers is an unacceptably high proportion of brainless, uncaring and filthy slobs.

My second prediction concerned the welfare of the fish. Many of the newer faces especially the younger ones were ill-equipped to fish for a delicate fish like a double-figure bream which will not tolerate abuse. We had retained bream for photographs until daylight, either in mammoth micromesh nets or carp sacks without problem. Some of the newcomers, however, either through ignorance or irresponsibility, crammed big bream into small keep nets that were highly unsuitable for them. Some fish were retained far too long in shallow water on hot days and the result was that bream started to turn up dead. This came to a head in the summer of 1985. For some reason that season saw a remarkable situation at TC in that a narrow band of water at the canal-bank end of the lake was weed-free, while the rest of the pit was choked. We had already established that big bream preferred to feed over areas that were naturally weed-free, and so it was predictable that this area would be where the fish would probably be located. In the event, every bream in the water remained in that small area for many weeks and during that time they became ridiculously easy to catch for the first time ever. Anglers who got to the two or three resident swims were guaranteed fish, many multiple catches resulted and my worst fears were soon realised. In October I was given the sombre news that over twenty double-figure bream had died that season alone, including at least four of the known thirteen-pounders. What an appalling tragedy. TC has never been the same water for bream since.

My last bream from TC and my biggest, was taken in my first visit of 1984 in early July. That was during a session when I was experimenting with sweetened caramel flavouring for bream and tench for the first time. On one rod I had kept faith in lobworm, but the other was baited with a cocktail bait of two casters and a large piece of caramel-flavoured flake. The loose feed was also laced with caramel and the tench loved it. During the two nights I was there I had no fewer than sixteen tench over that feed, with four six-pounders. Each one of the bites was a real butt ringer which was in complete contrast to the slow creep to the butt I experienced just before dawn on the Friday morning. This was one of only three bites that came to the lob and resulted in my last bream from TC, an immaculate fish weighing 12lb 4oz.

I had first began my experiments with bait flavourings for the TC tench in 1982 when I made several good catches on pineapple-flavoured maggots. In 1983 I started to use special pastes and had good catches on ones flavoured with maple cream and vanilla. But the most remarkable paste I made was almond-flavoured and coloured yellow. One session in particular was quite remarkable.

Three of us were fishing adjacent swims

for two days and there was no action to any of us, although tench could be seen rolling regularly. We were fishing either maggots or lobs, but on the second day I changed one of my rods over to fish almond paste. Within minutes I had my first bite and for the rest of that day and most of the next the tench would not leave me alone. I do not know exactly how many good bites I had during that session, but it must have been about fifty. I know that I landed over thirty tench. During this hectic action, my lobworm-baited rod yielded just one solitary bite and the anglers either side of me, still fishing their feeders, both blanked. That session was a real eye-opener and proved conclusively to me that on occasions, flavouring baits can bring quite spectacular results.

As well as developing specially-flavoured baits, I also began to use slowly-dissolving pastes following the lead given by Alan Smith. The same bait was used, but a small amount of very finely ground rusk was added to the mix. The amount of rusk used would determine the dissolution rate. In the summers of 1984 and 1985 the tench became more and more wary of anglers' baits, and these slowly-dissolving pastes produced me a fair few tench when traditional offerings were ignored. The attraction lay in the aura of flavouring that the slowly-dissolving rusk created around the perimeter of the ball of paste, and several fish were caught when the bait could have been little more than a pile of powder with a hook in the middle. As when I first began using flavoured pastes, these dissolving versions produced some tremendous runs and the most successful I used were almond, caramel and cough mixture.

I have not fished TC Pit since the summer of 1986, but during the intervening years there have been other changes in the fishing. The decimation of the bream stocks has seen the angling pressure down again to a more manageable level and I understand that the fishing is becoming quite pleasant again. Litter, however, is still a problem. Big tench still come out every season, most years seeing at least one nine-pounder, but there are many more small tench than there used to be. I think back to 1977 when it was rare to catch a tench under 5lb. Now, I know of several tench catches of upwards of twenty fish, where the majority are under 4lb. The occasional very big rudd and roach were always caught, but in the last two seasons many more big roach weighing over 2lb have figured in catches. I have even heard of a catch of six two-pounders in one night. Obviously that is a very exciting development and the situation warrants careful monitoring. The water still produces, as it always has, several big pike (up to mid-twenty pounders) every season, while quite a few good carp are just waiting for someone to put in a concerted effort after them. TC Pit is a water that I will always hold very dear to my heart, and I have a sneaking feeling that I have not finished with it yet. The pattern of the fishing may have changed for ever, but I am convinced that the water holds many more exciting secrets for us all.

17 Wensum Memories

It was not until my good friend Dave Plummer moved from his home town of Rotherham to Norwich that I fished the River Wensum. I had never really taken much notice of its press reports and although I knew it held big fish, I was occupied with other things. I did not feel that it offered any better than I already had considerably closer to home.

When Dave started to sort it out though, it was obvious that the average size of the chub was very high and he had several five-pounders in his first season. He wasted no time in inviting Trefor and myself to stay with him for a few days. The timing of that invitation could not have been better. In the early eighties, many of the lengths of the Cherwell and Leam from which Trefor and I had taken big fish were coming under intolerable pressure – obviously our own fault for being too successful – and we were finding it increasingly difficult to find

Trefor bends into a chub on the barbel syndicate water.

Trefor with a 2lb 10oz fish that had us fooled for a while. It is in fact a roach/bream hybrid.

peaceful fishing. Also, the Upper Ouse was in a rapid decline and the Wensum would provide a fresh challenge.

Our first trip to the Wensum confirmed that this was our kind of river: fairly narrow and intimate, not swamped with trees and rafts, but containing plenty of twists and turns and variations in current and flow rates to allow the mobile approach we love so much and which had proved so successful on all the other similar streams we had fished for chub.

That first trip saw two four-pounders to each of us and that was the first of many equally good days that winter. Those initial few weeks served as an apprenticeship which was to culminate in one of the most unforgettable weeks of chub fishing I have ever experienced. It was the last week of the season (in March 1982) and we had arrived in Norfolk to find the river in perfect trim. Fishing commenced at mid-morning on the Monday using our usual mashed bread and legered crust techniques, and I took good chub steadily throughout the day, taking no less than three four-pounders from one swim. In all I took seven chub during that first session, all over three pounds and with the top three at 4lb 1oz, 4lb 2oz and 4lb 4oz. Trefor had also weighed in with two with the largest at 4lb 6oz and we had some tremendous fishing to re-live in Dave's lounge that evening.

The following day was a singularly unsuccessful pike fishing sortie and we were back on the Wensum at dawn on Wednesday. That day was to prove the highlight of Trefor's week. The weather was foul, with non-stop heavy rain, and by dark I had only managed one fish of 3lb 14oz. Trefor had taken two three-pounders also and we were just contemplating calling it a day when I had a good pull which resulted in a cracking fish of 4lb 8oz, the best we had taken so far. It was not to remain the best for long. The rain had just returned with a vengeance when Trefor had a really savage bite which pulled the rod off the rest. After a good scrap he landed a magnificent fish of 5lb 4oz. Ten minutes later he was in again and soon another big chub of 5lb exactly was being admired. Naturally he was completely over the moon with that superb brace, the first time he had ever taken two fives in a session.

The Thursday dawned overcast but dry, and the river was not appreciably more coloured following the previous day's storms. Once again the chub were active, and I had another six fish again all over three pounds, with the top four at 4lb 2oz, 4lb 4oz, 4lb 9oz and 4lb 13oz. Trefor had a further three weighing 3lb 15oz, 4lb 7oz and 4lb 14oz. What a day's chub fishing!

Friday was to prove even more incredible, with ten fish evenly split between us and no fewer than seven of those chub being over 4lb – three to me and four to Trefor. Again Trefor just shaded me on size, taking the two biggest at 4lb 12oz and 4lb 14oz, my best being 4lb 11oz.

While the Wednesday evening had been the highlight for Trefor, Saturday was mine. The fishing had been so fantastic that all I needed to make it complete was my first Wensum five-pounder. We had decided to look at a different stretch for the morning session where the fish were reputedly even bigger than where we had been fishing previously. It was of a different character altogether – slow and steady and apart from the attractively wooded banks, totally featureless as far as current variations were concerned. Such stretches of the Cherwell and Ouse had often been found to hold the bigger fish. That day Trefor unfortunately blanked (an extremely uncommon occurrence) but I hit a purple patch, taking six nice fish again all over 3lb with two more four-pounders.

The second fish of the day made my week. I was presenting a bait in mid-river in the twenty-yard gap between two bankside, pollarded willows, and had cast progressively down the same line without success. I decided to increase my link weight to hold a bait further out in the current. I would cast past mid-stream and then attempt to induce a bite by lifting the bait from the bottom and rolling it inwards. The first cast to this new presentation did the trick. There was no response while the crust lay in mid-river, but as soon as it was lifted and started to bounce towards the near bank, it was taken viciously. Immediately I had a problem. I had not noticed that the line had thrown a double loop around my screw-in quivertip and I soon realised that I could not give line. I was in a real pickle as it was obvioiusly a very big chub I had hooked and therefore quite capable of either smashing my 6lb line or tearing the hook out in a direct pull. The rod bent alarmingly, the line became as taut as a guitar string and then, thankfully, the quivertip snapped and I was able to play the fish normally. Even then it gave me a high old tussle before it was netted expertly by Trefor. It was my personal best from the Wensum and weighed 5lb 7oz, and although I have since equalled it, I have yet to beat it.

It was the induced take technique that led to me equalling that chub on a March night in 1985. I was fishing the bottom swim of the barbel syndicate stretch below Costessy. I was not fishing for chub on that occasion, but for the large barbel for which the stretch was famous. In fact I was trying to avoid the large head of average chub that always inhabited that swim, and I was using a huge piece of luncheon meat – at least 1in (2.5cm) cube – mounted on a size 4 hook to 8lb Maxima. We were all experiencing very fast jabs from the chub that season, a great many having been taken accidentally on barbel tackle, and when I had fished the swim the previous evening I had lost count of the number of small bumps and pulls I had without a single positive indication.

Three of us were fishing that evening (Dave Plummer, John Bailey and myself) and after I had settled in the bottom swim once again, John told me that he had fished it much earlier in the afternoon and found much the same problem I had. Despite experiencing a multitude of inconclusive indications, he had not been able to put the

This 5lb 7oz fish was my first Wensum five-pounder.

hook into a single chub. I decided that for once I would not hold the rod, but fish off the rest as I was only interested in the barbel and these always gave a good solid thump. All the smaller indications to my large bait could be safely ignored. Any chub worth his salt would give a good pull anyway, or so I thought. The first bait had not been in place thirty seconds when the jabs and small plucks started and the rod top was barely still for a minute. For a while I was able to control myself and ignore the activity, but in the end it got too much for me. I decided to try and induce a bolder bite, reasoning that if I could hook a chub or two it might dissuade the others and leave the bait unmolested to await the hopeful arrival of an 'old whiskers'. Another clutch of fast jabs commenced and after the third bump I quickly wound the bait a foot upstream. The reaction was savage in the extreme, with the rod point being wrenched under water. I was not prepared for the resistance that followed. I had convinced myself that small chub, possibly as little as a pound in weight were responsible, but whatever was on the end of my line was considerably in excess of that. In fact, I was not at all sure at first that I had not hooked a barbel after all. Soon, however, those unmistakable thick white lips came into view and I netted an absolute cracker of a chub. It weighed 5lb 7oz and was a very memorable capture indeed.

Half an hour later and after John and Dave had kindly taken some photographs for me, John packed up and left while Dave and I settled down to fish into the dark hours. After a much appreciated coffee, I cast out again and sat back in my chair reflecting on the superb bonus fish I had just landed. The jabs and plucks had recommenced immediately the bait had settled again and for a while I let the fish get on with it. But then I decided to try the same dodge again. Amazingly the result was identical, another big chub whacking the rod around as soon as he saw the bait apparently escaping. That one weighed 5lb 2oz and gave me my first double 5lb chub catch from the Wensum. Dave's photographic expertise was again called upon and to the sounds of Dave describing me as a 'jammy bar steward', I grinned and posed in the time-honoured fashion.

At the start of the 1988 season, I had taken two 5lb chub in a day no less than four times during my career, twice from the Claydon Brook and once each from the Leam and the Wensum. Opening day of the new season saw that increased to five. I had decided to kick off the new season on the barbel trail at the syndicate water rather than have my traditional tench or carp start. I had arrived at tea-time on the 15th and spent the evening baiting all the areas where I had seen or caught barbel with corn and hemp. Fishing commenced at midnight and I stuck at it until well past dawn, but only achieved three very average chub.

After a good sleep in the van I was back on the river at midday, and again the first four hours were spent looking around and topping the bait up in all the swims. My first cast came at 5 p.m. in the swim at the top of the stretch where the big fallen willow hangs in the water. My bunch of sweetcorn grains sat there unmolested for over an hour, with me contentedly enjoying the glorious evening sunshine and then the line lifted and the quivertip arced towards the water. I saw a big chub kick as I struck and a few minutes later I was weighing a cracking fish of 5lb 6oz. What a great fish to have in the bag on 16 June.

Many hours later and well after dark, I was fishing about 200 yards downstream on the bottom bend of the syndicate stretch. Just as I was resigning myself to another barbel blank, I had two super fish in fairly quick succession – lovely barbel of 8lb 12oz and 9lb 11oz. And then I hooked another

Trefor returns the first of his many double-figure Wensum barbel.

big chub. That fish gave me a spectacular battle, leaping clear of the shallow swim three or four times. I could see that it was another five-pounder as soon as it lay in the net and the scales confirmed that. Another huge chub weighing in at 5lb 2oz had been the perfect end to an unforgettable opening day.

I made mention earlier of the Top Tree swim on the syndicate stretch, or the Point swim as it is now described. This has been one of the most reliable swims over the years, but it also reminds me of a very tragic day only three years ago. I had arrived at that swim from Coventry a little after dawn and as I was setting up my gear, I noticed a man wandering aimlessly up and down the river bank in the long meadow between the top of the stretch and Costessy Mill. I remember thinking it was early for a casual stroll, but when he went back up to the road I thought no more about it. I was soon engrossed in my fishing. Several hours later, I was quite startled by a voice behind me and turned to see Roger Miller, one of the syndicate members, standing there but in his official capacity as a police officer. His first words chilled me. 'Be on the look out for a body floating past' he said, 'there's an abandoned car by the mill with a suicide note on the front seat.' It transpired that a river authority scientist had taken an overdose of drugs and decided to end it all by jumping into Costessy Mill.

I can tell you that for the next two days I was on tenterhooks every time the rod pulled round, but nothing untoward turned up. We wondered whether it was a hoax at first, but when someone was reported missing it became horribly true. Shortly after that day (which was in late autumn) the winter floods came and then a protracted freeze-up which left the Wensum with ice margins for weeks. When they eventually thawed, the poor man's body was at last recovered and laid to rest. It had been in the water for several months. It saddens me to think that he may possibly have been the same man I saw walking the banks that morning. If only he had come and spoken to me.

Although there is no denying the superb quality of Wensum chub fishing, it is for the big barbel that I make the long journey to Norfolk these days. Most of my Wensum 5lb chub have been taken accidentally on large barbel baits. We had first become interested in the barbel after our fabulous last week's chubbing in March 1982 and from June of that year onwards we fished for those barbel intensively. Dave had already taken several doubles when Trefor and I achieved our first, in fact the first double-figure barbel either of us had ever caught from any water. I will never forget the circumstances. I was at home late one evening when the phone rang. It was a breathless Trefor, ringing from Norwich. 'I've cracked it' he shouted down the phone, 'is there any chance you can come out and photograph a fish for me? I've got a thirteen-and-a-quarter.' If you are going to beat a personal best, you might as well do it in style! To go and photograph the fish would have entailed a 300-mile round trip, which I would have been quite happy to do but for a very urgent business appointment I dare not miss the next morning. However, Dave Plummer was able to oblige and Trefor got his photographs. Back at home, he had his scales checked and found that they were reading half a pound heavy. To his eternal credit, no one need have known that apart from himself, but he immediately told me the bad news and amended the weight to 12lb 12oz. This unbelievable fish has now been named 'Beau' and is the same fish with which Dave holds the river record at 13lb 6oz.

An eleven-pounder taken early on in the season.

It was an extremely interesting night when Dave landed the barbel at that weight. Trefor and I were down for the last few days of the season, but Dave had not intended to fish for barbel that week. He and Derek Amies were going to hit the Thurne system for pike. However, Derek expressed a desire to catch his first ever barbel and Dave took him for an evening's fishing in the mill-pool itself. Trefor and I were ensconsed in the copse area and Dave had decided to give us plenty of room. A little after dark I had a seven-pounder with the prospects looking good for more bites when Dave materialised out of the blackness and stood next to me. He was out of breath and I will never forget the words he spoke to me. 'Hold on to your hat, but I've just had a thirteen-six' he said, 'Derek just can't believe it.' Nor could I, but the next morning there was the living proof emerging from the sack. It was Trefor's fish all right, but in absolutely tiptop condition. After the photographic session, it went back none the worse for its experience and has since been recaptured several times. It has, however, never been captured at over 13lb since that March night.

In 1984 Dave Plummer was involved in forming the syndicate that controlled the stretch until the end of 1988/1989 season and I was one of the lucky ones to be invited into that select group. I had yet to catch my first double and for three more seasons seemed destined never to achieve my target, not on the Wensum anyway. I had managed a solitary ten-pounder from the Stour but seemed as far away from my goal as ever in Norfolk.

By 1987, I was determined to break this hoodoo. I had by now taken over twenty barbel from the river, with a best at only 8lb 12oz. Surely my luck had to turn soon. It did in July of that summer, but for the worse! I had run out of my usual and reliable size 4 Au Lion d'Or hooks and had picked up a batch of alternative hooks of the same size. That was to result in the loss of no less than three doubles in two consecutive weeks. On the first trip I hooked a good barbel in the Copse swim, which I saw very clearly on the surface in the moonlight and which was a very big fish indeed. I had done the hard part and the fish was quite docile, but as it came towards the net the hook pulled out and the barbel sank slowly out of sight.

After that sickening experience I suppose I should have realised it might have been the fault of the hook, but I thought it was just one of those things. The following week, I was to pay dearly for my lack of foresight. All day long I had been baiting a swim in which could be seen clearly two big barbel, both definite doubles. It had been dark for perhaps an hour when I carefully lowered the first bait into that swim. Immediately, there was a rod-wrenching pull and a big barbel surged into mid-stream. The clutch yielded a couple of yards of line and then the hook pulled out. I was devastated but, trying to keep my composure, I put some more bait in the swim so that I could try again later for the other big fish I had seen. Several hours later I hooked that one. This second barbel fought tremendously hard, making several surging runs downstream in an attempt to gain the sanctuary of a raft of debris around some fallen branches. Three times I stopped the fish reaching his objective and when I thought he was mine at long last the hook pulled out again. That happened with only modest pressure on the fish. I have reverted to Au Lion d'Or hooks since and have never pulled out of another barbel.

A 4lb 12oz Wensum chub is hoisted ashore.

Success finally came in September of that year. I had been plagued by bootlace eels over the previous few weeks which had been taking my meat baits and had decided to concoct a bait based entirely on hemp seed. I came up with a hemp paste that I thought would give me a good chance of avoiding those wriggly little horrors. In the event, it worked better than I had hoped and I had a tremendous confidence booster when, on the very first cast, I had a strong pull and landed a 4lb plus chub. After dark that night, with the river about two feet up and coloured – perfect conditions in fact – three barbel over 6lb came to the bait and I was brimming with confidence as I baited swims for the second night's fishing.

It was just becoming dusk and I was sitting in a swim facing the old iron railway bridge over the river below the bottom of the syndicate water. That bridge is probably 30ft above the surface and my attention was distracted by a man appearing on the bridge parapet. I was fascinated as he started to undress and climb through the rails to balance on the narrow ledge at the side. That was an extremely dangerous thing to do at night in any event, but doing it over 2ft of fast floodwater was particularly foolhardy. As I watched he lowered himself over the edge and, wearing what appeared to be only underwear, started swinging backwards and forwards, holding on only by his fingertips. Just at that moment the line, which was lying over my index finger, gave a sudden vicious tug and the rod smashed round. I came back to the business in hand. In the rapidly gathering dusk I could see a very big fish powering through the rushes upstream of my position and for a few seconds it became snagged in them. Luckily this was a night when nothing was destined to go wrong and the fish came free without mishap. It still fought very hard for several more minutes, but never gave me any anxious moments and I was all smiles as I lifted the fish ashore. By the light of my little torch I confirmed a weight of 10lb 5oz and punched the air in triumph. Only after I had put the barbel in a sack to await a photographic session did I remember the would-be trapeze artist. When I looked back to the bridge, however, he had disappeared and so I have no idea what became of him. There are some mighty strange folk in Norfolk!

When the syndicate was formed, one of the first things that Dave tried to organise was extra car parking facilities. The car park we had been using was patronised by many courting couples and there had also been considerable vandalism, with several cars badly damaged. Consequently the farmer created a small car park near the top of the stretch for the members to use. The entrance was along a narrow winding lane, very dark at night with high trees and hedges both sides. As you drove through the gate there was a clearing of twenty yards up to a little side-stream. Over the tiny footbridge was about a 200-yard walk to the river, through reeds and nettles well over head height. Any one standing in that foliage only two yards from the edge of the car park could be hidden.

One winter's night two years ago, I had fished very late and packed up just after midnight. As I know the route through the undergrowth like the back of my hand, I never use a torch to light the way. The only illumination I had came from the brightly glowing Betalight on the end of my rod. As I approached the little footbridge, I could see a faint glow in front of me and soon realised that a courting couple were performing some kind of late night manoeuvres in a car parked right alongside the side-stream. As I emerged from the undergrowth by stepping up onto the high footbridge, there was a bloodcurdling scream and within seconds the car reversed at break-neck speed and careered out of the gate on two wheels. I could hear it howling off into the distance.

I was puzzled at first, but the more I thought about it, the more I realised that I probably made quite a frightening apparition in the pitch blackness. Out of total darkness, the first thing they would have seen was that eerie, disembodied green glow, apparently floating in mid-air, to be followed by a large dark spectre looming out of the undergrowth. I must have looked like the monster from the black lagoon! I bet that dampened their ardour!

Another amusing incident concerns my notorious clumsiness. It was mid-summer three seasons ago and I was fish-spotting in the area around the copse swim. A local angler had recognised me and we were chatting while we both peered for barbel. We both caught glimpses of fish in mid-river under the overhanging branches of the willow and I decided to climb the tree, from where I could be perched right above the centre of the river and look directly down at the fish. I had gone as high as possible to get the clearest view. My companion remained on the bank and we continued talking, with me telling him what I could see. I completely forgot where I was and went to take a step to the side. There was of course nothing but fresh air and fell off the branch on which I was standing. Instinctively my hands grasped out to grab something, and I clutched the large branch below me as I started to pass it. My momentum carried me right under the branch and back up the other side, and I ended up sitting on top of it. Anyone who knows me will testify that I am not really built for such arboreal acrobatics, but nonchalantly pretending that I had meant it all along, I lowered myself to my companion's side. He never said a word, but I could see he was impressed!

A very interesting week which began on the Wensum and ended over 200 miles away on the Bristol Avon, was the last week of the season in March 1989. When I arrived in Norfolk on Tuesday, 7 March, I was very disappointed to find the river running fairly clear and at normal level. We had experienced a lot of rain over the previous few days and I had expected to find a coloured river. Still, it was very mild with the promise of more rain to come, so conditions could have been a lot worse.

The fishing on that first night was very encouraging. On my very first cast just before dark, I landed a chub of 4lb 9oz, followed an hour later by another weighing just under 4lb. Later in the evening, I had two barbel bites in quick succession from adjacent swims. I somehow contrived to miss the first one and suspect it might have been a liner, but when I moved to the second swim an immediate strong pull resulted in a nice fish of 8lb 6oz. That was just before midnight and soon afterwards I was settling down for the night in my caravanette.

The following morning I was really in two minds as to what to do when I arrived at the river again. There had been a substantial drop in the water level (at least 6in) caused by the continuing work on the new weir at Costessy, and conditions now were not very promising for further barbel sport. The rest of that day seemed to provide confirmation of that conviction when, despite fishing until about 2 a.m., the only fish that rewarded my efforts were two 3lb chub.

On Wednesday morning I decided to give the river one more night and then make a decision whether I should move somewhere else. All day long I struggled with the steadily deteriorating conditions, and after twelve hours of fishing, I still had not had the slightest indication of a bite. At 1.15 a.m., completely out of the blue and as I was contemplating wrapping it up, I had a sudden lunge on the rod top and soon netted a hard-fighting barbel of 9lb 1oz.

An immaculate fish which weighed 12lb 6oz.

That super fish threw all my plans back into the melting pot again and I lay awake in bed for hours weighing up all the options. The following morning my mind was made up for me. I had given my wife the telephone number of the landowner on whose land I was parked in case she had to contact me for any reason, and just before I was going to leave for the river Fran rang. She was relaying a message from Trefor who was fishing the last week on the Bristol Avon. 'Trefor is waiting by a phone' she said, 'he's asked me to tell you that the river's very high and coloured and the barbel are going mad. He's had a lot of good fish already, and if you are struggling in Norfolk why don't you come down and join him. Also, he's just caught his best Avon fish of 11lb 10oz, and if you are going down he'll keep it in a sack for you to photograph it for him.' The decision was not difficult. The conditions were obviously poor on the Wensum and so I told Fran to phone Trefor back and tell him I was on my way.

Five hours and 200 odd miles later, on a wet and windy afternoon, I met up with Trefor and we headed off for the swim where two big barbel reposed in sacks. In the time it had taken me to reach him, he had caught another big fish of just under 11lb to complete a remarkable brace. Once the shots had been taken and the fish safely returned, Trefor filled me in on the fishing so far. It was my first sight of the Bristol Avon and what I could see was exciting. It was carrying quite a few feet of floodwater and Trefor told me that the barbel were feeding well. We spent the rest of the afternoon looking at a few areas of interest, before I decided where I would fish. I had no intention at all of fishing where Trefor had put in so much effort – I would leave that stretch for him to reap the rewards his work warranted. I was quite content to sort out another area for myself.

It was actually after dark when I made my first cast ever into the river. When I look back on it, that was a silly thing to do. A strange river in flood and after dark meant that I had no idea of the features and I was fishing hopefully rather than with any specific purpose in mind. The one fish I did catch, a good barbel of 7lb 14oz, could have caused me a tragic misfortune. The Avon has very steep banks in places, and with 4ft of fast floodwater it pays to watch your step carefully. Just after I had hooked the fish, I lost my footing on the steep bank and slid down the muddy slope. I only stopped myself from sliding into the river by grabbing hold of a large and thankfully tough clump of thick grass. It took me some time to work myself into a safe position from where to play and land the barbel, and even longer to clean off the thick mud with which I was covered. As the river was about 6ft deep at that point and moving strongly, I would not have fancied a nocturnal immersion in the middle of winter and wearing heavy waterproof clothing.

The next day I took the time and trouble to establish exactly what I had in front of me in all the swims I would fish for the rest of the week. Having done that, the next few hours were engaged in pre-baiting all the selected areas. As with the summer fishing, Trefor and I pre-bait with hemp in the winter in swims with a slacker than normal area where bait will settle. If a swim is left alone long enough after such an approach, the first cast into the slack or steady area will often yield an immediate bite.

I was to catch eight barbel on this first full day on the river, and when I finally retired to my bed I could look back on a fantastic day's fishing. The biggest of the fish I caught weighed 9lb 2oz and gave me one of my hardest fights with a barbel ever. It was taken from a clean gravelly glide, normally only inches deep and it used the extra water and flow rate to its maximum advantage. For over ten minutes it hugged the bottom, never very far away from me, but stubbornly refusing to yield. I really did think it was much bigger than it was. A winter barbel is undoubtedly a worthy adversary.

After that fabulous day the colour began to drop out of the river very rapidly and I started to struggle for bites. Apart from a crop of very small chub, I only managed another two average barbel before the season ended. Trefor must have cursed himself for ever phoning me, for I seemed to bring a curse down on him. After my arrival he never had another bite all season! I do not think he was unduly bothered. He had finished up with no fewer than eleven double-figure barbel in a few months, plus countless other big fish and once again was to take the Barbel Catchers Club award for the most outstanding season – a well-deserved honour.

My reward for driving over 200 miles to the Bristol Avon – a barbel of 9lb 2oz.

18 Norfolk Piking

FARCE ON HORSEY MERE

I suppose every angler has at least one of those days in his angling career when absolutely nothing goes according to plan. For sheer farce, it would be hard to beat a day's piking I spent at Horsey Mere way back in the late sixties. I was fishing with my old friends Phil Smith and Merv Wilkinson, as well as the late Peter Rayment.

We had arrived at the boat-yard well before daylight and quickly bundled all the gear into the two boats. Pete and Merv were sharing one boat and Phil and I the other. They were ready to go several minutes before us, and went off along the boat dike and out into the Thurne. When we came to start our motor, we encountered the first snag. It would not start and nothing we could do would persuade it. After perhaps half an hour of trying and becoming more frustrated, we were resigned to a long row when two other friends, Don and Trevor arrived. It transpired that Trevor knew quite a bit about outboards and within a couple of minutes, had got it going for us. Belatedly we set off. We had travelled a few hundred yards when we came across Merv and Pete waiting for us, obviously realising that something had gone wrong. Once we had relayed our story, we all set off again and for a few minutes there were no problems.

Because Merv and Pete were in a boat equipped with an inboard motor which was considerably more powerful than our outboard, they gradually pulled away and had just disappeared round a bend in the river when our outboard packed up again and we started to drift back the way we had come in the strong wind. We could not start the motor, whatever we tried and by the time we had stopped trying, we had drifted into thick weed. So we broke the oars out and had been rowing for perhaps ten minutes when Trevor and Don came up behind us. This time even Trevor had no joy with the outboard and so they hitched our boat up to theirs and towed us to Horsey Mere. At last we were ensconsed in a swim and were ready to commence fishing. We had already wasted a good hour and a half, and Don and Trevor left us with the promise that they would tow us back at night if we needed it.

There then followed an uneventful hour's fishing, until about 10.30 a.m., by which time the wind was becoming very strong indeed. It was then that we discovered that the anchor weight was not up to the job and we started to drift. To beat the drift, we drove the oars into the bottom, and lashed the boat to them. For a while this did the trick and then, without warning, one of the oars uprooted itself and started to drift away down the lake. Of course we had to retrieve it, so we pulled up the other oar, lifted the anchor and started to drift after it. Phil tried to start the motor and to our amazement it started. We had just overtaken the escaping oar when the motor died again and this time it refused to restart for a good four or five minutes, by which time we had drifted right to the other side of the mere in the heavy wind. It took about ten minutes to get back to our swim, steering into the teeth of the gale and by the time we got there we were both soaked with spray and short on temper.

By about midday, we had not had a run between us and decided to move to a pitch about fifty yards upwind of Pete and Merv. If we had known the trouble that was going to cause, we would not have bothered. Phil seemed to have got the hang of the outboard now, for it fired first time. When we got to the swim we wanted, we found that the wind, if anything, was stronger and even with both oars lashed to the boat it was impossible to keep still and we started drifting back down the mere. I think it was about ten seconds before we crashed into Merv's boat and when we did, two things happened. First, my keep net which was full of baits was dragged off the rowlock and promptly sank, and secondly, one of my rods shot into the air with the force of the collision and a treble hook caught in the lobe of Pete's right ear. The dead roach made quite an attractive ear-ring! There was a howl of pain from Pete as the treble tore out with the force of the drift and Merv spoke to us. I think it was 'you really must be more careful' or words to that effect!

As the baits in the net were the only ones we had, apart from a couple of very nondescript herrings that were lying in the bottom of the boat, we had to retrieve the keep net. But before we did, Pete suggested that we go to the other side of the mere and pick up a couple of large rocks that we could use as extra anchors. This was obviously a sensible idea, so off we went again. The motor behaved itself and we got there in a couple of minutes. There were plenty of rocks about, so we pulled the boat in close and I jumped out. I immediately sank past my knees in the most foul smelling mud, from which it took me a fair while to extricate myself. But I did manage to get two substantial rocks into the boat and we set off again. We had travelled about halfway back when the motor stopped again, and once more we found ourselves drifting down the mere. After about four or five tries Phil got the motor going, but as it was set on full throttle the boat leapt forward, unseating me so that I fell on my flask and smashed it, and knocked my Stewart box overboard which promptly sank.

While Phil steered the boat back to the swim, I tied one of the rocks on to the anchor rope. It was very sharp, but I had an old handkerchief to bandage the 4in-long gash that had suddenly appeared across the palm of my right hand. We went about thirty yards upwind of Merv and Pete's boat, cut the motor and started drifting back, keeping our eyes open for the net. As soon as we spotted it, I dropped the anchor and we started trying to retrieve it. We had been trying for perhaps three minutes when the boat was rocked by a particularly fierce gust of wind and the rock pulled off the anchor rope. We were off again! As we crashed into Pete's boat for the second time, I was starting to get really worried about Phil's hysterical laughter. We drifted about thirty yards downwind and then Phil restarted the engine and we went back to try again. I tied the second rock on to the anchor rope, but I did not have a second handkerchief to bandage the nasty cut that appeared on my left hand, so I had to use a bit of grimy old rag that I found at the bottom of my tackle bag.

This time there were no mishaps and we managed to get the net back. At long last, we settled down to do a bit of fishing and for two blissful hours there were no interruptions. We were not disturbed by the pike either!

Then we decided to move to another area, where we had seen some pike striking. This time nothing went wrong and we soon settled down again. After about an hour,

Phil had our only run. In keeping with the rest of the day, he missed it. We packed up well before dusk, completely demoralised and before we set off I threw my herrings overboard. The last one had sunk about a foot below the surface when a pike of about fifteen pounds shot from underneath the boat and grabbed it. I nearly threw the rock at it!

We had travelled about half-way back to the boathouse when the motor packed up again, once more when Pete and Merv were out of sight ahead. This time, Phil could not start it and in pitch darkness we started rowing which became considerably more difficult when the only torch we had between us failed. After about twenty minutes, we saw a light coming up behind us. To our immense relief, it was Don and Trevor again and once more we went on tow. We eventually arrived back at the boathouse at about 9.30 p.m., just as Merv and Pete were beginning to organise a search party.

Trefor with two lovely fish from Decoy Broad.

We did not do too badly at all on the return journey to Coventry. We got as far as Rugby before we ran out of petrol, and then we had to wait the best part of an hour for Merv and Pete to run into Coventry, pick up a can and bring it back to us. While we were waiting, Phil and I were questioned at length by two members of the local constabulary, who were convinced that we were loitering with criminal intent.

When Phil eventually dropped me at home it was 3.15 a.m. I threw my tackle down in the hall, stalked upstairs, undressed and, tired and disgusted with the day's performance, flopped into bed alongside my wife, who was sleeping peacefully. What happened? The bed collapsed! It is true, I swear it.

CHAOS ON DECOY BROAD

In the early eighties, Trefor West and I devoted a lot of the winter months searching for big Norfolk pike on both the Bure and Thurne systems. One of the waters that came to our attention was Decoy Broad, situated off the River Bure. Dave Plummer was the first to make us aware of it. At the time it was not producing a large number of pike, but the average size of those that were coming out was impressive. It had yielded several thirty-pounders and many twenties. In fact, on one of our Norfolk trips, John Watson had banked a 31¼lb specimen from Decoy on a day when Trefor and I had caught a few modest pike on the Bure.

It was a lovely secluded water, with fishing being allowed only from the boats provided by the club that ran the fishery. It was also controlled environmentally, with no outboard motors being allowed and no anchors permitted. No risk was to be taken of leaving ironmongery lying around the bottom, so instead of anchors, long ash poles had to be used fore and aft to which the boat was tied. These poles were provided by the club and were about 12ft in length. Driven into the lake bed at the prow and stern, they provided a very stable fastening point.

I consider myself to have been quite unlucky at Decoy in that I had several fish in the few trips I made there, but only had one double. The rest were jacks, and in a water where one out of every two fish had seemed to be twenty pounds plus, there were quite long odds against this.

The last time I fished the water, however, I was convinced that my luck was about to change. I had been tied up out in the middle since first light and was fishing four rods, two on each side of the boat. Each tackle was baited with a different deadbait under a surface float so I could see takes at the earliest possible moment, and therefore avoid deep-hooking. The floats formed a fanwise pattern around the boat. By using four rods I admit that I was breaking the rules, but I was to pay for my temerity later.

What had started as a very pleasant, calm morning rapidly deteriorated into a very wild day indeed. By midday, the sky was leaden and a heavy wind whipped across the broad, making the ash poles creak and groan under the rocking motion of the boat. I was getting soaked by the spray being tossed off the white-topped waves. And then, adjacent to one of the nearer floats, a very big pike turned over in the water – a fish that was definitely at least a good twenty. I was now keyed up and sure enough, a few minutes later, the same float slid away. Line disappeared against my loosely set clutch at a satisfyingly steady rate.

Just after I had wound down and struck into the pike, the sky darkened considerably and the wind strength picked up to gale force. Suddenly, the rear pole uprooted itself from the bottom and the boat began to swing backwards and forwards, pivoting around the front pole. For a fateful couple of minutes I hesitated. I was loath to put the rod down and secure the boat, as I was convinced that I had a very big pike on the end and consequently the inevitable happened. The pressure on the remaining pole was far too great and that came adrift as well. The result was total chaos. As the boat was moored side on to the wind, it began to spin round crazily in the water, drifting rapidly downwind as it did so. Obviously, as the boat spun round the floats remained where they were initially, with the result that the boat acted as a sort of gigantic cotton reel, tangling all four lines inextricably together and then towing them all behind me. By some miracle, the rod I was holding escaped the worst of the confusion and I played the fish as hard as I dare, so that I could land it and sort out the mess. With an almighty crash, my boat ploughed into the bankside trees, scatterig the rods and tackle everywhere and ripping a great hole in my wax jacket. But at least I was now stationary and I had the consolation that I had a very big pike on the end. Or so I thought. A few minutes later, my big pike turned out to be a seven-pounder that had both fought out of its skin and been towing a heavy branch around.

It is no exaggeration to say that it took me two hours to sort out the mess that day, by the end of which I was one very disgruntled angler. I have never fished Decoy Broad since.

THE SINKING FEELING ON THE BURE

Not long after we had decided to conduct a determined pike campaign in Norfolk, Trefor and I equipped ourselves with our own boat. We wanted the freedom of being able to fish at a moment's notice, without the hassle of having to pre-book boats before our intended trips. At the time we thought the one we purchased would be ideal for the job, but we were soon to find out that it was totally inadequate. It was a ten foot dinghy and came complete with trailer and outboard motor. It would revolutionise our pike fishing, or so we thought.

The weekend after its acquisition, we were packed and ready to go. I was already having misgivings. The long amount of time it took to secure the tackle in the boat and attach it to the trailer, had already suggested that it would not be so convenient as we had first thought. The long and slow journey from Coventry to the River Bure, and the length of time it took us to unship the boat from the trailer and prepare it for the actual fishing further enhanced these misgivings. Despite a very early start from Coventry, it was mid-morning before we were ready to go, but at last everything was set and we pushed off from the bank, heading downriver towards the general area of Wroxham Broad.

When Trefor and I had first clambered into the boat, a further problem had been uncovered. With all the tackle on board and ourselves, there was very little freeboard above the water line. Obviously it was really only a one-man boat, but we had to make the best of it. Even with the tackle trimmed to a bare minimum, I felt the boat not to be entirely safe, especially if a good wind sprang up while we were on an exposed water.

Despite our reservations, we fished quite happily for several hours, even managing to troll the river successfully. We worked quite well as a team, taking it in turns to row the boat and attend to the rods. After each take, we would change places and by mid-afternoon we had caught several small pike. We had even managed to stand up in the boat for a little deadbait spinning without mishap. The only really hairy moment we experienced was when a large cruiser came past far too fast and we came close to being swamped by the wash.

And then, in mid-afternoon disaster struck. We were moored close to a boat dike that was a well-known hot spot, fishing static deadbaits while we had a break from the more active methods. One of my floats went away and I found myself playing not a big pike, but one that certainly gave a good account of itself. As it came in towards the boat, Trefor leaned out with the net. I am not really sure what happened next. I remember sliding along the seat and I think that I must have been temporarily unbalanced by the slight tilting of the boat as Trefor netted the pike. Of course, the shifting of my weight further unbalanced the boat which made Trefor fall forward as well. All the weight was now on one side and the inevitable happened. Water began to flood in and we were in imminent danger of totally capsizing. My problem was that, as I had slid along the seat my legs had become wedged under it, and for a while I could not move. For a critical few seconds there was little I could do to right the situation, as I was struggling to free myself. It was Trefor who rescued us from what could have been a much nastier situation. With great presence of mind, he flung himself face down across to the other side of the boat in an attempt to balance the load. It was all very dramatic, but it worked and a few minutes later the boat was stable again. Now there was only an inch or two of freeboard, as we were carrying about 2ft of water as well as all the gear. There was also a very irate pike swimming around, still attached to the hooks. All in all it was a scene of total chaos. The saving grace of course was that we were close to the bank and very gingerly we transferred all the sodden tackle and clothing on to it. With the boat completely empty of equipment, we then began baling, and within half an hour had restored some semblance of order.

Looking back on the incident now I can see the funny side, but it certainly was not funny at the time and we were lucky to escape so lightly. The stupid thing is that it was all so predictable. We both knew that the boat was dangerously overloaded when we first embarked, but we chose to ignore it. It is a mistake I will never repeat. When we returned to Coventry, I vowed that I would never fish out of the boat again, unless I was on my own. I never did and that one trip to the Bure was the only time Trefor or I ever used it.

FINAL TRIUMPH ON THE THURNE

The winter following that Bure fiasco I equipped myself with another boat, but this time one that was definitely man enough for the job. The lessons had been learned well. Andy Barker and I had jointly purchased a 14ft-long, very sturdy clinker-built craft, with a draft deep enough to ensure an adequate load-carrying capacity, as well as being virtually impossible to capsize. It would also be kept moored in Norfolk wherever we intended fishing. In the pike season of 1984/1985, all our efforts were to be concentrated on the Thurne in the

A long and lean seventeen-pounder for Trefor.

A cracking brace of Broadland pike.

Martham area, and our boat was kept padlocked in the small boat dike that empties adjacent to Martham Ferry. The fishing would obviously be much more convenient with no trailer to worry about. The only drawbacks were the possible problems of vandalism or theft, but the boat was well insured and we felt the risks to be ones worth taking. As it was, that pike season saw no problems of that nature whatsoever, and I fished the Thurne extensively from October until March. The boat has subsequently been stolen from the dike, but that is another story!

The Thurne had long had a reputation for being a very slow pike water, and I found nothing different when I embarked on my campaign. By late February, I had only managed to net a handful of pike, with the biggest two at 17lb. What kept me going back, of course, were the massive pike that were known to inhabit the water. Several thirty-pounders had been caught that season, along with Neville Fickling's record fish of over 40lb. I had twice fished with Dave Plummer when he had caught twenties and I had caught only jacks, so I knew it was only a matter of time before I too latched into a monster. I had come very close in early February when I had pulled out of a pike at very close range that looked every ounce of 30lb.

Towards the end of February, there was a severe freeze in Norfolk, with the Thurne and the broads being completely frozen over for about a fortnight. At the start of the third week, a warmer air-stream came in and I reasoned that by about the Thursday, the ice should have gone and I would be able to fish water that had been undisturbed during the Arctic conditions. A phone call to Dave Plummer reinforced my decision and he agreed to meet me on the river at 2 p.m. on Thursday afternoon. Along with Neville Fickling, Dave had a cruiser booked for the week.

All week I looked forward to the trip and I pulled out of my drive in the very early hours, with the intention of arriving on the banks of the Thure so as to be fishing at first light. All the regulars on the river had told me that the dawn period was one of the most reliable for the big pike. For the first twenty miles or so of my journey everything went to plan, but as I travelled into Northamptonshire, I hit fog and the further east I went the thicker the fog became. With still well over 100 miles to drive, I was reduced to little more than twenty miles an hour, so bad were the conditions. Twice I stopped the car with the full intention of aborting the trip, but both times I persuaded myself to carry on. I knew that conditions could be perfect on the Thurne, and that was all the incentive I needed.

It was well after day-break when I eventually arrived at my destination and I hurriedly loaded the boat. In my haste to get going, I flooded the outboard motor and could not start it whatever I tried, so there was a further half-hour delay while I removed the plug and dried it out. When I was purring down the boat dike towards the Thurne itself at long last, I was in a sour mood. The fates appeared to be conspiring against me.

Worse was to follow. All that week, I had had an area in mind that I intended fishing, the spot where I had lost the big fish a few weeks previously. As the days had passed, I had convinced myself that I would definitely catch a very big pike from that spot. To reach it entailed a long trip up the Thurne, almost as far as the entrance to Martham North Broad. However, I had only motored about 200 yards upriver when I noticed pack ice ahead. Although it was quite mild now, the ice had been so thick that it was taking a lot longer to melt than I had envisaged. On reaching the edge of this

A 24lb 8oz fish from Martham North Broad.

ice, I realised that I would be going no further. The ice stretched from bank to bank and although it probably was not very thick by now, it would be foolhardy to attempt to break through it with the boat and risk damaging it or the outboard. I was now totally disgruntled and jumped out of the boat and walked a long way upstream to see if there were any open areas. I must have walked about half a mile and the ice was unbroken the whole way.

On the walk back to the boat, it occurred to me that the conditions could actually provide ideal fishing. The boat was moored in an area that had perhaps been ice-free for only a few hours, which meant that any pike in the area would not have seen an angler's bait for a couple of weeks. I was the only angler on the river that morning, so I could be first to cash in if any big pike were on the prowl. As I set up my gear, all the enthusiasm came flooding back and I was soon sitting with a hot cup of tea, watching two floats. The first supported a paternostered roach tethered at the edge of the ice, while I fished a free-swimming crucian livebait on the other. On this tackle, I used a heavily greased line to ensure that the bait covered as much water as possible without undue hindrance, and forty yards of water were searched very thoroughly without response. I did, however, have the encouragement of a four-pounder quite early on, on the paternostered bait.

As the morning wore on, the air temperature began to climb very rapidly in conjunction with a steadily strengthening breeze. By about midday, there was a constant cracking and creaking as the ice started to break up and by about midday it was melting very quickly. I remember looking at my watch at 12.30 p.m., by which time the ice had all but disappeared. It was at this time that the possibilities really began to excite me. I could now fish water that had become accessible literally only minutes previously, and I decided to take my free rover 100 yards upstream, and cover every inch of water back to the boat. I would then move up 100 yards and repeat the process. In this way, I was confident that I would attract a big pike eventually.

I fished my crucian livebait to a logical pattern. What I would do was lower it at my feet and search the near-bank margins first of all. The bait was then worked to midstream, and finally along the far-bank rush beds. Having covered the area thoroughly in front of me, it was then time to walk twenty paces downstream and work the bait down towards me. In an hour, I had perhaps covered eighty yards in this way. The float approached an area on the far bank where there was a little bay in the rushes, and then an almighty vortex appeared in the surface of the water and the float disappeared. The take was spectacular and awe inspiring. So great was the displacement of water that it had to have been caused by a very big fish, and my mouth went dry with anticipation.

The events of the next few minutes are permanently etched on my memory and provided some of the most heart-stopping action of my angling career. After the take, the pike had sulked on the bottom for perhaps a minute while I debated what to do for the best. The big pike I had lost a few weeks earlier had done the same thing and I had struck that one prematurely. It had the bait across its jaws only and had come unstuck. I wanted to prevent that happening again, and yet I am paranoid about deep-hooking big pike. They are far too precious to risk damaging by irresponsible angling. The pike, however, solved the dilemma for me. As I was taking in the slack line a monstrous shape rose to just under the surface, a shape I could see clearly was at least 4ft long, and then it took off downstream at top speed. I remember telling myself out loud to stay calm. So close under

My 32-pounder is unhooked.

Looking on as Dave Plummer weighs my 32lb fish.

the surface was the fish that the wake it made was very impressive, and in fact it resulted in one of the most comical sights I have witnessed in angling. A pair of mallards were swimming along, minding their own business, about fifteen yards downstream. As the pike bore down on them, I could almost read their minds. As if to say 'let's get the hell out of here', they both took off in a panic and collided head-on in mid-air. In a great cloud of feathers, they both fell into the water on their backs, whereupon they started fighting, as if each was blaming the other for the débâcle.

I now had more serious things on my mind. Never had I experienced a pike that had gone so fast or fought so hard. It was truly a memorable battle, but eventually the fish was circling a few yards out. Cautiously, I coaxed it over the net and then I began to lift. At that moment, I went numb as the net refused to budge. The sunken mesh was caught fast on a snag and no amount of tugging would release it. For what seemed an eternity the pike lay across the arms of the net, regaining its strength and then it slowly slithered away and shot downstream once again. I was utterly powerless to prevent it and at that moment I was convinced that I was destined to lose yet another monstrous pike. I now knew that the fish on my line weighed well over 30lb. It took all my powers of self-control to let the pike run against a light pressure, and when it stopped I knelt down on the grass and reached underwater with my left hand in an attempt to free the mesh. Being careful to maintain a tight line, I groped around for several minutes before I was able to release the net. During this time the pike thankfully behaved itself and I was able to play it back quite easily. The second attempt proved successful and I was soon kneeling beside the fish of my dreams, a 30lb pike.

My personal best to date – the 32lb 1oz fish I took from the Thurne.

When I lifted its head, I could see that the fish was quite deeply hooked. Unlike the big one I had hooked and lost, this one had obviously gulped the bait straight down. For a short while, I endeavoured to extract the trebles, but it was a job that really required two sets of long-handled forceps and four hands. I realised that it would be much easier if there were two of us on the job, and as I knew Dave Plummer was joining me shortly, I disconnected the trace and placed the fish in a sack to recover while I waited for him. With such a big valuable fish, I wanted to take no risk whatsoever that it should come to any harm. That was certainly the right decision, because the hooks were out in short order after Dave's arrival and the pike went back none the worse for its experience.

That magnificent Thurne pike weighed 32lb 1oz and is still my personal best at the time of writing, as well as being the only thirty-pounder of my career. It is a fish I shall never forget.

19 My First Double

One of my principal targets at the start of the 1986 season was a barbel of over 10lb in weight. Irritated at my continual failure to catch a double, I decided that this called for a determined campaign on the Dorset Stour. Perhaps a change of venue would improve my luck with the species as I certainly seemed to be jinxed with the big Wensum fish. Since I had first started to fish seriously for the Wensum barbel in 1981, I had taken twenty-six fish, with the biggest an 8lb 12oz specimen. There is of course nothing wrong with an eight-pounder, but I could reasonably have expected one or two doubles from over twenty barbel on the Wensum, where it would appear par for the course that about one fish in six weighs over 10lb.

I had not fished much of the Dorset Stour before apart from Throop Fisheries which I knew well. However, reports of some exceptional fish from upriver and some exciting information from my good friend Stef Horak, who had fished the Stour extensively, meant that when I arrived on the bank for my first trip in August 1986, I was tingling with anticipation.

A good part of that first trip was spent looking around and generally acquainting myself with the characteristics of the stretch to which I intended to devote my attention. The water was low and clear, the fish being easy to spot and I decided eventually to confine my efforts to four swims. Each one consisted of a smooth gravel patch adjacent to streamer weed, and by baiting each with hemp seed, any barbel in the vicinity should be attracted out from under the cover. After half an hour, barbel were avidly feeding in two of the areas and in one of the swims were two fish that looked well into double figures. I had found what I was seeking.

It did not take me too long to find something that I was certainly not seeking. The river appeared carpeted with eels, and it did not seem to matter what bait I put on the hook – the eels loved them all. That first trip was one of total frustration and although I managed one barbel, an eight-pounder on a lump of meat at dusk, the eels nearly drove me scatty. Talking to Stef later, he confirmed that this is a constant problem in the summer months on the Stour, and one to which there is no complete answer.

The only way to minimise the problem was to restrict the use of meaty baits. Fishing a maggot hookbait in conjunction with a feeder load of maggots, for instance, would act like a magnet for eels, whereas a maggot hookbait fished over a carpet of hemp may stay unmolested long enough for a barbel to find it. The mistake I had made was feeding loose maggots as well as hemp, which meant that the swims were full of eels and any hookbait I tried was immediately attacked. It was a mistake I would not make again.

For the next two months I fished the Stour every week, sometimes making the long journey from Coventry for just one day's fishing. Several more barbel rewarded my efforts, but by mid-October the eight-pounder taken on my first trip remained the biggest fish of the present campaign. Even in mid-October that year, the river was low and clear and the nights were getting very cold. As I drove back after one fruitless session, I decided that the next week I would go piking. I would come back to the Stour when there was some rain to colour and raise the river.

But it is strange how things work out sometimes. I had not been home more than an hour when the phone rang. It was Stef enquiring whether I fancied a couple of days on the Stour next week, as he had a couple of days' holiday available! I must admit that I did not take too much convincing, and in the early hours of the following Thursday morning I picked up Stef and we set off once again for Dorset.

When we started fishing that morning, I did not fancy our chances one little bit. If anything the river was lower and clearer than ever, coupled with the fact that there had been a slight frost – hardly what I would describe as good barbel conditions. Nevertheless, when the early morning mist had cleared and the sun had broken through, it was a pleasant enough day, although singularly unproductive. At its close, Stef had had the grand total of two bites, yielding a small chub and a 4lb barbel, while my sorry contribution consisted of pulling out of a medium-sized barbel as I attempted to heave it clear of a clump of streamer. It was, however, a very enjoyable day. Stef is very good company and we talked fishing late into the evening, over quite a few beers.

When we were asleep in my car in the early hours of the morning, it transpired

Stef Horak with a 10lb Stour barbel.

that I must have had perhaps one too many beers. At about 2 a.m. I had to dive out of the car to be as sick as a dog under the hedge. I thought I was dying. The next morning I felt only marginally better and when I looked out of the window to see the first really hard frost of the winter, the last thing on my mind was barbel fishing. I admit quite openly that had I been on my own I would have come home. Apart from the fact that I felt so rough, conditions were now obviously hopeless for barbel. However, Stef wanted to fish and he had booked a holiday especially for the trip, so off we headed back to the river. Stef was full of optimism, while I was vowing that this time I would definitely turn teetotal!

By the time we had walked to the swims we had baited the previous day, the cold frosty air had cleared my head considerably and I was feeling a lot better. I even started to generate some enthusiasm as I lowered five droppers of hemp and one of casters into my 4ft-deep swim. Just after I had finished the baiting, Stef stopped by for a brief chat and as we stood talking, there was a distinct flash of coral pink over the hemp. At a little over four feet, the swim was a fraction deep to see the fish clearly, but an occasional sighting of the pectorals and a large tail told us that it was quite a big fish that had taken up residence. Frost or no frost, here was one fish at least that appeared willing to feed.

Very carefully, I lowered my hookbait of two casters on a size 12 hook to a 2-foot 6lb hooklink. I was using a small Drennan feeder with the holes opened out, allowing free dispersion of the hemp in the current. For over an hour I sat there, concentrating intently. Every so often, the barbel would flash and I really was on the edge of my seat. Despite all that the bite, when it came, still took me by surprise as it was so sudden. One moment the rod was lying still and unmoving in my hand, the next it was bent double with the clutch whining, as something big and powerful surged through the streamer bed.

Seconds after that initial plunge, everything jammed solid and nothing I could do would shift the fish. I could clearly see my swimfeeder caught at the root of the downstream clump of streamer. Obviously, as the fish had raced downstream the feeder had been forced progressively further up the line.

After some considerable time pulling from every conceivable angle, I became convinced that the fish had gone and that I was simply snagged in the roots. I was on the point of pulling for a break when there was another lurch on the rod and a further two yards of line were taken against the clutch. The barbel was still there!

As I shouted to Stef to come and give me a hand, there were several more short buzzes from the clutch, but the swimfeeder still remained clearly in view at the base of the streamer. I now had no way of knowing exactly how much line the fish had taken, or even in which direction it had travelled. There was only one solution to the dilemma we faced. One of us had to go in and free the line and as I had the important job of holding the rod, Stef drew the short straw!

With the sharp frost the previous night, it was not the ideal day to go for a swim and it was quite fascinating to observe the different shades of blue on Stef's flesh. The swim was also slightly deeper than we had estimated and he disappeared up to his neck as he gingerly waded out to the offending streamer clump. Feeling around with his feet he located the line and as he did so, there was another savage wrench on the rod top and a few more yards of line were lost. When the run had stopped, Stef carefully lifted the line to the surface, bringing with it the entire root of streamer. It appeared that the line completely encircled the root and it was then obvious that the barbel, after the

My first double – 10lb 9oz taken from the Dorset Stour.

initial downstream surge, had made an abrupt turn and headed back upstream. Agonisingly slowy, he cleared the line from the fronds one by one, while I kept the rod as high as possible to keep the line free of further snagging.

As the line came free at last, there was a fast run and the now unencumbered line rocketed upstream. So fast did it move that Stef had to duck under water quickly to avoid the line going around his throat and garrotting him!

At long last, I was in direct contact with the fish, which I now knew was a good thirty yards upstream of where I had first hooked it. The drama was by no means over. That fish fought tremendously hard, staying deep for a good ten minutes within about five yards of me, and as it came up in the water Stef and I could see clearly that it was a good double. For a few more minutes it stubbornly refused to come any closer and I had my heart in my mouth. I had the size 12 hook on my mind and knew that I dare not attempt to bully the fish, although the temptation to do so was almost overpowering. Eventually, however, my patience was rewarded and a magnificent barbel rolled into the landing net exactly one hour after I had first hooked it. Mere words simply cannot express my elation at that moment. After the many thousands of hours searching for a double figure barbel, my ambition had finally been realised.

It is the sign of a good friend that Stef was as pleased as I and his face was wreathed in smiles as, through chattering teeth, he announced 10lb 9oz. I shook him warmly by the hand. Without his assistance that barbel would certainly have been lost.

20 Three Weeks at Redmire

All anglers of my generation were brought up on the writings of the legendary Richard Walker. As well as being an exceptional angler, Dick's writing style was masterly. So infectious was his enthusiasm for fishing in general and fishing for big fish in particular, and so much of the excitement of big fish hunting did he convey in his articles, that he is rightly considered the father of modern specimen hunting. Little did he realise, when his buzzer sounded in the early hours of that dark September morning of 1952, that he was about to change the face of angling for ever.

Dick's account of the capture of his record carp is arguably one of the most famous angling articles ever written, confirming that big fish could indeed be caught by design, and bringing to the angling public's notice the name of this new carp angling Mecca, Redmire Pool.

As a boy, I eagerly devoured every word of his accounts of the tussles with the Redmire monsters. In my mind's eye, I had a picture of the Willow pitch, Inghams and Pitchfords Pit. How I wished I could fish that magical place. Little did I realise at the time that, over thirty years later, I was to have my wish fulfilled.

In August 1985 I walked onto Redmire Dam for the first time. It was the middle of a sunny afternoon and Dave Plummer was to join me later, but for the time being I had Redmire to myself. I was immediately affected as others had said I would be. I was totally overawed and stood on the dam for ages just drinking it all in. There in front of me, all my boyhood dreams had come to life. I remember thinking that a man would have to be devoid of soul not to be captivated by such a beautiful lake.

I suppose I stood there for about twenty minutes, and in that time many great carp glided silently through the surface layers, lazily basking in the afternoon sunshine, as indeed some of these very same fish must have done all those years before when Dick Walker and Pete Thomas first visited Redmire. Most of them appeared to be commons, but I spotted three big mirrors, one right at my feet alongside the old punt. Almost certainly, the mug shots of these three carp appeared somewhere in my copy of *Redmire Pool*, that marvellous book by Len Arbery and Kevin Clifford on this jewel of carp fisheries. I had the book with me, and with it I was able to identify all the

First impressions.

The famous stool overlooking the shallows at Redmire.

swims that have become so famous over the years.

It was just as I had finished a tour of the water that Dave Plummer arrived. As with myself, it was his first visit and he was also totally mesmerised. For ages we stood on the dam talking. Neither of us was in a hurry to get the tackle out of the cars; for the time being it was enough simply to be there.

By early evening, however, it was time to attend to the particulars of setting up the gear for our four-day stay. Over a can of beer it had been decided that Dave would fish the Evening pitch, while I would fish the famous swim that had captured so much of my boyhood imagination, the Willow pitch. A fine drizzle had started as I ferried my gear over the dam, and by the time my pitch was arranged to my satisfaction, it was raining steadily and the wind strength was increasing. The pleasant afternoon sunshine was now a distant memory as heavier and more ominous clouds rolled in from the west.

In the gathering dusk, with a hot meal inside me and three pop-up tutti frutti hookbaits in position, I lay on my bedchair listening to the howling wind and the sound of the rain drumming on the bivvy. Again, my mind drifted back to the famous names that had occupied that very spot over the past thirty odd years. I was to find out days later that my first night at Redmire Pool coincided with the date of Richard Walker's death. It was I suppose fitting that such a sad day should be marked by such a black, miserable and sombre night.

Dawn the following morning was equally wet and uninspiring, and as I warmed my hands around the first cup of tea of the day, one of my rods was away on a fast run. With barely suppressed excitement I picked it up, engaged the pick up, waited for the line to tighten and then struck. I connected with thin air. My first run at Redmire, and I had missed it. I felt devastated.

Before I had had chance to re-bait, I heard one of Dave's alarms sound on the opposite bank and watched him go into action. Shorty after, he had a very small common on the bank, a fish of about three pounds. Not long after, he had its twin and then he missed a third run. I started to feel a little better. If the small commons had become active, perhaps it was one of those I had missed.

By mid-morning, the heavy rain had reverted to a fine intermittent drizzle and both Dave and I baited two other areas towards the shallows on our respective banks. In my case, I had baited the In-Willow swim with hemp containing a handful of blue cheese-flavoured boilies, and right in the shallows I prepared an area with a couple of pints of a special bean that Dave wanted to try out. I never did get a run on one of those beans, but early afternoon did at least yield my first Redmire carp, a spectacularly fighting 8lb common that picked up a double blue cheese boilie offering.

When dawn broke on our last morning, Dave and I could look back on four enchanting days at Redmire. We had not caught much, Dave having managed a further four small commons and I a further two, but it did not matter that much anyway. However, there was to be an explosive finale. Not long after dawn, Dave had a slow run which he struck and played quite casually at first, obviously expecting another small common. It was only when the fish made a twenty yard run that Dave started to take it seriously. That carp fought very hard before it was eventually netted, a beautiful mirror of just over 22lb. It was a lovely fish and, amazingly, one whose photograph we could not find in *Redmire Pool*.

That statement, however, could not be made about another big fish that lay in Dave's net just thirty incredible minutes later. That one weighed 23lb and was a well-known resident affectionately called 'Raspberry'. Redmire had reserved its drama until the last act.

Soon, it was time to go. We wound in our baits as we had cast them out four days previously, in pouring rain. As I slowly drove up the hill to the farm cottage, crossed the famous cattle grid and rejoined the outside world, I wondered whether I would ever fish Redmire again. Fervently, I hoped so.

Unbelievably, I was to get my wish only a few short weeks later. I had a phone call at the office from Clive Diedrich, who controlled the fishing at that time. 'There is a free week at Redmire at the beginning of October' he said, 'if you and Dave fancy a return trip.' Did we fancy a return trip, he must be joking! I couldn't wait.

Unluckily for Dave, business pressures meant that he had to cry off the trip at the very last moment, and thus it was that I arrived on the banks of Redmire Pool on a still, misty October morning for a week's

The Willow pitch.

carp fishing on my own. To have Redmire to myself for a whole week was a paradise I could hardly have contemplated as a boy. For several hours I looked round the pool, lying still and mysterious in its colourful autumn garb. There was no sign of fish activity, apart from a large burst of very fine bubbles in front of the Willow pitch which I attributed to eels, and eventually I decided that my first point of attack would be from the swim known as the Stumps. With no visible fish activity to guide me, this swim would allow me to cover as large an area of the pool as possible.

On this trip, I had decided to put down a large bed of tiger nuts and fish over them with nuts on one rod and pop-up boilies on the other two. The baits were fished off the bottom in the hope of avoiding eels as much as possible. The first few hours I spent fishing provided the bulk of the action I was destined to enjoy on that trip. No more than ten minutes after my baits were in position and I was brewing up the first cup of tea of the evening, the rod baited with the tiger nuts was away. Under the still, dark water, the line was streaking away and the rod plunged around in my hand as a big fish kited left under the marginal trees. Seconds later, the rod top sprang back – I had pulled out.

As it turned out, I had little time to be despondent. I had not even completed re-baiting when my middle rod was shaking in the rests with an Optonic screeching. As I struck, a tremendous bow wave headed for the shallows at top speed, with the clutch whining. As the fish neared the dangerous brambles on one of the far-bank islands, I increased the finger pressure on the spool and applied as much side-strain as the tackle would stand. With only feet to spare, the carp turned and headed back just as fast up the lake towards the dam. From that moment on, however, I never allowed it to get close to any other snags, and it was a case of patiently playing it backwards and forwards until it was close enough to net. As soon as it sagged in the folds of the mesh, I knew I had a twenty-pounder, and a 20lb common at that which was a long hoped for dream. In fact, the fish did not weigh as much as I thought, but at 20lb 12oz it was still immensely satisfying.

A Redmire star. Dave Plummer with 'Raspberry'.

Photographs taken, baits re-cast and with a fresh cup of tea in my hand, I lay back on my bedchair in the gathering dusk bathing (as the poets would have it) in a rosy glow of contentment. Whatever else happened, the session was a resounding success. I would have been quite content that evening if nothing else had happened, but in actual fact the action was only just beginning. In the next two hours, I was to have a further four runs. The first yielded a small common, the second was missed and the last two resulted in two other lovely common carp of 16lb 10oz and 18lb 14oz. What an incredible first evening. I slipped into my sleeping bag at about midnight a very happy man indeed.

That fantastic evening was not to be followed by more of the same, because there were then two completely blank days and nights in the Stumps. Just after dawn on Thursday morning, I moved my gear into the Evening pitch. The previous evening the first big fish I had seen roll since my arrival on Monday morning had showed itself at the edge of the branches in that swim. The first twenty-four hours in this new position also proved uneventful, but I was well entertained by the antics of a whole swarm of blue tits which continually raided my tiger nut bucket. It was still calm, misty and totally peaceful, and anyone who knows Redmire will agree that, for a carp angler, it is as close to heaven on earth as you can get.

The session ended with a bang, just as it had begun. On the Friday morning, with only a few hours to go before I had to leave, I had three runs in very quick succession. Again the first two were from small commons and I landed fish of about seven pounds apiece. The last one turned out to be an exceptionally scrappy double of 14lb exactly, a common again. It proved to be nowhere as big as I had thought it was when I was playing it, but what a memorable tussle that carp gave me. There is no doubt at all that those Redmire commons are beautiful and magnificent creatures in every respect.

If my first two weeks at Redmire were memorable because they were the realisation of all my boyhood dreams, the third and last week I was to fish there, in autumn 1986, was memorable for very different reasons. I had arrived at mid-morning on Monday, on a very humid and heavily overcast day. It was as still as the grave and the first thing I saw after I had parked my car inside the compound was one of the famous big mirrors roll about thirty yards out from the Evening pitch. There was other activity in the form of bubbling and smoke-screening and my decision on choice of pitch had been made for me. I was fishing on my own again, Andy Barker this time having to back out at the last minute, and as I set up I could barely suppress my excitement. What did the water have in store for me this week?

I was soon to find out. By about mid-afternoon, the very calm conditions had been replaced by quite a stiff breeze and as the clouds overhead rapidly darkened, the breeze picked up force. By about 4 p.m. it was as black as night, the wind was now gale force and then the heavens opened. I have never experienced rain as sustained and torrential as I did that night on the banks of Redmire Pool. All thoughts of fishing were forgotten as I lay in my sleeping bag listening to the howling wind and thunderous downpour. I was praying I would not get a run and, to be honest, I probably would not have heard the Optonic if I had had one.

The next morning the rain was still heavy, although the wind had moderated mercifully, and as I looked around the water the sight was incredible. Everywhere was a sea of red mud, and the water was the most vivid crimson. So hard and unremitting had the rain been in the night that the sluice at the side of the dam was temporarily unable to cope and floodwater was actually running over the dam itself. Dave (the gamekeeper) joined me as I was looking around and he told me that in all his years on the estate, he had never known a storm like it. Apparently, there had been substantial damage caused to the roofs of several buildings by the gale.

View of the day and the Old Pipe swim, taken from Bramble Island.

By about midday, the rain had all but stopped and I re-cast all three baits with reels that sounded like stirrup pumps, before embarking on an attempt at tidying up the muddy chaos that my bivvy had become. I then cooked myself a very enjoyable hot meal and, as dusk was approaching, settled down for the night. It was calm once again, and exceptionally warm and muggy – the kind of night when you are expecting something to happen at any time.

At about midnight, with nothing having transpired to disturb my dark, still world, I climbed into my sleeping bag and wearily closed my eyes. To the sound of a distant hunting owl, I was soon asleep and so I remained until a little after 3 a.m. when I was awoken with a start by the most violent shaking of the bivvy on the side on which I was sleeping. It was almost as if a large dog had taken the material in his mouth and was trying to rip a hole in it. I shot out of the bivvy to investigate the cause of the commotion, and as I did so the shaking stopped abruptly. It was a litle unnerving, especially as I soon established that there was no apparent cause for the phenomenon. I was totally alone, there was not a breath of wind and I soon convinced myself that it must have been a large animal. Perhaps a fox or badger had stumbled into the material.

Back in my bivvy, I decided to have a brew up before retiring to bed once more and while I was waiting for the kettle to boil I became aware for the first time of how incredibly cold it had become inside my shelter. It was weird. Outside it was a very warm, humid night, but the bivvy felt as though it had been refrigerated. At first I put it down to condensation, but even then it was unnaturally chilly. Once I had made my tea, I wandered down to the Stumps swim with it to warm my feet up. I was perhaps only there for three or four minutes, but it was long enough for me to realise the tremendous temperature difference between that area and my bivvy. In the space of only about forty yards of bank, it felt as though the temperature difference was about twenty degrees Fahrenheit.

Convincing myself that it was obviously some freak atmospheric condition, I was soon once more ensconsed in my sleeping bag and was soon asleep. Three times, however, in the next hour I was awoken suddenly by what felt like a blast of freezing air across my cheek, and the third time it was so startling that I sat bolt upright on my bedchair. I noticed two things almost instantaneously. The first was that the bivvy was now like an icebox, and the second was a large black shadow that crossed and then recrossed the open door of the camp. To say that I was now distinctly uneasy would be putting it mildly, and without further ado I gathered up my sleeping bag and walked with it to the car, only about twenty yards away. Having locked myself in, I lowered the passenger seat, made myself as comfortable as possible and then slept the rest of the dark hours without further interruption.

I tried to make sense of it all the following morning and even tried to convince myself that I had imagined it. But deep down I knew that I had not. The shaking of the tent and the intense cold had been only too real. What I did know was that I had now lost all interest in fishing and simply did not want to spend another night at the water alone. Not long after day-break, I packed my gear in the car and set off, or rather I tried to set off. The torrential downpour had left the car parking area so muddy that there was no way that I could drive through the gate and into the field beyond, especially as that manoeuvre involved a right angle turn going uphill. I struggled for half an hour but to no avail, and so I was forced to go and find Dave, who eventually arrived with the tractor to pull me out. At long last, I was on my way home three days early, and this time I had no regrets about leaving Redmire.

The interesting postscript to this story is that at the time I had never read or heard of the strange occurrences that have been attributed to the Evening pitch by various anglers. It was many months later at a NASA conference, when I was talking to Len Arbery and his son Tony, that Len said something that took my mind back. He mentioned a night when he too had experienced feelings of intense cold in his bivvy, and it was so marked in his case that articles inside the camp were actually frosted the next morning – and this was in summer!

On 11 October 1989, I read in the *Angling Times* of the most frightening phenomenon in the Evening pitch to date, one so shocking that a priest was called in to perform an exorcism. Ricky Richardson was camping in the swim with his son at night and a hideous apparition with green staring eyes materialised at the bivvy door and stared in on them. Other anglers from different parts of the lake heard their screams and when they arrived found Ricky cowering in shock at the back of the camp. When I read that story, my mind went back to that particular night in 1986. If I had seen the same spectre, it would definitely have been a case of breaking out the brown trousers!

21 The Queenford Phenomenon

I was privileged in the autumn of 1983 to be present when Alan Wilson took his fabulous catch of four thirteen-pounders from TC Pit, and I truly believed that it was a catch of bream that would never be equalled. There were few waters known where the average size of the bream came anywhere near that of TC and certainly only one or two that had the potential of producing a near fourteen-pounder – even those only produced an occasional specimen. No, Alan's catch would remain unsurpassed, perhaps for ever.

Little did I realise that only a few months later I was to become involved with a water that has changed the complexion of big bream fishing in this country for all time, and where a thirteen-pounder has proved to be a below-average specimen. Strangely enough it was Alan's TC catch that began the chain of events. A few weeks later an article by Phil Smith appeared in the angling press describing the events of that fabulous night, and Phil mentioned that I had captured the fish on video. At that time, video equipment among anglers was still very rare and Phil's article aroused considerable interest. I had several phone calls requesting more details, one from a man named Alastair Nicholson.

That first conversation led to a firm friendship and in May 1984 he and I, in the company of Trefor West, drove down to Deans Farm for a look around. Alastair and his friends had been catching big tench and bream from Deans for several years and Trefor and I had been invited down to join in the fun. On the journey we passed Queenford, and quite casually Alastair announced that he was going to catch a record bream from the water! I pressed him for more details and he told me that a friend had recently found a dead bream in the margins that weighed almost thirteen pounds.

Alastair's prophecy came remarkably true with the very first bream that he landed from the water, after many blank nights. It weighed 13lb 14oz, 2oz above the official TC record of Alan Smith. I will never forget how excited he sounded when he telephoned me the news. During that conversation he told me that Amey Roadstone Corporation (ARC), who owned the water, had not been slow in recognising the potential and after negotiations with himself and Joe Taylor of Bicester, they sanctioned the formation of a limited membership night syndicate. Joe was given the task of making the necessary arrangements and only a few days after the capture of the first Queenford bream, the syndicate places were filled. I was pleased to be one of the lucky few.

Only three more bream were caught that season, but what bream they were! On the second weekend following the syndicate's formation, Alastair caught a fish that made the big fish world buzz with excitement. Phil Smith has told me that Alastair appeared behind him at about midnight and quite nonchalantly announced that he had landed a huge bream, which he felt may beat the newly established record of 15lb 6oz, a fish that had been taken from one of the Cheshire meres by Tony Bromley. As Phil is chairman of the NASA record fish committee, Alastair could have had no one in attendance better qualified than Phil and after a short and agonising wait, Phil declared 15lb 6oz, equalling the Cheshire capture. There was now no doubt whatsoever that in Queenford we had stumbled across a gold-mine. This was further confirmed only a week later when I had my first session at the venue. Again, the only man to catch fish was Alastair – two more monsters gracing his landing net, immaculate bream of 14lb 12oz and 14lb 14oz.

Alastair's four fish of 1984 were the only bream taken that season although the syndicate fished many long fruitless hours, but the following season saw more of the members coming to terms with the fishing. Several more very big fish were taken, culminating in John Knowles taking the record with a fish of 15lb 10oz, which was again witnessed by Phil. It was at this time that we realised that the water was even more special than we had first imagined. As far as we could ascertain, all the big bream that had so far been caught were different fish!

I never actually fished Queenford in the 1985/1986 season, being totally sidetracked by carp, but I renewed my acquaintance with the water in July 1986. That season I was determined that I would bank one of those impressive bronze slabs. Two or three nights a week for six weeks I fished hard, with nothing to show for my efforts except small perch and one tench. During that period though, I did have two fascinating sessions, although they both ended in blanks. In late July I was fishing the road bank with Phil Smith and Joe Taylor, and on the second night of a three-day stint I

One of the 14lb bream that started it all.

A 2lb Queenford perch.

must have had over fifty line bites, varying from a few inches to real butt ringers. It was non-stop almost throughout the entire night and Joe had even stopped fishing to sit with me. Whatever I tried was to no avail and when the indications finally petered out after dawn I retired to my sleeping bag, one very frustrated angler.

Very similar indeed was a session two weeks later off the north bank. This time the liners took place over two nights. On the Thursday night I had perhaps six indications, but on Friday the activity was frenzied. Phil had arrived to fish for his fortnight's holiday and I advised him, as I was leaving the following morning, that it would be sensible to move into my swim when I left. At least we could be certain that it contained fish. All night long Phil and I sat together drinking endless cups of tea, and all night long the activity continued unabated. Most of the movements were obviously liners, but I did have several that took the bobbins to the butt nice and slowly, and begged to be struck at. Every time though, I struck into fresh air. I found out later that Phil had had liners himself the following two nights but then, in the early hours of Sunday morning, one of the indications proved to be the real thing. Although that fish was lost after a few seconds, it was followed by two more positive bites, yielding bream of 13lb 7oz and 15lb 3oz. Those two fish gave me tremendous encouragement and although I was still on a Queenford blank, I was confident that I was getting close to my first success. It was closer than I thought.

My first Queenford bream came on my twentieth night of fishing the water, in August 1986 and the circumstances of its capture are somewhat bizarre. I had settled into a swim on the Thursday afternoon known to the syndicate members as Flanders' Bar, on account of the fact that Andy Flanders had taken the first bream from it. A cast of only about twenty-five yards puts the bait on a very hard gravel plateau about 6ft deep, but the cast has to be accurate. The bar is only a few yards wide and about 3ft deep, before dropping off on all sides to much deeper water. The shelf on the right is much gentler than on the left and I was fishing one bait on this slope, as well as one on the peak of the plateau. Both rods were baited with lobs which were air injected to make them waver a few inches off the bottom above an appealing carpet of mixed corn, casters and hemp seed.

Almost as soon as darkness had fallen, indications started on both rods and until about 2 a.m., I was on the edge of my seat in a state of pent-up expectation. I was convinced that among all the small lifts and twitches the positive bite that would signal the arrival of my first Queenford bream would occur. At around midnight the activity was intense, with eight or nine fast liners occurring in the space of about twenty minutes. The promise remained unfulfilled, however, and I was a disappointed angler when I finally climbed into my sleeping bag at about 3 a.m. The Optonics had been silent for over an hour.

About half an hour after day-break, I was awoken by an alarm as one of the bobbins twitched and jerked its way to the butt ring. The nature of the bite told me what was responsible and sure enough, a few minutes later a small perch was being returned. About an hour later, another identical bite yielded an even smaller perch and I assessed that my chance of bream had now gone.

At about 7.30 a.m., I decided to cook myself a breakfast and pretty soon my bivvy was filled with the delicious aroma of frying eggs and sausages. Just after I had sat down to tuck in, one of the bobbins twitched up two inches, dithered for a few seconds and then dropped back. It was obviously another small perch and so I ignored it. A minute later, the bobbin dropped to the floor and then jerked its way back to its original position. I still ignored it and carried on with my meal. There were no further indications for at least three minutes, and then the bobbin rose to the butt in a series of half inch jumps. My half-eaten breakfast was put to one side and I struck into what I expected to be a feeble resistance. As I connected, something shot across the swim at great speed, taking me by surprise.

It was then that I was convinced that the fish was a jack pike – the bite had been typical. Nothing annoys me more than jacks taking carefully placed baits intended for worthier quarry and I heaved and hauled for all I was worth, dragging the fish unceremoniously towards me. I was half hoping the pike would bite me off; my eggs and sausage were going cold. In short order, the fish was alongside the marginal bushes to the left of the swim and then it rolled showing a great deep expanse of bronze flank – I had been wrong. I broke out into a cold sweat when I thought about the way I had played that bream, but luckily my surprise did not lead me to make any mistakes, as it might well have done. When the scales registered 13lb 2oz it was a moment of pure elation. I deserved that fish for the effort I had put into the water, but not for the ham-fisted way in which I had played it. It does, however, sum up the magic of Queenford in that you really do not know what the next bite may produce.

That thirteen-pounder was the only bream I was to catch in the 1986/1987 season, and that was exactly what was to happen in the following season. This time, however, success was to be achieved on the very first night at the fishery in June. If only I had known that, I could have packed up while I was ahead!

Again, I had arrived on a Thursday afternoon to find I had Queenford to myself. It was a wet, windy and dismal day, and once

My first success – a 13lb 2oz bream.

more I settled into Flanders' Bar. At about tea-time, Andy Flanders joined me and moved into the Cyanide swim, so called because every bream that has ever been hooked in there has come adrift. That was about forty yards to my left.

This time I was presenting baits on two different bars simultaneously, one on the plateau where I had caught the thirteen and the other on another shallow bar I had located about fifty yards out. The high point of that feature is so hard that it feels like a granite outcrop and is barely 5ft deep. Both areas were baited heavily with brown breadcrumbs laced with liquid molasses. This mixture also contained two pints of casters, four pints of hemp and three tins of corn.

As soon as it was fully dark, the wind dropped completely and the lake became flat calm. Under the heavy cloud cover there was no moonlight and the motionless Betalight bobbins glowed extra brightly on that black night. Despite the persistent drizzle it was very warm and humid, and I sat outside in waterproofs. I could not settle; I just knew something was going to happen that night. Sure enough, at around midnight, I had a sudden very fast liner to be followed quickly by two more. Ten minutes later the bobbin was a blur and the Optonic screaming as the reel began to backwind very rapidly indeed. As I struck, the rod slammed over and the fish surged some thirty yards to my left, taking line against the now engaged clutch. The bite and the way the fish was fighting convinced me that I had hooked one of the water's carp.

Things were not looking good. The fish was pulling so hard that I was not able to win back any line, and it was slowly kiting into the heavy tangle of bushes and trees that lined the bank to my left. The banks of Queenford are quite high and I jumped down into the margins and waded out as far as I dare to the edge of the trees where the bottom drops off quite quickly. Laying the rod over, parallel to the water, I applied maximum side-strain. I dare not yield another inch of line and the Tricast rod bent as never before. I was expecting the 6lb Maxima to part at any moment. For a few heart-stopping seconds all was stalemate and then the fish began to yield grudgingly a yard at a time.

A 14lb 3oz specimen, taken at midnight.

When I had started to regain some line, I began to have visions of actually landing the fish and then I realised that my landing net was on the high bank, about 15ft behind me. At the top of my voice I shouted for Andy to come and help, but to no avail. Through all my yelling, Andy slept peacefully. Only about ten yards from me the fish found a snag, obviously an underwater branch judging by the unmistakable grating sensation on the line. For several moments I exerted greater and greater pressure, but the fish was immovable. It was then that I made the vital decision. If the fish should come free, I would be unable to land it anyway. I therefore placed the rod on the rest, still well bent, and sprinted back to retrieve the landing net. Nothing had moved on my return. There was nothing for it but to haul and hope, and I bent more and more into the snag. Suddenly, the rod lurched back in my hand and the line fell slack. Disappointed, I began to wind in and then the rod thumped over again as I caught up with the fish swimming strongly back offshore – it had broken free of the snag and was still attached to the line.

From then on it was plain sailing. Constant side-strain brought the fish into the open water in front of me and at long last I was able to net it. I breathed a long sigh of relief. Only now could I see that I had a bream, and in the beam of my small torch it looked absolutely enormous. I unhooked the fish and before weighing it went to fetch Andy to be a witness. He was still sleeping like a baby, and only came round when I yelled about two inches from his right ear;

how he hears an Optonic in the night is totally beyond me!

A few moments later, Andy announced that my second Queenford bream weighed in at 14lb 3oz, a male as evidenced by the numerous spawning tubercles adorning its head. That fight was one of the most memorable I have ever had from any fish. From a stillwater bream, even a big one, it was quite exceptional.

While it is generally agreed among the syndicate members that we have learned very little about what controls the movements and whereabouts of the bream at any time, there is one thing that now seems crystal-clear. Our experience shows that the bream do not appear to feed over areas with any substantial amount of bottom weed. What is more, they do not appear to respond to swim clearance and heavy baiting, as do tench. Many of us have tried clearing weed off good-looking features, but to date not one bream has resulted from these tactics. The most startling example of this is a swim that Alan Wilson created three years ago. He found a fairly substantial bar which was heavily weeded. After weed clearance the swim really was superb and Alan fished it hard for several weeks, keeping the bar regularly cleared and baited. He never had a sign of a bream, but the interesting fact was that a very short distance from him a very small bar, which was naturally weed-free, produced several fish that summer.

Nowadays, we use this knowledge at the start of each season to assess those areas we believe most likely to produce bream. In this regard, the 1988/1989 season was particularly interesting, as it was perhaps the worst season for weed since the syndicate was formed. All of the swims on the north and south banks were badly affected, whereas in previous seasons they had been mainly weed-free and had produced a large percentage of the captures. For about 100 yards offshore from the west bank, however, the bottom was virtually weed-free, and this was where we all concentrated our efforts. I remember well the fascinating readings I obtained with my newly-acquired Humminbird echo-sounder. From virtually every point on the west bank, I could go out over a clean gravel bottom for about a hundred yards or so and then suddenly come up against a wall of weed. By August that year, weed mats covered the surface of the water everywhere apart from that west bank area. This led to this bank being more intensively fished than ever before. Some weeks, every available swim was taken and several features were located that had not been known about before.

Derek Quirk moved into just such a swim in July 1988. He had been on the water for several days without success, but little did he realise that he was about to make angling history. A few hours later he had landed five bream for an incredible total weight of 72lb 2oz. They weighed 15lb 9oz, 15lb 8oz, 14lb 6oz, 14lb 6oz and 12lb 5oz, surpassing Alan Wilson's TC catch that I had thought invincible. After that epic catch, a few more big bream were taken in fairly quick succession by several anglers, usually as single captures. By mid-August they had reverted to their more normal elusive selves and for a period of two weeks not a single bream was landed.

When I arrived on the last Thursday in August for a two-day session, I had already decided that this was to be my last of the summer; I was getting the urge to move on to some big barbel. For the first time that season, I had the water to myself and I moved immediately into Knowles' Bar. This was a famous swim where John Knowles took his previous record of 15lb 10oz, and is one of the more substantial features on the fishery. Surprisingly, despite being a member of the syndicate since its inception, it was the first time I had ever fished the swim.

Scanning the water for signs of life.

Once I had set up my camp I spent quite a while paddling around in my boat, eyes glued to my Humminbird screen. This device certainly makes location of the bars so much easier and once I had placed my swim markers to my satisfaction, I sounded all the other bars along the west bank. As well as the well-known features, I also covered a multitude of smaller ones, and it is hardly surprising that we catch the bream so rarely. Picking the right feature on any particular night is largely a lottery.

That day, I had a very interesting occurrence. The Humminbird screen showed up very few fish traces, but there were three substantial ones a foot off the bottom over the shallowest point of Knowles' Bar. They need not have been bream, of course, and there was no guarantee that they would stay there, but it was encouraging none the less.

Over the previous fortnight, Phil and I had been discussing the merits of heavy baiting for the Queenford fish. We had both made the same two observations. First, whenever a bream was caught and the angler concerned baited at all heavily for a second night, he almost invariably blanked. Secondly, although captured bream often regurgitated corn and caster shells, there was never any sign of hemp, although most of us were using it in quantity. The obvious conclusion was that the bream were not feeding on it and if that were the case, was the hemp actually acting as a deterrent rather than an attractant? We had known for some time that the bream ate corn in fair quantities, and the most successful bait for three seasons had been a lobworm and corn cocktail. In the 1988/1989 season, many of us had been experimenting with double-hook rigs, keeping faith with lobs on one hook but using corn, casters or flake, or cocktails of the same on the other. I find it very interesting that, although every bream deposited corn in the carp sack, every fish took the lobworm hookbait rather than the smaller one. (As I write this, that pattern has just been broken by Derek Quirk's magnificent sixteen-pounder, which accepted a corn and caster cocktail.)

That Thursday night I formulated my plan of action. I would bait with three tins of corn only using double-hook rigs carrying lob/corn and corn/caster respectively. If there was no action the first night, I decided to put in no further bait at all for the second – I would merely assume that no bream had visited the area to eat the corn. If any came in on Friday night, any additional free feed would lessen the chances of one of them picking up my hookbait.

Throughout Thursday night I was fully alert, expecting something to happen, but I was not rewarded with a solitary bleep for my lonely vigil. The only occurrence of any interest was the sight of quite a large tench rolling almost on top of one of my markers. Even the dawn period failed to provide a little light relief in the form of perch twitches. Friday passed uneventfully, as most of the daylight hours at Queenford do, and at tea-time I was joined on the bank by Pete Coates, who elected to fish about a hundred yards down the bank to my right. This was the swim that had produced the epic catch to Derek Quirk.

As dusk rapidly approached, I was in a dilemma. I had decided beforehand to introduce no further bait the second night if the first was blank, but there had been one or two water birds diving over the swim. I wondered if they had eaten all the corn but in the end I decided to stick to my predetermined plan of action, although I was far from confident.

After the little sleep I had had the previous night, I was very tired and retired to my sleeping bag at about 11 p.m. There had been no indications of fish activity whatsoever. At some time around 12.30 a.m., I was awoken with a start by the sound of an Optonic screaming, and as I looked out of the bivvy I could see the nearer bobbin jammed in the butt ring. That bright, still, moonlit night meant that I could see easily the reel handle spinning furiously. I was out of the camp like a shot, and soon standing on the high bank with the rod well bent and a powerful fish taking line. That first headlong rush must have taken everything out of the bream, because once it had been turned the fish was played in quite easily. The only anxious moment came when it made one last effort as it was approaching the net and tangled my other line. Luckily it came free after only a few seconds and soon an enormous fish was wallowing in the folds of my capacious net. When I had the full expanse of the fish in the beam of my large torch, I could see that as well as being the most pronounced two-tone fish I had ever seen, it was also easily a personal best. It looked simply colossal. It is hard for me to describe the euphoria when I recorded a weight of 15lb 2oz.

After I had sacked the fish and re-cast, I went down the bank to tell Pete the good news. He was fast asleep when I arrived, and so I did not bother to wake him; I would wait until dawn. That was to lead to quite an amusing confusion. At a little after dawn, Pete appeared at my bivvy door and said 'That's another fifteen-pounder in the bag then.' I wondered how he knew and so I asked him. It was his turn to look puzzled. What had transpired was that later in the night Pete had also landed a big fish, of 15lb 11oz, and had come down the bank to tell me. This time I was asleep and Pete had decided to wait until dawn as well! That night was very significant in that as well as those two fish being the last that were caught that season, it was the first time ever when two big fish had been caught from different swims on the same night.

In August 1989 Phil Smith compiled a complete list of all bream caught from Queenford and the statistics make very interesting reading. A total of eighty-six bream have been taken to date, of which only four have been under double figures, with the smallest taken being 9lb 3oz. The remainder have comprised 9 ten-pounders, 4 eleven-pounders, 7 twelve-pounders, 22 thirteen-pounders, 19 fourteen-pounders, 20 fifteen-pounders and a top fish of 16lb exactly. The average weight of fish taken so far has been a remarkable 13lb 8oz.

When we delve into the figures, even more interesting facts emerge. Just considering the fifteen-pounders alone, photographic evidence shows that the majority are different fish which tells us that there is a far bigger head of fish in Queenford than we had imagined. As far as we can tell, there have only been three recaptures among the fifteens and the most recent has given rise to considerable excitement. In the early days of the 1988/1989 season, Geoff Dixon took a tremendous fish of 15lb 10oz, which was carrying a fair quantity of spawn. That fish was recaptured by Phil Smith in August 1989, completely spawned out, but it weighed 15lb 14oz. The conclusions are obvious – the fish are still demonstrating a good growth rate and we are convinced that a new bream record from Queenford is imminent. One of the most easily recognisable bream in the fishery is the one that John Knowles took at 15lb 10oz three years ago. That fish was carrying no spawn and has never been recaptured. When and if it is, that is a bream that could once again command the headlines.

It is interesting to speculate how big the bream could possibly grow in Queenford. There have now been sufficient taken to form a fairly accurate idea of the potential. I have been told that, in any brood of mature fish, the range of weights can easily be plus or minus thirty per cent of the average specimen. In any animal species, there are those individuals that are poor feeders and those that are greedy feeders, coupled with the added complication of varying metabolic rates. Looking at the Queenford average of 13lb 8oz, it is easy to calculate that this would give a range of bream from about nine pounds to about eighteen pounds.

Analysing statistics can reveal some fascinating facts. For instance, although the average (mean) weight of the fish has been 13lb 8oz, the numerical average (median) has been 13lb 14oz, in that there have been forty-three bream caught at or above this weight and forty-three below it. Interestingly, the first Queenford bream ever caught weighed 13lb 14oz. I said at the time that unless Alastair Nicholson was exceptionally lucky, it was statistically likely that his first bream would prove to be average for the water. That has turned out to be a remarkably accurate assessment. The discrepancy between the mean (13lb 8oz) and the median (13lb 14oz) I believe provides further evidence to indicate that, although we have caught a handful of fish at the low end of the spectrum (nine- and ten-pounders) we have yet to bank a fish at the top end. Let me now stick my neck out and say that within two years, one of the Queenford members will land a bream of over 17lb – it is just a matter of time.

Phil's statistics also show that to be successful at Queenford you need a reasonable amount of time available for fishing, and need to be of the correct temperament – unless you are very lucky. I would contend that my own results are about average, with three bream landed to date from a total of forty-five nights on the water. The important point is that I have caught bream on three different nights which obviously means that I have had bream bites only one night in every fifteen. I make this point because, if a bream is caught it is then very possible that it will be followed by others, and this fact can create distortions that lead to those outside the syndicate believing the fish to be easier to catch than they really are. All my fish have been singletons, as have the majority of Queenford fish, but occasionally anglers have been in the right place at the right time to take catches of up to five

A personal best to date at 15lb 2oz.

fish. It is interesting to look at the results of the two men who have taken more bream than anyone else – Phil Smith and Derek Quirk. In Phil's case, he has caught bream on nine different nights although he has had a total of fourteen fish. Phil tells me that he has fished Queenford for a total of around 120 nights all told. Catching fish on only nine of them puts the pace of the fishing more into perspective, and is very similar to my average of three successful nights from forty-five fished. We see a similar story behind Derek's catches. Although he has taken thirteen fish, he has only made catches on six different nights. Looking at the number of nights he has fished (around eighty), we again see a similar ratio to mine and Phil's.

What Phil's list also shows is the influence of luck, both good and bad, on each member's success at the water. It has to be emphasised right from the start that I believe angling skill to have little relevance. All of the syndicate members are quite capable of locating the various features, baiting them and then placing hookbaits accurately. Most of the swims are now well known and it really is only a matter of being in the right swim on the right night. If the bream are in your swim, they are not that difficult to catch. Knowing which is going to be the right swim on any particular night is an ability we would all like to acquire! I will not accept that any of us have been lucky in catching fish at Queenford. Without exception, all the syndicate members have fished long and hard for the fish they have taken. Several, however, have been extremely unlucky. Joe Taylor himself, who has fished the water for a great many nights has yet to catch his first bream and the same goes for Leon Tandy. Leon fishes constantly with Jeff Mills and they have fished the same swims for the same number of nights, yet Jeff has taken five bream while Leon has taken none. Jeff has undoubtedly earned his fish, but Leon can certainly claim to have been desperately unlucky. It has not been a kind water either for Alan Wilson – although he has taken two Queenford fish, he has put in well over 100 nights for them.

Where good and bad luck has played more of a part is in the sizes of the fish taken by individual members. In this regard, two of the unluckiest men have been Gary Brandwood and Andy Flanders. Both have done very well, taking seven bream apiece and yet both have only taken one fish each weighing over 14lb. A total of twenty members have only taken seventeen fish below 12lb in weight and incredibly, Gary and Andy between them have had eight of these. A reverse situation is found with Derek Quirk. Derek has certainly earned every fish he has caught, but I believe he has been fortunate in the average size of his fish. Of his thirteen bream, no fewer than nine have been over 14lb, with an incredible six fifteen-pounders. The average Queenford bream has been 13lb 8oz and Derek's average has been 14lb 4oz – no wonder he likes the water!

Index

Arbery, Len 210

barbel 30, 44–50, 77–91, 92–5
Barbel Catchers Club 44, 189
Barker, Andy 107–15, 176, 195
Betalights 27, 28, 154
Black Horse pit 132–5
blood baits 26
bream 149–50, 167–78, 212–22
Bristol Avon 188–9
Brown, Ray 42–3, 148
bullheads 65
bulls 23–4, 68
Bure, River 194–5

carp 96–115, 154–7, 205–11
crucian 25–7, 154–7
carp syndicate water 102–7
Cassien, Lake 107–15
Cherwell, River 43, 54–91
chub 17–23, 34–5, 54–68, 69–77, 116–24, 147–53, 179–89
Clattercote Reservoir 36–7
Claydon Brook 8–24, 55, 128, 147
Coates, Peter 219
Coventry Specimen Group 30–5, 36, 42–4, 54, 96–7, 151
crayfish 8, 10, 54–68, 147–53
Cuttle Mill 100–1

Deans Farm 142–6
Decoy Broad 192–3

Fawsley Park 25–9
Flanders, Andy 214, 216
flavourings 144–5, 177–8
floating crust 65–8

Garnafailagh Lake 51–3
ghosts 80–1, 209–11

Hardwick pit 135, 137
Hawk Lake 154–7
Horak, Stef 201–4
Horsey Mere 190–2

induced takes 61, 181, 182
Ireland 51–3

Jones, Terry 37, 43, 170

Killinure, Lough 51–3
Knowles, John 213

Leam, River 116–31
lift float 26, 39, 154
loosefeeding 76–7, 124–5, 144, 166, 168
Lush, Simon 87–91

margin fishing 100
Marlborough Pool 98–100
Martham 195–200

Napton Reservoir 36, 96–8
Nicholls, Mick 44
Nicholson, Alastair 79, 142, 212–13

Ouse, Great 55, 60, 147–53
Oxford Debate 162

perch 10–17, 128–31, 173
Plummer, Dave 79, 179–89, 196–200, 205–7
pike 132–41, 190–200
potatoes 41

Queenford Lagoon 105, 212–22
Quirk, Derek 217–22

Rayment, Peter 12, 42, 92, 190–2
Redmire Pool 80, 205–11

Ree, Lough 51–3
reservoirs 36–8, 138–41
roach 27–9, 124–8
Royalty fishery 92–5
rudd 51–3
Rushey Weir 45–7

Severn, River 47–50
slugs 65
Smith, Alan 174–6, 212
Smith, Phil 38, 43, 174–6, 190–2, 212–22
Stour, River 30–5, 201–4
Sywell Reservoir 37–8

Taylor, Fred J. 148
Taylor, Joe 44, 212–22
TC pit 77–8, 158–78
tench 36–41, 51–3, 158–78
Thames, River 45–7
Thomas, Pete 148
Throop 10, 30–5
Thurne, River 195–200
trotting 72–4

Upton upon Severn 49–50

Walker, Richard 22, 60, 147–9, 205–6
water-skiers 137–8
Wensum, River 179–89
West, Trefor 27, 31, 37–8, 43, 47–9, 54–68, 69–77, 94–5, 97–8, 116–31, 132–8, 142–5, 150–3, 158–74, 179–89, 193–5
Wilkinson, Darryl 140–1
Wilkinson, Mervyn 22, 37, 42, 51–3, 92–4, 132–3, 151, 162, 190–2
Wilson, Alan 174–6, 217
Wobbeking, Rolf 163–4